MICROECONOMIC PROBLEMS
Case Studies and Exercises for Review

FIFTH EDITION

Companion volumes by Edwin Mansfield
MICROECONOMICS: THEORY AND APPLICATIONS, FIFTH EDITION
MICROECONOMICS: SELECTED READINGS, FIFTH EDITION

MICROECONOMIC PROBLEMS

Case Studies and Exercises for Review

FIFTH EDITION

EDWIN MANSFIELD
University of Pennsylvania

W · W · NORTON & COMPANY

NEW YORK · LONDON

Published simultaneously in Canada by Penguin Books Canada Ltd.,
2801 John Street, Markham, Ontario L3R 1B4.

PRINTED IN THE UNITED STATES OF AMERICA.

Library of Congress Cataloging in Publication Data
Mansfield, Edwin.
    Microeconomic problems.
    1. Microeconomics—Problems, exercises, etc.
    2. Microeconomics—Case studies. I.
Title. HB172.M35   1985   338.5   84-22766

    ISBN 0-393-95406-4

W. W. Norton & Company, Inc.,
500 Fifth Avenue, New York, N.Y. 10110
W. W. Norton & Company Ltd.,
37 Great Russell Street, London WC1B 3NU

1 2 3 4 5 6 7 8 9 0

Contents

Preface to the Fifth Edition vii

Part 1. Introduction 1
 1. The Nature of Microeconomics 1
 2. Demand and Supply 10

Part 2. Consumer Behavior and Market Demand 26
 3. The Tastes and Preferences of the Consumer 26
 4. Consumer Behavior and Individual Demand 44
 5. Market Demand 61

Part 3. The Firm: Its Technology and Costs 80
 6. The Firm and Its Technology 80
 7. Optimal Input Combinations and Cost Functions 98

Part 4. Market Structure, Price, and Output 119
 8. Price and Output under Perfect Competition 119
 9. Price and Output under Pure Monopoly 147
 10. Price and Output under Monopolistic Competition 161
 11. Price and Output under Oligopoly 171

Part 5. Markets for Inputs 186
 12. Price and Employment of Inputs under Perfect Competition 186
 13. Price and Employment of Inputs under Imperfect Competition 199

Part 6. General Equilibrium, Welfare Economics, and
    Political Economy 211
 14. General Equilibrium Analysis and Resource Allocation 211
 15. Welfare Economics 226
 16. Public Goods, Externalities, and the Role of Government 238

Part 7. Intertemporal Choice and Decision-Making Involving Risk 250
 17. Intertemporal Choice and Technological Change 250
 18. Decision-Making and Choice Involving Risk 263
 19. Appendix: Linear Programming 281

Preface

As in its previous editions, *Microeconomic Problems: Case Studies and Exercises for Review*, fifth edition, continues to provide a comprehensive set of questions which covers the entire range of topics taught in intermediate-level microeconomics courses. The inclusion of empirical material as well as problems and cases based on real-world situations demonstrates to students the power of microeconomic theory as an aid to decision-makers in both the private and public sectors of the economy. The result is a combination of theory on the one hand with measurement and application on the other. Based on student response to the previous editions of the study guide, this seems to be an approach that provides an effective tool for learning microeconomic theory. In all, over 1,000 questions are included in the present edition of this book.

While the basic structure of the fifth edition of *Microeconomic Problems* remains the same, there have been notable changes:

• About one-half of the case studies are new. Practically all of these cases are based on new empirical data.

• The book has been reorganized, in accord with the changes in my textbook. The material on linear programming has been brought together in an appendix at the end of the book. The rest of the material in what formerly were Chapters 8 and 9 is now included in Chapter 8.

• About 20 problem sets are new or altered in form.

The organization of *Microeconomic Problems*, fifth edition, is designed to provide students with a combination of materials which allows them both to review their grasp of basic concepts and to test their ability to apply those concepts. Each chapter contains four parts. The first is a case study. This is followed by a second part which contains some twenty to thirty problems and short essay questions. These questions vary in difficulty, but only a few (labeled as advanced) require mathematics beyond basic algebra. A third part amounts to a self-test; it covers the main points of the chapter in about thirty completion, true-false, and multiple-choice questions. The fourth part offers a list of key concepts for review. In addition, brief answers are provided at the end of each chapter for practically all of the questions. Some of these answers are of necessity truncated and incomplete. However, they will provide sufficient feedback to students to enable them to gauge their own progress.

I am indebted to many instructors for their comments and suggestions. In particular, my thanks go to Harvey F. Brazer of the University of Michigan, Donald C. Cell of Cornell College, Daniel Fletcher of Denison University, Douglas Needham of James Madison University, and Wesley Yordan of the University of Colorado. Also, I want to thank Anne Williams, whose questions were the basis for several problems included here.

Philadelphia, 1984

E. M.

MICROECONOMIC PROBLEMS
Case Studies and Exercises for Review

FIFTH EDITION

Part 1 INTRODUCTION

CHAPTER 1 The Nature of Microeconomics

Case Study: Should the U.S. Establish Its Own MITI?

After World War II, Japan's Ministry of International Trade and Industry (MITI) played an important role in guiding the nation's industrial development. According to many accounts, it provided government aid (such as subsidies and tax reductions) for industries that were expected to grow rapidly (so-called sunrise industries) and adjustment assistance for those that were declining (sunset industries). In recent years, electronic computers, lasers, robotics, and biotechnology are some of the industries that MITI and others regard as sunrise industries. In the computer field, MITI has allocated over $500 million to try to beat the U.S. to the development of a new generation of computers. Research is being carried out on advanced computer architecture and artificial intelligence, among other things.

During the 1980s, a substantial number of American politicians and business executives, impressed by Japan's rapid economic growth since World War II, proposed that the United States government should intervene in a similar way.

a. If you were asked to argue in favor of such intervention, what points would you make? What arguments do you think are made by the proponents of such intervention?

b. If you were asked to argue against such intervention, what points would you make? What arguments do you think are made by the opponents of such intervention?

c. Can microeconomics shed light on a question of this sort?

Problems and Review Questions

1. A baguette is a long, thin, crispy loaf of French bread. From the French revolution to 1978, the price of a baguette was controlled by the French government. Then it was decontrolled, and it rose to about 40 cents in 1980. In late 1980 Albert Rodriguez, a baker in southern France, cut the price to about 22 cents. Afterwards bakers everywhere were following his example.*

   a. According to a Parisian baker, "It is going to kill the small-business man. It will mean going to a system of commercial baking in a huge central factory. You have got to pay the baker and his costs." What is this baker's implicit assumption about the relationship between the size of a bakery and its cost per baguette?

   b. In December 1980, some of Mr. Rodriguez's competitors tried to sell baguettes outside his shop for 11 cents each. Why do you think they did this?

   c. Most of Mr. Rodriguez's customers ignored Mr. Rodriguez's competitors, when they tried to sell baguettes outside his shop for 11 cents each. Why do you think they did this?

   d. What are some of the principal inputs required to produce baguettes?

   e. If you were assigned the task of constructing a model to predict whether a particular baker would cut the price he or she charges for a baguette, what factors would you stress?

2. As part of the Revenue Act of 1978, Congress passed a tax credit for families that invest in solar energy equipment. For example, if a family spends $10,000 on solar energy equipment, it can reduce its income tax by $2,200. (For expenditures up to $2,000, the tax credit is equal to 30 percent of the expenditure.) The Office of Tax Analysis of the U.S. Treasury Department, in analyzing this proposal, estimated that the cost of heating a 1,850-square-foot house over a 20-year period with solar and other types of heating systems was as follows:

Type of heating system	Cost (dollars)
Solar	12,907
Electric furnace	5,440
Electric resistance	4,968
Oil	3,659
Gas	2,582

    a. Some observers feel that solar energy will play an important role in solving our energy problems. How does the price system determine how rapidly the use of solar energy will spread?

    b. Based on the information provided above, how rapidly do you think that the use of solar energy will spread?

    c. What reasons can you give for the government's intervening in this way to encourage the use of solar energy?

    d. Will this tax credit cut the income tax liabilities of the poor more than those of the rich?

    e. Construct a model to predict what type of heating system a consumer will install in a new house.

3. In June 1981, about 7.7 percent of the labor force was unemployed. How can anyone say that labor is scarce?

4. On most questions of policy, one can find disagreements among economists. Does this prove that economics is not a science?

5. If a certain proposition holds true for a part of a system, must it hold true for the whole system? For example, suppose that a farmer will benefit from producing a larger crop. Does it follow that all farmers will benefit from producing a larger crop? Explain.

6. In evaluating the accuracy of their statements, should one distinguish between (1) economists' descriptive statements, propositions, and predictions about the world and (2) their statements about what policies should be adopted? Explain.

7. According to Adam Smith, "Monopoly . . . is a great enemy to good management." What do you think he meant? Do you agree or disagree?

*For further discussion, see "In France, Price War Cuts Cost of Bread," *New York Times* (December 21, 1980).

8. In aeronautical engineering, models of an airplane are used to investigate its aerodynamic properties in a wind tunnel. Must such models have seats for passengers? Must they be hollow? What functions must they serve?

9. According to Alfred P. Sloan, who was president of General Motors from 1923 to 1937 and chairman of its board of directors from 1937 to 1956, "The great difference between the industry of today as compared to that of yesterday is what might be referred to as the necessity of the scientific approach, the elimination of operation by hunches."* Indicate how microeconomics plays a role in this more scientific approach to management.

10. What concerns does economics deal with? What is the difference between microeconomics and macroeconomics?

11. Give several examples of the particular types of problems that microeconomics helps to solve.

12. Is microeconomics concerned solely with the solution of practical problems? Give examples of questions that are dealt with in microeconomics that do not take the form of practical problems. In what sense is microeconomics like mathematics?

13. Define human wants. What role do human wants play in microeconomics?

14. Define economic resources. What role do economic resources play in microeconomics?

15. Describe the various types of economic resources.

16. Define technology. Is there any difference between science and technology? If so, what is the difference? What role does technology play in microeconomics?

17. Describe the four basic tasks that must be performed by any economic system.

18. How does our system determine the level and composition of output in the society?

19. How does our economic system allocate its resources among competing uses and process these resources to obtain the desired level and composition of output?

20. How does our economic system determine how much in the way of goods and services each member of the society is to receive?

21. How does our economic system determine the rate of growth of per capita income?

22. What is a model? Can the usefulness of a model be deduced from the realism of its assumptions? Why do economists use models?

*A. Sloan, *Adventures of a White Collar Worker* (Garden City, N.Y.: Doubleday), 1941.

-3-

23. What considerations must be taken into account in judging or evaluating a model?

24. Are the models contained in this book sufficiently accurate to solve all of the problems faced by governments and firms? Have all of them been tested completely? Are they the best available at this time?

Completion Questions

1. National defense is an example of a _____ good. Such goods (will, will not) _____ be provided in the right amounts by private industry, so _____ tends to intervene.

2. Economics is concerned with the way in which _____ are allocated among alternative uses to satisfy _____.

3. Microeconomics deals with the economic behavior of _____ _____.

4. Wants _____ from individual to individual and over time for the same person.

5. Resources are used to produce _____.

6. There are two types of resources: economic and _____.

7. Resources are often classified as land, labor, and _____.

8. Technology is directed toward _____ ; science is directed toward _____ _____.

9. In a free-enterprise economy, _____ choose the amount of each good that they want, and _____ act in accord with these decisions.

10. In our system, the income of each individual depends largely on how much he or she owns of each resource and _____.

11. A nation's rate of growth of per capita income depends on the rate of growth of its resources and the _____ _____.

True or False

_____ F 1. When economists refer to goods as being scarce, they mean that these items are monopolized by a few people. If goods were distributed equitably, there would be no problem of scarcity.

_____ F 2. Models generally are not useful in practice; if they were, they would not be called models.

_____ T 3. Microeconomics is helpful in promoting an understanding of the powerful modern tools of managerial decision-making.

T _____F____ 4. The lawyer who argues an antitrust case, and the judge who decides one, must both rely on and use the principles of microeconomics.

_____F____ 5. Microeconomics is concerned only with solving practical problems.

_____F____ 6. Economic resources always have a zero price.

_____F____ 7. There usually is only one way of producing a commodity so it is easy to figure out which way is best.

_____F____ 8. The price system plays some role, but only a minor one, in allocating resources in a free-enterprise economy.

_____F____ 9. In the acquisition of new weapons, society relies exclusively on the price system.

_____F____ 10. A model cannot be useful if it simplifies and abstracts from reality.

_____F____ 11. Models are used by economists, but not physicists.

_____T____ 12. One reason for using a model is that it may be the cheapest way of getting needed information.

Multiple Choice

1. In choosing among alternative models, economists generally have the strongest preference for models that
   a. have assumptions that are close to exact replicas of reality. *abstract*
   b. predict better than any other that is available. ✓
   c. have few assumptions and are as simple as possible, even if they cannot predict very well.
   d. are detailed and complex, with every available fact and figure included.
   e. all of the above.

2. Microeconomics is concerned with
   a. optimal production decisions.
   b. pricing policy. ✓
   c. optimal resource allocation. ✓
   d. antitrust policy. ✓
   e. all of the above.

3. In a free-enterprise economy, profits and losses are
   a. the stick used to eliminate less efficient firms.
   b. the carrot used to reward the proper decisions.
   c. both a and b.
   d. neither a nor b.
   e. always equal to zero.

4. If a model is to be any good, it must
   a. make assumptions that are exact replicas of reality.
   b. refrain from referring to things that are not directly measurable.
   c. predict phenomena in the real world reasonably well.
   d. all of the above.
   e. none of the above.

Key Concepts for Review

Economics	Capital
Microeconomics	Technology
Macroeconomics	Tasks performed by an economic system
Human wants	The price system
Labor	Models
Land	Model-building

Answers

Case Study: Should the U.S. Establish Its Own MITI?

a. Some people believe that the price system does not work in a sufficiently dependable and timely fashion. Also, they argue that the government is already intervening in a variety of ways, and that what is needed is to coordinate its policies and make them more efficient.

b. Many people are skeptical of the ability of government agencies to forecast which industries will grow rapidly and which will decline. MITI itself has made a considerable number of mistakes in this regard. More basically, these people believe that the price system will allocate resources more effectively than government intervention of this sort.

c. Microeconomics shows the way in which the price system allocates resources and the conditions under which government intervention of various kinds can be justified. Clearly, a knowledge of these matters is essential in thinking about questions of this sort.

Problems and Review Questions

1. a. This baker is assuming that the cost per baguette falls as the size of the bakery increases.
   b. They did it to cut Mr. Rodriguez's sales and to punish him for cutting his price.
   c. They did it because they suspected that, once Mr. Rodriguez's competitors had hurt his business and brought him into line (or put him out of business), they would raise their price to its original level. As one of Mr. Rodriguez's customers said, "We know that at his place it will still be [22 cents] tomorrow."
   d. Flour, services of ovens, fuel, services of bakers, water, shortening, yeast.
   e. The probability that a particular baker would cut its price would be expected to be directly related to how profitable he or she believes such an action to be.

2. a. The price system allows consumers and producers to decide whether or not they want to use solar energy. If potential users are willing to pay the amount required to use solar energy, they will adopt it; otherwise they won't. In general, one would expect that if other types of heating systems are cheaper, most consumers and firms will not adopt it.
   b. It probably will not spread very fast because it seems to be much more expensive than other types of heating systems.
   c. The government may feel that there are social benefits from switching to solar energy (and thus reducing our dependence on foreign oil) that are not reflected in a comparison of the costs to the consumer of solar energy with those of other types of heating equipment.
   d. The direct impact on the taxes of the rich will probably be relatively greater, since few poor people can afford to install solar energy.

   e. It seems likely that the consumer would choose the least costly type of heating system that will be appropriate for his or her house. Thus the choice will depend on the relative costs of various types of heating systems, among other things. ⟶ *where consumer lives*

3. Despite the fact that some labor is unemployed, labor is scarce. Certainly, the quantity of labor is not unlimited, and labor's price is nonzero.

4. No, because most of the disagreements stem from differences in ethical and political views.

5. No. This is the so-called fallacy of composition.

6. Yes, because the latter statements reflect the value judgments of the economist.

7. He meant that a monopolist, having succeeded in freeing himself from competition, is likely to take things easy, and worry less about efficiency.

8. No.

   No.

   They must provide information that is useful in predicting the characteristics of the final airplane.

9. It helps to indicate how firms should analyze their production, marketing, and financial problems in order to increase their profitability.

10. Economics is concerned with the way in which resources are allocated among alternative uses to satisfy human wants. Microeconomics deals with the economic behavior of individual units like consumers, firms, and resource owners; macroeconomics deals with the behavior of economic aggregates such as gross national product and the level of employment.

11. Business firms are constantly faced with the problem of choosing among alternative ways of producing their product. One type of problem that microeconomics can help to solve is: which technique will maximize the firm's profits?

   Firms are also faced with the problem of pricing their product. Another type of problem that microeconomics can help to solve is: which price will maximize the firm's profits?

   Society as a whole must decide how it wants to organize the production and distribution of goods and services. Microeconomics can sometimes be useful in helping to indicate what changes society would be justified in making in this system.

   Public policy must also be concerned with the structure of individual markets and industries. Microeconomics plays an important role in helping to illuminate antitrust cases and to solve problems in this area.

12. No.

   Why is steak more expensive than hamburger? Why are physicians paid more than carpenters? How will an increase in the price of margarine affect the amount of butter purchased by Mrs. Smith? Why are there so many producers of wheat and so few producers of automobiles?

   Pure mathematics is not concerned with the solution of particular problems, but it has turned out that various branches of mathematics are of great value in solving practical problems. This is true as well of much of microeconomic theory. Also, microeconomics, like mathematics, is extremely important as a basis for understanding the world around us and for further professional training.

13. Human wants are the things, services, goods, and circumstances that people desire.

   Human wants—or, more precisely, their fulfillment—are the objective at which economic activity is directed. *UTILITY* *fulfillment*

14. Resources are the things or services used to produce goods which can be used to satisfy wants. Economic resources are scarce, and thus have a nonzero price.

   The essence of "the economic problem" is that some resources are scarce and must be allocated among alternative uses. If all resources were free, there would be no economic problem.

15. Land is a shorthand expression for natural resources.

   Labor is human effort, both physical and mental.

Capital includes equipment, buildings, inventories, raw materials, and other nonhuman producible resources.
16. Technology is society's pool of knowledge regarding the industrial arts.
    Yes. Pure science is directed toward understanding, whereas technology is directed toward use.
    Technology sets limits on the amount and type of goods that can be derived from a given amount of resources.
17. First, an economic system must allocate its resources among competing uses and combine these resources to produce the desired output efficiently.
    Second, an economic system must determine the level and composition of output.
    Third, an economic system must determine how the goods and services that are produced are distributed among the members of society.
    Fourth, an economic system must determine the rate of growth of per capita income.
18. Consumers choose the amount of each good that they want, and producers act in accord with these decisions. Also, the production of some goods is a matter of political decision.
19. The price system is used to indicate the desires of workers and the relative value of various types of materials and equipment as well as the desires of consumers. To firms, profits are the carrot and losses are the stick. In addition, the government intervenes directly in some areas like weapons acquisition.
20. The income of an individual depends largely on the quantities of resources of various kinds that he or she owns and the prices he or she gets for them. In addition, the government modifies the resulting distribution of income by imposing progressive income taxes and by welfare programs like aid to dependent children.
21. The rate at which labor and capital resources are increased is motivated, at least in part, through the price system. Increases in efficiency, due in considerable measure to the advance of technology, are also stimulated by the price system. But the government plays an extremely significant role in supporting research and development.
22. A model is composed of a number of assumptions from which conclusions—or predictions —are drawn.
    No.
    The real world is so complex that it is necessary to simplify and abstract if any progress is to be made. A model may be the cheapest way of obtaining needed information.
23. The most important test of a model is how well it predicts. Another is whether its assumptions are logically consistent. Another important consideration is the range of phenomena to which the model applies.
24. No.
    No.
    Yes, according to a consensus of the economics profession.

Completion Questions

1. public; will not; government
2. resources; human wants
3. individual consumers, firms, and resource owners
4. vary
5. goods and services
6. free
7. capital
8. use; understanding

9. consumers; producers
10. the price of each resource
11. rate of increase of the efficiency with which they are used

True or False

1. False   2. False   3. True   4. True   5. False   6. False   7. False   8. False   9. False
10. False   11. False   12. True

Multiple Choice

1. *b*   2. *e*   3. *c*   4. *c*

CHAPTER 2 Demand and Supply

Case Study: In Vino Veritas

In 1979, the weather conditions in many parts of Europe were ideal for cultivating grapes. In France, there was a record output of more than 2.2 billion gallons of wine. In Bordeaux, wine-makers took about 10 million gallons of wine off the market in an attempt to buttress the price of their wine.* However, another way that industries can attempt to protect themselves against reductions in the price of their product is to prevail on the government to establish a price floor. Suppose that the French government had decreed that Bordeaux wine could not be sold in 1979 at less than its 1978 price.

a. If the market demand curve for Bordeaux wine was the same in 1979 as in 1978, would such a price floor have raised the price above the equilibrium price that otherwise would have prevailed?

b. If such a price floor raised the price, would the price increase result in an increase in the total amount of money received by the Bordeaux wine-makers?

Problems and Review Questions

1. According to unofficial estimates by economists at the U.S. Department of Agriculture, the market demand curve for wheat in the American market in the early 1960s was (roughly) as follows:

Farm price of wheat (dollars per bushel)	Quantity of wheat demanded (millions of bushels)
1.00	1,500
1.20	1,300
1.40	1,100
1.60	900
1.80	800
2.00	700

In the middle 1970s, the market demand and supply curves for wheat in the American market were (roughly) as follows:

Farm price of wheat (dollars per bushel)	Quantity of wheat demanded (millions of bushels)	Quantity of wheat supplied (millions of bushels)
3.00	1,850	1,600
3.50	1,750	1,750
4.00	1,650	1,900
5.00	1,500	2,200

*For further information concerning economic aspects of the wine trade, see "Wine Talk: A Blow to the Law of Supply and Demand," *New York Times*, May 7, 1980.

a. If the market demand curve in the middle 1970s had remained as it was in the early 1960s, can you tell whether the farm price of wheat in the middle 1970s would have been greater or less than $2.00? Explain.

b. Did a shift occur between the early 1960s and the middle 1970s in the market demand curve for wheat? If so, was it a shift to the right or the left, and what factors were responsible for this shift?

c. What was the price elasticity of demand for wheat during the middle 1970s if the price was between $3.00 and $3.50?

d. Suppose that the government had supported the price of wheat at $4.00 in the middle 1970s. How big would have been the excess supply? What would have been some of the objections to such a policy?

2. The following two demand curves, D_1 and D_2, are parallel straight lines:

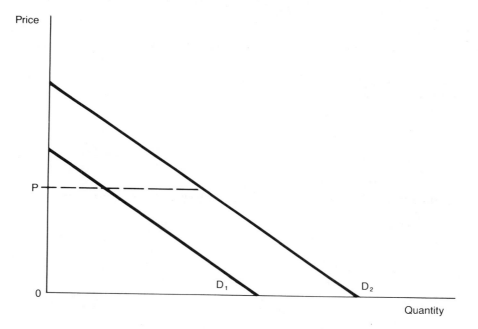

Prove that, if the price is held constant (say, at OP), the price elasticity of demand is *not* the same if the demand curve is D_1, as it is if the demand curve is D_2.

3. If both the demand and supply curves in a competitive market shift to the right, one can predict the direction of change of output but not of price. If the supply curve shifts to the right, but the demand curve shifts to the left, one cannot, without further knowledge, be certain about the direction of either the price or the quantity change. Do you agree with this statement? Explain.

4. *a.* The demand curve for beer is

$$Q_D = 500 - 5P$$

where Q_D is the quantity demanded of beer (in millions of barrels per year) and P is its price (in dollars per barrel). If the supply curve for beer is a vertical line at $Q_S = 400$ million barrels of beer per year, what is the equilibrium price of a barrel of beer?

  b. Under the conditions described in part (*a*), what would be the effect on the price of a barrel of beer if a tax of $5 per barrel is imposed by the government on beer?

5. *a.* The supply curve for butter is

$$Q_S = 100 + 3P$$

where Q_S is the quantity supplied of butter (in millions of pounds per year) and P is the price of butter (in dollars per pound). If the demand curve for butter is a vertical line at $Q_D = 106$ millions of pounds per year, and if the government imposes a price floor of $1 per pound on butter, will there be an excess supply or excess demand of butter, and how big will it be?

  b. If the government's price floor is set at $3 per pound, will there be an excess supply or excess demand of butter, and how big will it be?

  c. Under the conditions described in part (*a*), what is the price elasticity of demand for butter? Do you regard this as a realistic value for this price elasticity? Explain.

6. Suppose that the number of bicycles demanded in the United States in 1985 at various prices is as follows:

Price of a bicycle (dollars)	Quantity demanded per year (millions of bicycles)
80	20
100	18
120	16

  a. Draw three points on the demand curve for bicycles in the graph below.

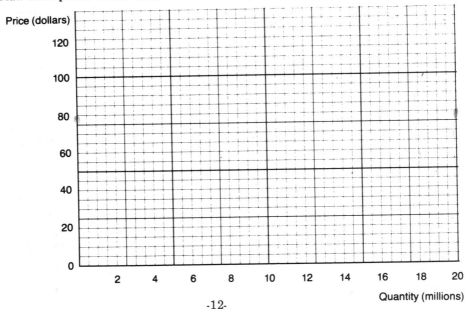

b. Calculate the arc price elasticity of demand when (1) the price is between $80 and $100 and (2) the price is between $100 and $120.

7. Suppose that the relationship between the quantity of bicycles supplied in 1985 in the United States and the price per bicycle is as follows:

Price of a bicycle (dollars)	Quantity supplied per year (millions of bicycles)
60	14
80	16
100	18
120	19

a. Draw four points on the supply curve for bicycles in the graph below.

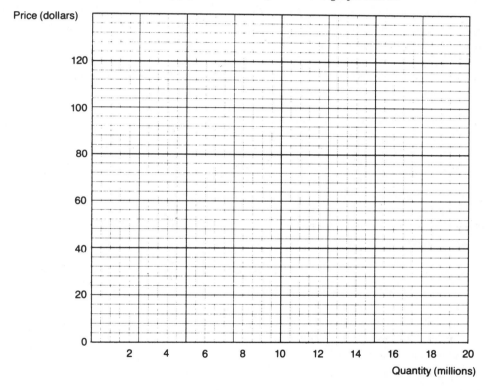

b. Estimate the price elasticity of supply when the price is between $80 and $100.

c. Based on the data presented here and in the previous question, what is the equilibrium price of a bicycle in the United States?

d. If the price is $80, will there be an excess demand? An excess supply?

e. If the price is $120, will there be an excess demand? An excess supply?

8. The government imposes an excise tax of $40 on each bicycle (in the previous problem). Then it decides to set a price ceiling of $100 on the price of a bicycle. Will there be a surplus or shortage of bicycles? If so, how big a surplus or shortage? (Hint: Use the data in question 6.)

9. Suppose that the demand curve for cantaloupes is

$$P = 120 - 3Q_D$$

where P is the price per pound (in cents) of a cantaloupe and Q_D is the quantity demanded per year (in millions of pounds). Suppose that the supply curve for cantaloupes is

$$P = 5Q_S$$

where Q_S is the quantity supplied per year (in millions of pounds). What is the equilibrium price per pound of a cantaloupe? What is the equilibrium quantity of cantaloupes produced?

10. Suppose that the government puts a price floor of 80 cents per pound on cantaloupes. How big will be the resulting surplus of cantaloupes, based on the data in the previous problem? What measures can the government adopt to cut down on this surplus?

11. Do you think that the market demand curve for rubber is more price elastic in a period of 10 years than in a period of 10 days? Explain.

12. Do you think that the market supply curve for rubber is more price elastic in a period of 10 years than in a period of 10 days? Explain.

13. Suppose that the market demand curve for fish shifts to the right. Does this mean that consumers are willing to buy more fish than previously at any given price? Does it mean that a given quantity of fish put on the market will now bring a higher price?

14. If the market demand curve for cocoa shifts to the left, does this mean that less money will be spent on cocoa?

15. Is it likely that the market demand curve for cocoa will shift to the right because of a technological innovation that reduces the cost of producing cocoa? Explain.

16. Suppose that a plague attacks the nation's beef cattle, but has no effect on its pork production. What effect will this have on:
    a. the market supply curve for pork?
    b. the market demand curve for pork?
    c. the equilibrium price of pork?

17. Suppose that a major increase occurs in the cost of producing hogs (but not in the cost of producing beef). What effect will this have on:
    a. the market supply curve for pork?
    b. the market demand curve for pork?
    c. the equilibrium price of pork?

18. Suppose that the transit authority in a major city permits a large increase in fares on bus, subway, and trolley lines. Do you think that this will shift the market demand curve for taxis in this city to the left or to the right? Explain.

19. Define a market. Must the market demand curve for a commodity always slope downward to the right?

20. Describe the difference between the point elasticity of demand and the arc elasticity of demand.

21. "Since the actual price does not equal the equilibrium price, it is useless to figure out the equilibrium price." Comment on this statement, and indicate whether or not you agree with it.

22. "In order to protect the poor, it is essential that the price of natural gas be kept at its existing level. Any increase in price would only go into the pockets of the rich." Comment on this statement, and indicate whether or not you agree with it.

23. "The laws of supply and demand are immutable. No one, including the government, can affect a commodity's demand curve or supply curve." Comment on this statement, and indicate whether or not you agree with it.

24. C. Nisbet and F. Vakil estimated the demand curve for marijuana among students at the University of California at Los Angeles in 1972. The estimated demand curve for a representative student (who was in the market for the drug) is shown below:

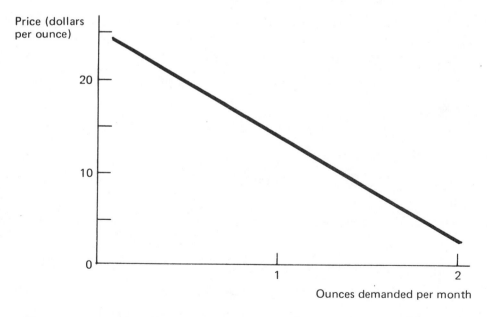

a. How many ounces per month of marijuana were demanded by the student when the price was $10 per ounce? $15 per ounce?

b. What was the arc elasticity of demand when the price was between $10 and $15 per ounce?

c. In recent years, the United States government has intensified its efforts to restrict the inflow of marijuana in order to cut back the supply, thus increasing the price. If the price were driven sky-high, would this affect the market demand curve for marijuana? If so, in what way?

d. If marijuana were legalized, what effect would it have on the market supply curve for marijuana?

e. If research were to indicate that marijuana causes birth defects, what effect would it have on the market demand curve for marijuana?

Completion Questions

1. If the price elasticity of demand for refrigerators is 2, and the price of a refrigerator increases by 1 percent, there will be an (increase, decrease) _____ of about _____ percent in the amount spent on refrigerators.

2. The market demand curve for grade-A widgets is a vertical line at a quantity of 1,000 units per year. The price elasticity of demand for grade-A widgets equals _____ .

3. The equation for the market supply curve of grade-A widgets is $P = 0.1Q$, where P is the price (in dollars) of a grade-A widget and Q is the output (in units per year) of grade-A widgets. The price elasticity of supply of grade-A widgets equals _____.

4. Based on the information in Questions 2 and 3, the equilibrium price of a grade-A widget equals _____ .

5. Based on the information in Questions 2 and 3, the equilibrium output of grade-A widgets equals _____ .

6. If the government sets a price floor of $150 for a grade-A widget, the excess supply of grade-A widgets will be _____ , based on Questions 2 and 3.

7. If the government sets a price ceiling of $80 for a grade-A widget, the excess demand of grade-A widgets will be _____ , based on Questions 2 and 3.

8. If a tax of $1 is imposed on each grade-A widget, the effect is to increase the equilibrium price of a grade-A widget by _____ , based on Questions 2 and 3.

9. If a tax of $10 is imposed on each grade-A widget, the effect is to reduce the equilibrium output of grade-A widgets by _____ units per year, based on Questions 2 and 3.

10. If the price elasticity of demand for gasoline is 0.50, a _____ percent increase in the price of gasoline will be required to reduce the quantity demanded of gasoline by 1 percent.

11. If the actual price of gasoline equals the equilibrium price, the difference between the quantity of gasoline supplied and the quantity of gasoline demanded equals _____ _____ .

True or False

_____ 1. No equilibrium price nor equilibrium quantity exists if a good's demand curve is a vertical line and its supply curve is a horizontal line.

_____ 2. The demand curve for a free good (a good with a zero price) must be a horizontal line.

_____ 3. If actual price exceeds equilibrium price, there is a tendency for actual price to rise.

_____ 4. A shift to the right of the market supply curve tends to increase the equilibrium price.

_____ 5. A product's market demand curve generally slopes upward and to the right, if the product's price elasticity of demand is very large.

_____ 6. The slope of the market demand curve equals the price elasticity of demand.

_____ 7. In any market, the seller alone determines the price of the product that is bought and sold. Since the seller has the product, while the buyer does not have it, the buyer must pay what the seller asks.

_____ 8. If the price elasticity of demand for a good is infinite, a tax on this good will reduce the equilibrium price of the good.

_____ 9. If the price elasticity of demand for a good is infinite, a tax on this good will increase the equilibrium price of the good.

_____ 10. If the price elasticity of demand for a good is zero, a tax on this good will increase the equilibrium output of this good.

_____ 11. If the price elasticity of demand for a good is zero, a tax on this good will reduce the equilibrium output of this good.

_____ 12. If the price of coffee goes up, it is likely that the market supply curve for tea will shift to the right.

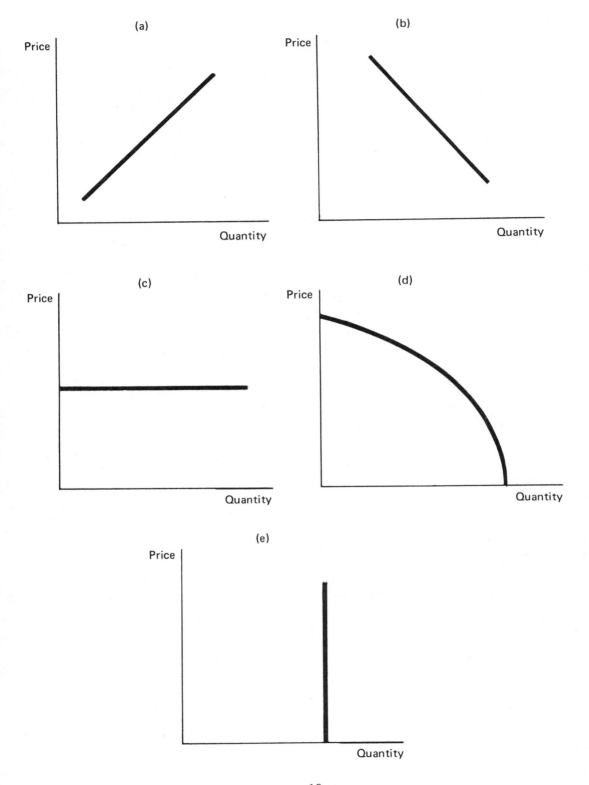

(a)

Price

Quantity

(b)

Price

Quantity

(c)

Price

Quantity

(d)

Price

Quantity

(e)

Price

Quantity

-18-

Multiple Choice

1. If President Ronald Reagan were to announce that the government would no longer allow private parties to buy gold (so that the government would be the sole buyer) and if he were to announce that the government would buy any and all gold at $500 per ounce, which of the diagrams on page 18 would represent the demand curve for gold in the United States?

   C

2. Suppose that the market demand curve and the market supply curve for asparagus are as shown in the graph below.

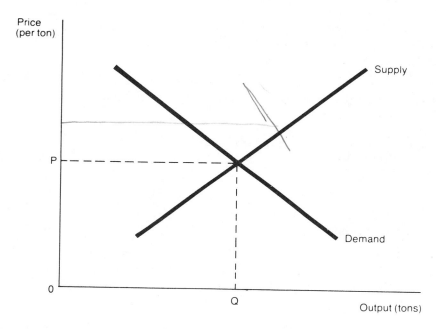

   If the government sets a price floor equal to 2P per ton, the result will be:
   a. a reduction in the quantity of asparagus supplied.
   b. an excess supply of asparagus.
   c. a shift to the right of the market supply curve for asparagus.
   d. all of the above.
   e. none of the above.

3. In the previous question, if a government report indicates that asparagus contains important, hitherto unrecognized ingredients that can safeguard health and prolong life, the result is likely to be:
   a. a shift to the right in the market supply curve for asparagus.
   b. a shift to the left in the market supply curve for asparagus.
   c. a shift to the right in the market demand curve for asparagus.
   d. all of the above.
   e. none of the above.

4. If the government imposes a tax of $1 per ton on asparagus, it is clear from the diagram in Question 2 that the equilibrium price of asparagus will:

a. fall.

b. increase by $1.

c. increase by less than $1.

d. increase by more than $1.

e. be unaffected.

5. If the price of broccoli falls considerably, the result is likely to be:

a. a shift to the right in the market demand curve for asparagus.

b. a shift to the left in the market supply curve for asparagus.

c. a shift to the left in the market demand curve for asparagus.

d. an increase in the equilibrium price of asparagus.

e. none of the above.

6. If the price of broccoli falls considerably, and if the government freezes the price of asparagus at the level prevailing before the fall in the price of broccoli, the result is likely to be:

a. a surplus of asparagus.

b. a shortage of asparagus.

c. a shift to the left in the market supply curve for asparagus.

d. a shift to the right in the market supply curve for asparagus.

e. none of the above.

Key Concepts for Review

Market demand curve

Market supply curve

Equilibrium

Equilibrium price

Surplus

Price elasticity of demand

Price elasticity of supply

Price ceiling

Price floor

Shortage

Answers

Case Study: In Vino Veritas

a. If the market demand curve for Bordeaux wine was the same in 1979 as in 1978, and if the 1979 market supply curve for Bordeaux wine (S_{79}) is to the right of the 1978 supply curve (S_{78}), the situation is as shown on the graph on the next page. The equilibrium price in 1979 would be OP_0, and the price floor would be OP_1 (since this was the 1978 price). Thus the price floor would be above the equilibrium price.

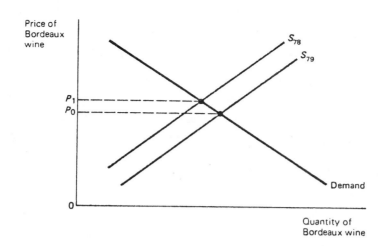

b. Whether such a price increase would result in an increase in the total amount of money received by the Bordeaux wine makers depends on the price elasticity of demand for their wine. For example, if this price elasticity equals one, such a price increase would have no effect on the amount of money they receive. To see this, note that the total amount of money they receive is the quantity of wine sold multiplied by its price. If the price elasticity of demand equals 1, a 1 percent increase in price results in a 1 percent decrease in quantity sold. Thus the total amount they receive is not affected by the price increase. (More will be said on this score in Chapters 4 and 5.)

Problems and Review Questions

1. *a.* It is impossible to tell. At $2, the quantity demanded would have been 700 million bushels, but we are not given the quantity supplied at $2. If it were greater than 700 million bushels, the equilibrium price would have been less than $2; if it were less than 700 million bushels, the equilibrium price would have been greater than $2.

   b. Yes. At $3, the quantity of wheat demanded during the 1960s would have been less than 700 million bushels, if the demand curve was downward sloping to the right. During the 1970s, 1,850 million bushels were demanded at $3. Thus the demand curve seemed to shift to the right. The reason was increased foreign demand due partly to poor harvests in the Soviet Union, Australia, and Argentina, as well as devaluation of the dollar.

   c. $\eta = -\dfrac{(1,850 - 1,750)}{(1,850 + 1,750)/2} \div \dfrac{(3.00 - 3.50)}{(3.00 + 3.50)/2} = 0.36$

   d. 250 million bushels. The problems involved in such farm supports are discussed in more detail in later chapters. Such surpluses have been an embarrassment, both economically and politically. They suggest that society's scarce resources are being utilized to produce products that consumers do not want at existing prices. Also, the cost of storing these surpluses can be large.

2. As pointed out in footnote 6 of the text, the slope of the demand curve does not equal the price elasticity of demand. While the slope is the same if the demand curve is D_1 as it is if the demand curve is D_2, the price elasticity is not. Specifically, whereas dQ_D/dP and P are the same under these circumstances, Q_D is not the same, so the price elasticity is not the same. (Q_D is quantity demanded, and P is price.)

3. The first sentence is correct. The second sentence is incorrect; one can be certain that price will fall.

4. *a.* Since the quantity supplied must equal the quantity demanded if equilibrium is achieved

$$500 - 5P = 400$$

or

$$100 = 5P$$

which means that $P = 20$. Thus, the equilibrium price is $20 per barrel.

   b. No effect, because the supply curve would be unaffected by the tax.

5. *a.* In equilibrium, $Q_S = Q_D$, so

$$100 + 3P = 106$$
$$3P = 6$$
$$P = 2$$

Thus the equilibrium price is $2 per pound. Since this exceeds the government's price floor, there will be no excess supply or excess demand of butter.

   b. If $P = 3$, the quantity supplied equals $100 + 3(3) = 109$, and the quantity demanded equals 106, so the excess supply equals $109 - 106$, or 3; that is, it equals 3 million pounds per year.

   c. Zero.
   No, because decreases in the price of butter are almost certain to increase the quantity demanded.

6. *a.*

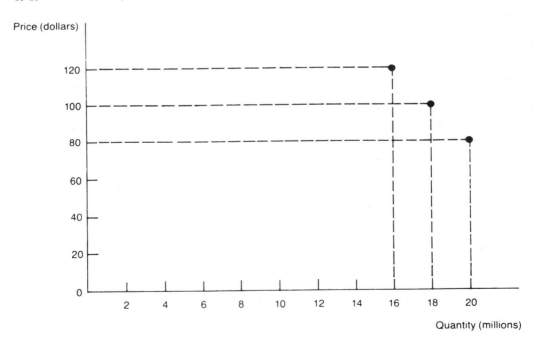

-22-

b. $\eta = -\dfrac{(20-18)}{(20+18)/2} \div \dfrac{(80-100)}{(80+100)/2} = \dfrac{2}{19} \div \dfrac{20}{90} = 0.47$

$\eta = -\dfrac{(18-16)}{(18+16)/2} \div \dfrac{(100-120)}{(100+120)/2} = \dfrac{2}{17} \div \dfrac{20}{110} = 0.65$

7. a.

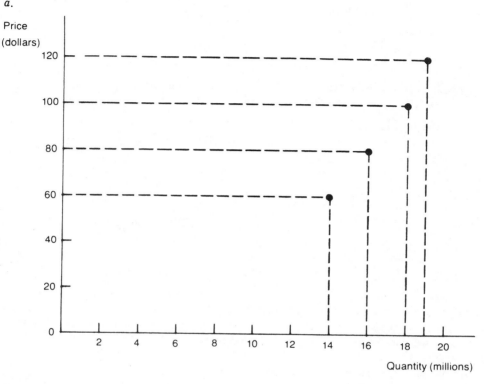

b. $\eta_s = \dfrac{18-16}{(18+16)/2} \div \dfrac{100-80}{(100+80)/2} = \dfrac{2}{17} \div \dfrac{20}{90} = 0.53.$

c. $100.

d. Excess demand.

e. Excess supply.

8. With the excise tax, the supply curve is

Price (dollars)	Quantity supplied
100	14
120	16
140	18
160	19

Thus the equilibrium price of a bicycle is $120, since at this price the quantity supplied equals the quantity demanded. If the government sets a price ceiling of $100, there will be a shortage of 4 million bicycles per year, since the quantity demanded will equal 18 million while the quantity supplied will equal 14 million. (See the data in Question 6.)

9. Since the quantity supplied must equal the quantity demanded, we have two equations to be solved simultaneously:

$$120 - 3Q_D = 5Q_S$$
$$Q_D = Q_S$$

Letting quantity equal Q, it follows that

$$120 - 3Q = 5Q$$
$$120 = 8Q$$
$$15 = Q$$

Since $P = 5Q$, it follows that $P = 75$. Thus the equilibrium price is 75 cents and the equilibrium quantity is 15 million pounds per year.

10. From the previous problem

$$P = 120 - 3Q_D$$

or

$$3Q_D = 120 - P$$
$$Q_D = 40 - 1/3\,P$$

Also, $Q_S = 1/5P$. Thus, if $P = 80$, $Q_D = 40 - 80/3 = 13\,^1/_3$, and $Q_S = 80/5 = 16$. Consequently, $Q_S - Q_D = 16 - 13\,^1/_3 = 2\,^2/_3$, which means that the resulting surplus equals $2\,^2/_3$ million pounds per year. To reduce this surplus, the government could attempt to reduce the amount of cantaloupes produced by farmers or expand the demand for cantaloupes.

11. It is likely to be more price elastic in a period of 10 years because consumers will have more time to adapt to changes in the price of rubber.

12. It is likely to be more price elastic in a period of 10 years because producers will have more time to adapt to changes in the price of rubber.

13. Yes. Yes.

14. Yes, if the supply curve for cocoa slopes upward to the right.

15. No. Such an innovation would be expected to influence the supply curve, not the demand curve, for cocoa.

16. *a*. None.
    b. It will shift to the right.
    c. It will increase.

17. *a*. It will shift to the left.
    b. None.
    c. It will increase.

18. It may shift them to the right because bus, subway, and trolley transportation is a substitute for taxis.

19. A market is a group of firms and individuals that are in touch with each other in order to buy or sell some good.
    No.

20. The point elasticity of demand refers to a case where the change in price is small; the arc elasticity of demand refers to a case where the change in price is not small.

21. Since the actual price tends to move toward the equilibrium price, it is useful to figure out the equilibrium price, because this helps to indicate whether the actual price will rise or fall.

22. This statement is obviously a vast oversimplification of the effects of such a price increase. For example, an increase in price might increase natural gas supplies which might be socially beneficial.

23. The government can influence a commodity's demand or supply curve by subsidies, taxation, and other means.

24. a. About 1.3 ounces per month at $10. About 0.9 ounces per month at $15.

  b. Let P_1 = $10, Q_1 = 1.3 ounces, P_2 = $15, and Q_2 = 0.9 ounces. Then the arc elasticity equals

$$- \frac{(1.3 - 0.9)}{(1.3 + 0.9)/2} \div \frac{(10 - 15)}{(10 + 15)/2},$$

  or 0.91.

  c. Such an increase in price would reduce the *quantity demanded*, but it would *not* shift the demand curve . In other words, there would be a *movement along* the demand curve from a point corresponding to the current price to a point corresponding to a sky-high price, but no *shift* in the demand curve.

  d. Legalization would probably shift the market supply curve to the right. Suppliers could supply more at a given price because their costs would be lower. They would no longer have to pay for secrecy and protection, and the risks would be less.

  e. It would shift to the left for obvious reasons.*

Completion Questions

1. decrease, one
2. zero
3. one
4. $100
5. 1,000 units per year
6. 500 units per year
7. 200 units per year
8. $1 per unit
9. zero
10. 2
11. zero

True or False

1. False   2. False   3. False   4. False   5. False   6. False   7. False   8. False   9. False
10. False   11. False   12. False

Multiple Choice

1. *c*   2. *b*   3. *c*   4. *c*   5. *c*   6. *a*

*For further discussion, see C. Nisbet and F. Vakil, "Some Estimates of Price and Expenditure Elasticities of Demand for Marijuana among U.C.L.A. Students," *Review of Economics and Statistics* (November 1972).

Part 2 CONSUMER BEHAVIOR AND MARKET DEMAND

CHAPTER 3 The Tastes and Preferences of the Consumer

Case Study: Nuclear-Powered vs. Conventionally Powered Aircraft Carriers

During recent years, a basic decision confronting the United States Navy has been whether to build nuclear-powered or conventionally powered aircraft carriers. Suppose that the effectiveness of the United States Navy would be the same if the navy had each of the following combinations of numbers of aircraft carriers of each type.

	Number of aircraft carriers	
Combination	Nuclear-powered	Conventionally powered
A	4	9
B	5	6
C	6	4
D	7	2

Suppose too that the price of each nuclear-powered aircraft carrier is more than double the price of a conventionally powered aircraft carrier.

a. Can you suggest how the theory of consumer behavior might be applied to this case? How would utility be defined? Who would be the consumer? What determines the consumer's budget line?

b. Given the (hypothetical) data presented above, can you prove that some of the combinations of numbers of aircraft carriers of each type are nonoptimal?

c. Suppose that the people who are closely involved in this decision prefer nuclear-powered carriers because they are large and impressive and more consistent with their idea of what the "warship of the future" should look like. If these people are influenced by such considerations, as well as by the data presented above, is this a violation of the assumptions underlying the theory?

d. In the table above, what would be the meaning of the marginal rate of substitution? To maximize the effectiveness of the navy, what should be the value of the marginal rate of substitution?

Problems and Review Questions

1. The fact that each person consumes many different goods supports the theory of diminishing marginal utility. Explain.

2. A consumer has budgeted a total of $100 to spend on two goods, X and Y. She likes to consume a unit of good X in combination with a unit of good Y. Any unit of good X that she cannot consume in combination with a unit of good Y is useless. Similarly, any unit of good Y that she cannot consume in combination with good X is useless. If the price of a unit of good X is $5 and the price of a unit of good Y is $10, how many units of each good will the consumer purchase?

3. John Jones has 2 fifths of scotch and 2 fifths of gin. His friend Bill Bailey (who, as is well known, sometimes must be beseeched to come home) has 1 fifth of scotch and 2 fifths of gin. The marginal utilities of each good are shown in the table below. For example, to Jones, the marginal utility of the first fifth of scotch is 20 utils, the marginal utility of the second fifth of scotch is 18 utils, the marginal utility of the third fifth of scotch is 15 utils, and so on.

| John Jones | | | | Bill Bailey | | | |
| Scotch | | Gin | | Scotch | | Gin | |
Number of fifths	Marginal utility	Number of fifths	Marginal utility	Number of fifths	Marginal utility	Number of fifths	Marginal utility
1	20	1	30	1	15	1	7
2	18	2	25	2	14	2	5
3	15	3	20	3	13	3	3
4	10	4	15	4	11	4	1

a. Will Jones be better off if he trades a fifth of his scotch for a fifth of Bailey's gin?

b. Suppose that Jones decides to ask for two of Bailey's fifths of gin in exchange for a fifth of his scotch. Would Bailey be better off to accept this deal than none at all?

4. Suppose that, if a family is eligible for food stamps, it pays $100 per month for $200 worth of food. The price of a pound of food is $5; the price of a pound of nonfood items is $3.

a. Draw a family's budget line on a graph where the quantity of food consumed per month is measured along the horizontal axis and the quantity of nonfood items consumed per month is measured along the vertical axis, if the family has a cash income of $300 per month and it is not eligible for food stamps. Use the grid below.

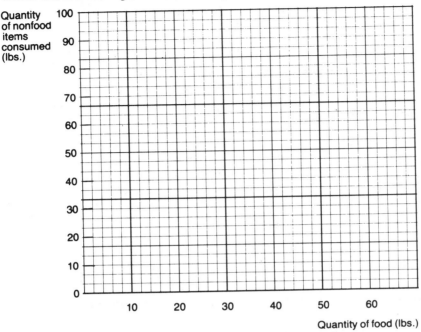

b. Draw (in the grid below) the family's budget line under these conditions if it takes part in the food stamp program described above.

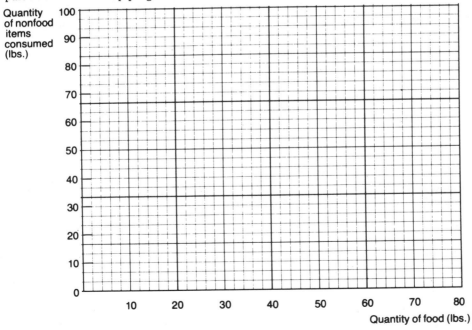

c. Under what circumstances would the family be better off if it were given $100 per month in cash, rather than in food via the above food stamp program?

5. Suppose that James Gray spends his entire income on goods X and Y. The marginal utility of each good (shown below) is independent of the amount consumed of the other good. The price of X is $100 and the price of Y is $500.

	Mr. Gray's Marginal utility (utils)	
Number of units of good consumed	Good X	Good Y
1	20	50
2	18	45
3	16	40
4	13	35
5	10	30
6	6	25
7	4	20
8	2	15

If Mr. Gray has an income of $1,000 per month, how many units of each good should he purchase?

6. In the diagram below, we show one of Ellen White's indifference curves and her budget line.
   a. If the price of good A is $50, what is Ms. White's income?
   b. What is the equation for her budget line?
   c. What is the slope of the budget line?
   d. What is the price of good B?
   e. What is her marginal rate of substitution in equilibrium?

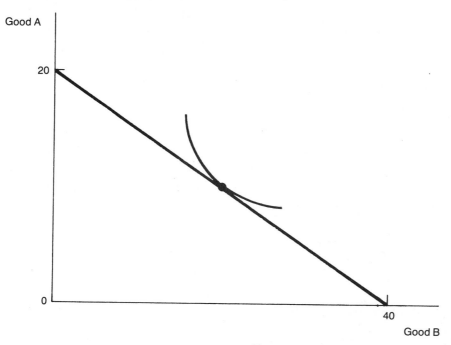

7. Suppose that in 1985 consumers in San Francisco pay twice as much for apples as for pears, whereas consumers in Los Angeles pay 50 percent more for apples than for pears. If consumers in both cities maximize utility, will the marginal rate of substitution of pears for apples be the same in San Francisco as in Los Angeles? If not, in which city will it be higher?

8. According to *Business Week*, American wine producers "are encouraged by the whole changing social role of their product."* Specifically, the American consumer has become much more attuned to wine. How does the growing acceptance of wine by American consumers affect their indifference curves between wine and other kinds of alcoholic beverages?

9. In recent years, great numbers of Americans have traveled to Europe. What effect do you think that this has had on American tastes for wine? How could you test your hypothesis?

10. What are the basic assumptions that economists make about the nature of consumers' tastes?

11. Draw the indifference curve that includes the following market baskets. (Use the grid on the next page.) Each of these market baskets gives the consumer equal satisfaction.

Market basket	Meat (lbs.)	Potatoes (lbs.)
1	2	8
2	3	7
3	4	6
4	5	5
5	6	4
6	7	3
7	8	2
8	9	1

Business Week, February 23, 1974, p. 70.

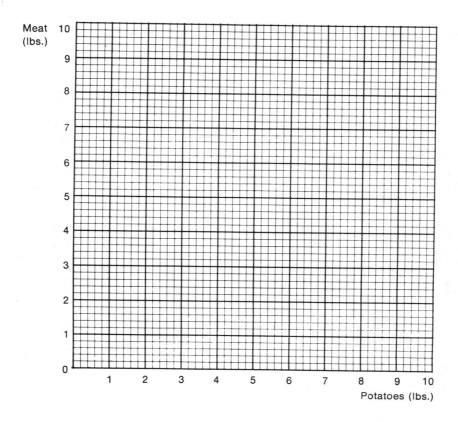

Meat (lbs.) — Potatoes (lbs.)

12. In the previous question, what is the marginal rate of substitution of potatoes for meat? How does the marginal rate of substitution vary as the consumer consumes more meat and less potatoes? Is this realistic?

13. Define utility. How does cardinal utility differ from ordinal utility; which concept is generally used by economists today?

14. Suppose that the consumer has an income of $10 per period and that he or she must spend it all on meat or potatoes. If meat is $1 a pound and potatoes are 10 cents a pound, draw the consumer's budget line.

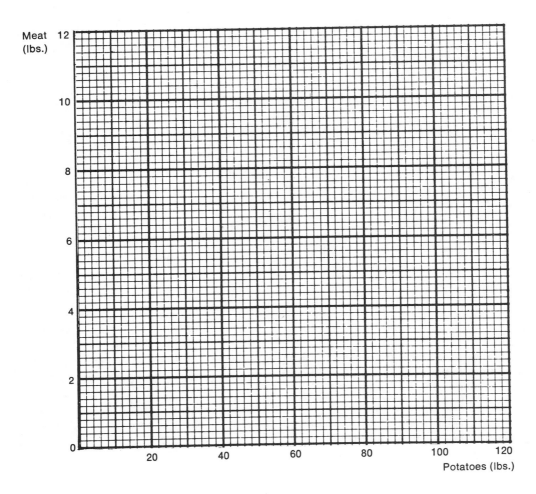

15. In the previous case, what will be the budget line if the consumer's income increases to $12? What will be the budget line if the consumer's income is $10, but the price of meat increases to $2 per lb.? What will be the budget line if the consumer's income is $10, but the price of potatoes increases to 20 cents per lb.?

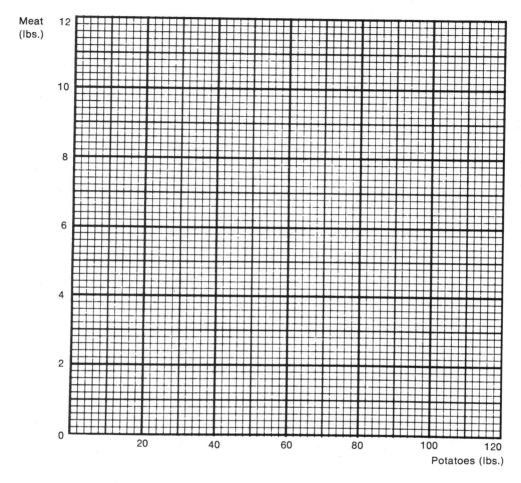

16. What is meant by the theory of revealed preference? Can it be used to measure indifference curves? Is it really a practical measurement technique?

17. What determines consumer tastes and preferences? What is meant by conspicuous consumption?

18. (*Advanced*) Suppose that Mrs. Brown has $50 to be divided between corn and beans and that the price of beans is 50 cents per lb. What will be the relationship between the price of corn and the amount of corn she will buy, if her utility function is $U = \log Q_c + 4 \log Q_b$, where U is her utility, Q_c is the quantity of corn she consumes (in lbs.), and Q_b is the quantity of beans she consumes (in lbs.)?

-33-

Completion Questions

1. If the prices of goods Y and X are both $5 per unit, and if the marginal utility of good X is twice that of good Y, the consumer should buy (less, more) _____ of good X and (less, more) _____ of good Y.

2. All other things equal, the rational consumer is assumed to prefer _____ of a good to _____ of a good.

3. All market baskets possessing the same utility are said to be on the same _____ _____ curve.

4. The negative of the slope of the tangent to an indifference curve is termed the _____ _____ .

5. The rational consumer attempts to _____ his utility subject to a _____ constraint.

6. The condition for consumer equilibrium is that the budget line be _____ _____ an indifference curve (if some of both commodities is consumed).

7. If the rational consumer always prefers more of a good to less, it follows that all indifference curves have a _____ slope.

8. If the marginal rate of substitution of good X for good Y at constant utility decreases with increases in the quantity of X, then the indifference curve is _____ .

9. One of the most important determinants of a consumer's behavior is his or her _____ _____ .

10. The three basic assumptions an economist makes about the nature of consumer tastes are: If the consumer is presented with two market baskets, he or she can decide _____ _____ . If the consumer prefers oranges to bananas and bananas to apples, then he or she _____ . The consumer always prefers _____ of a commodity to _____ of it.

11. Different market baskets on the same indifference curve should be given the _____ values of utility.

12. Market baskets on higher indifference curves should receive _____ utilities than market baskets on lower indifference curves.

True or False

_____ 1. If the total utility from consuming caviar is 5 times the number of ounces of caviar consumed and the total utility from consuming hot dogs is 2 times the number of hot dogs consumed, the consumer should buy caviar, not hot dogs.

_____ 2. A consumer who is rational equates the marginal utility of all goods consumed.

_____ 3. Two indifference curves can intersect only when one of the goods being studied is a high-priced item.

_____ 4. Economists generally assume that indifference curves always lie above their tangents.

_____ 5. Indifference curves are always concave to the origin.

_____ 6. The marginal rate of substitution of good X for good Y is the number of units of good X that a customer will accept instead of good Y to increase his or her satisfaction.

_____ 7. Utility theory assumes that market baskets on higher indifference curves have higher utilities.

_____ 8. Any numbers can be attached to a set of market baskets to represent utility so long as market baskets higher up on the same indifference curve have higher values.

_____ 9. If a consumer's income rises, he or she will probably buy the same amount of a good.

_____ 10. The shape of a consumer's indifference curve is generally assumed to be unaffected by price changes.

_____ 11. A person's tastes are like his or her fingerprints: They don't change.

Multiple Choice

1. David Howe has 8 hours to spend during which he can either play backgammon or read. The marginal utility he obtains from an hour of reading is 8 utils. The total utility he obtains from 1, 2, 3, 4, and 5 hours of backgammon is as follows:

Hours	Total utility
1	20
2	33
3	40
4	40
5	35

If he maximizes utility (and if he can allocate only an integer number of hours to each activity), he will spend
a. 4 hours playing backgammon and 4 hours reading.
b. 3 hours playing backgammon and 5 hours reading.
c. 2 hours playing backgammon and 6 hours reading.
d. 1 hour playing backgammon and 7 hours reading.
e. none of the above.

-35-

2. If point B lies above and to the right of point A on a two-commodity indifference map, and the indifference curve passing through point A is characterized by a utility level of 1, then the utility level of the indifference curve passing through point B has utility:
   a. greater than one.
   b. equal to one.
   c. less than one.
   d. equal to zero.
   e. equal to infinity.

3. Modern microeconomic theory generally regards utility as
   a. cardinal.
   b. ordinal.
   c. independent.
   d. Republican.
   e. Democrat.

4. The consumer is likely to find the market basket that maximizes his or her utility
   a. immediately.
   b. if time is allowed for him or her to adapt and learn.
   c. never.
   d. if he or she has studied economics.
   e. none of the above.

5. The theory of revealed preference is
   a. a practical technique to measure indifference curves.
   b. a useless and discredited version of utility theory.
   c. a means of demonstrating how indifference curves can, in principle, be determined.
   d. none of the above.
   e. all of the above.

6. A basic assumption of the theory of consumer choice is that
   a. the consumer tries to get on the highest indifference curve.
   b. the consumer tries to get the most of good Y.
   c. the budget line is concave.
   d. none of the above.
   e. all of the above.

Key Concepts for Review

Indifference curves	Equilibrium
Marginal rate of substitution	Indifference map
Convexity	Market basket
Utility	Revealed preference
Cardinal utility	Conspicuous consumption
Ordinal utility	Determinants of tastes
Marginal utility	Rationality
Budget line	Advertising and selling expenses
Money income	

Answers

Case Study: Nuclear-Powered vs. Conventionally Powered Aircraft Carriers

a. The various combinations can be viewed as points on an indifference curve, as shown below:

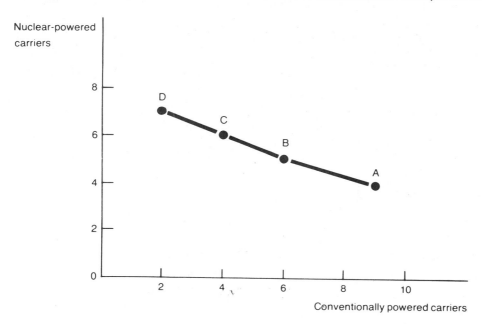

Utility would be defined as effectiveness of the navy. The consumer would be the navy (or the Defense Department or the American people). The budget line would be determined by the total amount of money allocated for aircraft carriers (of either type) and the relative price of each type of aircraft carrier.

b. If the price of a nuclear-powered aircraft carrier is more than double the price of a conventionally powered aircraft carrier, the budget line must have a slope that is between −1/2 and zero. Such a budget line could be tangent to the indifference curve shown above at points *B* or *A*, but not at points *C* or *D*. Thus, combinations *C* or *D* seem to be poorer than combinations *B* or *A*. Another way of proving this is to note that, when we move from combination *B* to combination *C* or *D*, we must increase cost (since a nuclear-powered aircraft carrier is assumed to cost more than twice as much as a conventionally powered aircraft carrier), but the effectiveness is the same.

c. No, but the indifference curves representing these people's tastes (not the indifference curves representing navy effectiveness) may be the relevant ones in shaping the decision.

d. The marginal rate of substitution is the number of aircraft carriers of one type that can be substituted for one aircraft carrier of the other type with navy effectiveness (or some other measure of utility) held constant. It should be set equal to the ratio of the prices of the two types of aircraft carriers.

Problems and Review Questions

1. If a consumer received increasing marginal utility from a good, he or she might spend all of his or her income on this good.

2. The consumer's budget line is as shown below, since she has $100 to spend, and the price of a unit of good X is $5 and the price of a unit of good Y is $10. Clearly, she can buy 20 units of good X if she buys only good X, or 10 units of good Y if she buys only good Y, or any combination of quantities of good X and good Y on this line. If she is rational, she will choose the point on this budget line that is on her highest indifference curve. Two of her indifference curves (1 and 2) are shown in the graph below. Since any unit of good X that she

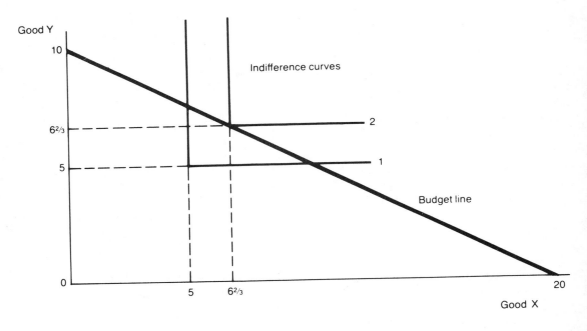

cannot consume in combination with a unit of good Y is useless and since any unit of good Y that she cannot consume in combination with a unit of good X is useless, her indifference curves have the shape shown above. (For example, indifference curve 1 shows that, if she purchases 5 units of good X and more than 5 units of good Y, her satisfaction is the same as if she purchases 5 units of each. Similarly, this indifference curve shows that, if she purchases 5 units of good Y and more than 5 units of good X, her satisfaction is the same as if she purchases 5 units of each.) Given the shape of her indifference curves, it is obvious from the graph that she will achieve her highest indifference curve if she purchases $6\frac{2}{3}$ units of each good.

3. *a.* Since the marginal utility of the second fifth of scotch to Jones is 18 utils and the marginal utility of a third fifth of gin to him is 20 utils, the change in his total utility if he trades a fifth of scotch for a fifth of gin is $20 - 18$, or 2 utils. Thus, Jones would be better off if he makes this trade.

b. If Bailey gives up two fifths of gin, his total utility will decrease by 7 + 5, or 12 utils (since the marginal utility of the first fifth of gin is 7 utils, and the marginal utility of the second fifth of gin is 5 utils). If he gains one fifth of scotch, his total utility will increase by 14 utils (since this is the marginal utility to him of a second fifth of scotch). Thus, the exchange of two fifths of gin for one fifth of scotch will change his total utility by 14 – 12, or 2 utils. Thus, Bailey would be better off to accept this deal than none at all.

4. *a.*

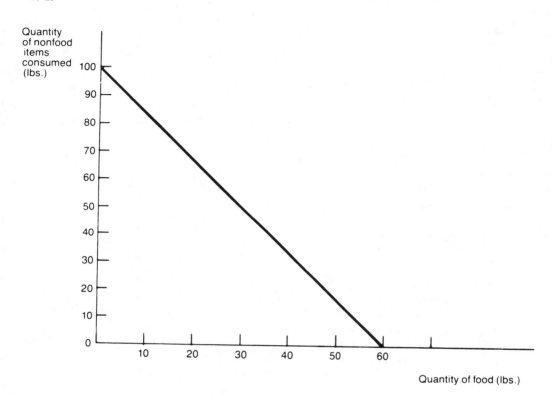

b.

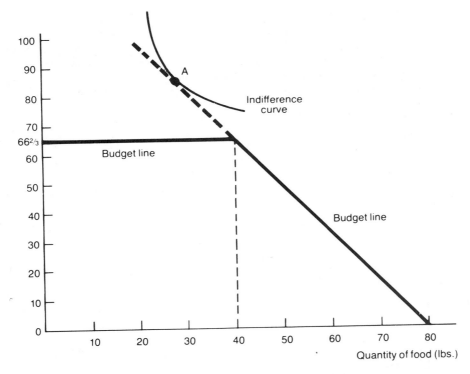

c. The family would be better off with $100 in cash if its indifference curves were such that it could reach its highest indifference curve by choosing point *A* in part (b) above. Point *A* would be on the family's budget line if it received $100 in cash; it is not on the family's budget line under the food stamp program.

5. He should set the ratio of the marginal utility of good X to its price equal to the ratio of the marginal utility of good Y to its price. If he buys 5 units of good X and 1 unit of good Y, the total amount spent is $1,000, and this condition is met, since for each good this ratio equals 1 util ÷ $10.

6. *a.* $1,000, since the budget line intersects the vertical axis at 20.

   b. $Q_A = 20 - 0.5 Q_B$, where Q_A is the quantity consumed of good A and Q_B is the quantity consumed of good B.

   c. −0.5.

   d. It must be $1,000 ÷ 40, or $25.

   e. 0.5.

7. No.
   Los Angeles, because the price of a pear divided by the price of an apple is higher in Los Angeles.

8. Consumers value wine more highly. They may be willing to exchange more of other types of alcoholic beverages for a pint of wine.

9. By coming into contact with wine in France, Italy, and other European countries, American travelers have become exposed to wine, and many have found that they liked it. Possibly one could test this hypothesis by analyzing the buying habits of people before and after trips abroad to determine if there were any evidence of a change in tastes.

10. First, we assume that the consumer can decide whether he or she prefers one market basket to another or whether he or she is indifferent between them.

Second, we assume that the consumer's preferences are transitive.

Third, we assume that the consumer always prefers more of a good to less.

Fourth, we assume that, by adding a certain amount of one of the goods to the market basket that is not preferred, we can make it equally desirable in the eyes of the consumer.

11. The indifference curve is drawn below:

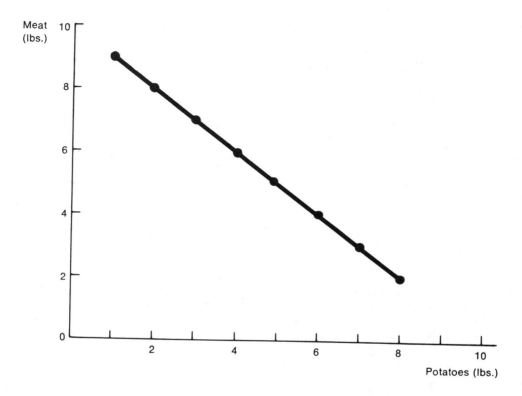

12. 1.

It does not vary at all, at least in tnis range.

No.

13. Utility is a number that indicates the level of enjoyment or preference attached to a market basket.

In the case of ordinal utility, no particular meaning or significance attaches to the scale which is used to measure utility or to the size of the difference between the utilities attached to two market baskets. In the case of cardinal utility, it is assumed that utility is measurable in the same sense as a man's height or weight is measurable.

Ordinal utility.

14. The consumer's budget line is drawn below:

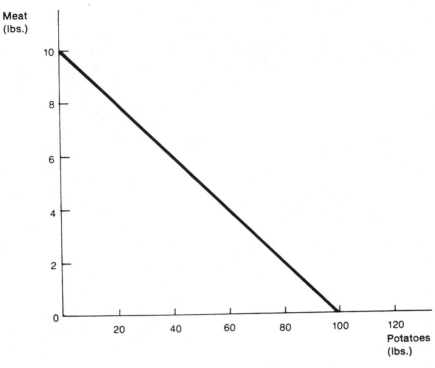

15. Under the first set of circumstances, the budget line is *A*. Under the second set of circumstances, it is *B*. And under the third set of circumstances, it is *C*.

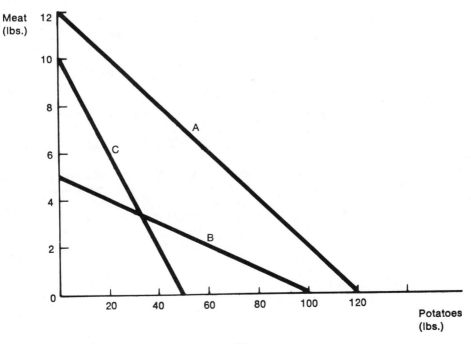

16. The theory of revealed preference deduces a consumer's preferences by looking at what he or she actually chooses under particular sets of circumstances.

    Yes, in principle.

    No.

17. A consumer's tastes depend on his or her age, education, experience, and observation of others, as well as on advertising and other selling expenses, and sometimes on price.

    Conspicuous consumption refers to cases where goods are consumed because they are expensive and quality is judged by price.

18. If P_b is the price of beans and P_c is the price of corn, $P_b Q_b + P_c Q_c = 50$. Since $P_b = 0.50$, $0.5 Q_b = 50 - Q_c P_c$. Also $\partial U/\partial Q_b \div P_b = \partial U/\partial Q_c \div P_c$, which means that $\dfrac{4}{Q_b} \div 0.5 = \dfrac{1}{Q_c} \div P_c$. Thus, $\dfrac{8}{Q_b} = \dfrac{1}{Q_c P_c}$, or $Q_c P_c = Q_b/8$. Since $Q_b = 100 - 2 Q_c P_c$, $8 Q_c P_c = 100 - 2 Q_c P_c$, or $Q_c P_c = 10$. Thus the relationship is $Q_c = 10/P_c$.

Completion Questions

1. more, less
2. more; less
3. indifference
4. marginal rate of substitution
5. maximize; budget
6. tangent to
7. negative
8. convex
9. tastes [or his or her income]
10. which he or she prefers; prefers oranges to apples; more; less
11. same
12. higher

True or False

1. False 2. False 3. False 4. True 5. False 6. False 7. True 8. False 9. False
10. True 11. False

Multiple Choice

1. *c* 2. *a* 3. *b* 4. *b* 5. *c* 6. *a*

CHAPTER 4   Consumer Behavior and Individual Demand

Case Study: The Benefits from a New Highway

A state is considering building a new highway. John Marshall lives and works near the site of the new highway. He makes a number of trips each month between towns A and B. If the new highway were built, it would reduce the cost of each such trip from 30 cents to 20 cents. The graph below shows Mr. Marshall's individual demand curve for trips between towns A and B.

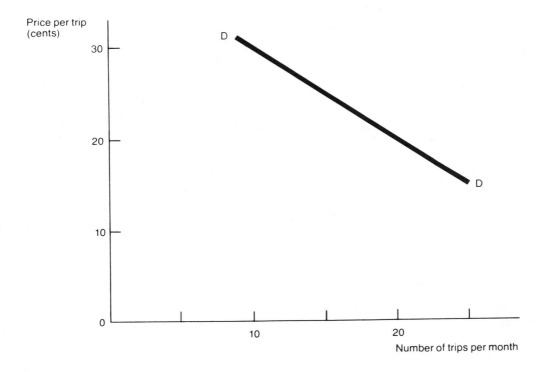

As indicated, Mr. Marshall would make 10 trips per month when the price of a trip is 30 cents.

A state legislator asks Mr. Marshall whether he favors the construction of the new highway. Mr. Marshall replies that it would save him $1 per month, since he makes 10 trips per month between towns A and B, and the saving per trip is 30 cents minus 20 cents, or 10 cents. Thus, he says that the most that he would be willing to pay is $1 per month in taxes to support the new highway. If he is not asked to pay more than this amount, he favors the construction of the new highway. Otherwise he opposes it.

Do you agree with Mr. Marshall's reasoning? If not, what changes would you make in his argument?

Problems and Review Questions

1. A Laspeyres price index tends to exaggerate increases in the cost of living because it does not take into account the possibility that the consumer will tend to shift from goods that become increasingly expensive to goods that remain relatively cheap. Do you agree? Why or why not?

2. Mildred Martin has an income of $1,000 per month, which she spends entirely on goods A and B. The graph below shows her equilibrium positions when the price of good B is $20 and $50.

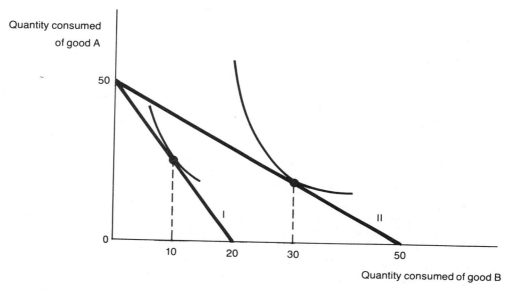

   a. Give the coordinates of two points on her demand curve for good B.
   b. Will these two points be on this demand curve, regardless of the price of good A? If not, what price of good A is assumed here?

3. A consumer's utility function is:

$$U = 20xy$$

   where U is the consumer's utility (in utils), x is the amount of good X consumed per month, and y is the amount of good Y consumed per month.
   a. If the consumer is consuming 5 units of good Y per month, what is the marginal utility of good X?
   b. Can you answer question (a) without knowing how many units of good X the consumer is consuming?
   c. Is this utility function realistic? What "law" does it violate?

4. Suppose that a government agency must allocate its entire budget of $2 billion only to roads or to mass transit or to a combination of both. Suppose that each mile of mass transit costs $10 million and each mile of road costs $5 million. The government agency's indifference curves (I_1, I_2, I_3) are as follows:

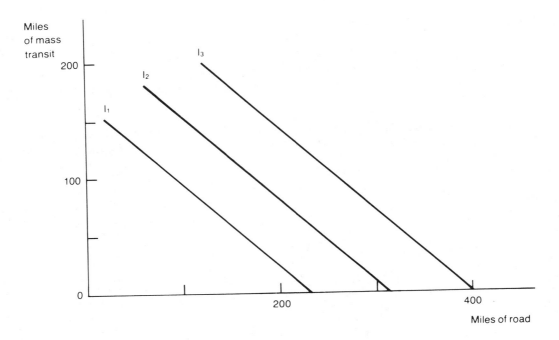

Miles of mass transit (y-axis), Miles of road (x-axis)

a. What is the optimal number of miles of road that this agency should fund?
b. What is the optimal number of miles of mass transit that this agency should fund?
c. In this case, is the optimal "market basket" at a point where the budget line is tangent to an indifference curve? If not, why not?

5. Suppose that all consumers pay 10 cents for a telephone call and 15 cents for a newspaper (and that all consumers purchase some of both goods).
   a. If all consumers are maximizing utility, is it possible to determine each consumer's marginal rate of substitution of telephone calls for newspapers?
   b. Suppose that a local economist applies for a grant to estimate this marginal rate of substitution, his or her proposed procedure being to ask a sample of consumers. Can you suggest a simpler procedure?
   c. Based on these facts alone, can you estimate this marginal rate of substitution? If so, what is it?

6. According to some observers, typical Irish peasants in the nineteenth century were so poor they spent almost all their income for potatoes. When the price of potatoes fell, they could get the same amount of nutrition for a smaller expenditure on potatoes, so some of their income was diverted to vegetables and meat. Since the latter also provided calories, they could even reduce their consumption of potatoes under these circumstances. If this is true, were potatoes
   a. a normal good?
   b. an inferior good?
   c. a good exhibiting Giffen's paradox?

7. Calculate the Laspeyres and Paasche indexes for a family that consumes the following amounts of bread and clothing (and no other goods) in 1980 and 1985.

	1980	1985
Amount consumed of bread (pounds per month)	100	140
Amount consumed of clothing (units per month)	120	130
Price of bread (per pound)	30 cents	50 cents
Price of clothing (per unit)	30 dollars	40 dollars

8. According to Karl Fox, "An increase of 10 percent in the farm price of the 'average' food product would be associated with something like a 4 percent increase in the retail price and perhaps a 2 percent decrease in per capita consumption."* Is the price elasticity of demand different at the farm level than at the retail level? Why?

9. James B. Hendry has pointed out, in connection with the demand for fuel, that "Fuel-burning equipment tends to be specialized and costly, and changeovers are generally not made frequently." † What are the implications of this fact for a household's demand for fuel?

10. Show why, if the consumer is to be in equilibrium, the marginal rate of substitution of good X for good Y must equal the ratio of the price of good X to the price of good Y.

11. Suppose the following relationship exists between a consumer's income and the amount of eggs he or she consumes.

Income ($ per week)	Eggs (no. per week)
100	12
150	24
200	36
250	42
300	48

Graph the consumer's Engel curve for eggs below:

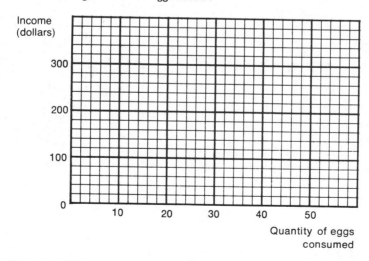

*K. Fox, "Commercial Agriculture," Committee for Economic Development, November 1962, p. 66.

†J. B. Hendry, "The Bituminous Coal Industry," in W. Adams, *The Structure of American Industry* (New York: Macmillan, 1961), p. 98.

12. Describe the factors that will influence the shape of a consumer's Engel curve for a particular good.

13. Describe what is meant by a price-consumption curve. How can it be used to help determine the individual demand curve?

14. In the case of John Jones, the relationship between the price of eggs and the amount that he will purchase is shown below:

Price of eggs (cents per dozen)	Quantity of eggs consumed per week
50	15
60	14
70	13
80	12
90	11
100	10

Plot John Jones's individual demand curve for eggs in the graph below:

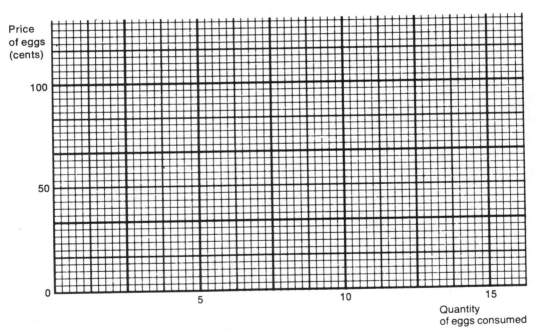

15. Suppose that a 1 percent increase in the price of pork chops results in Mrs. Smith's buying 3 percent fewer pork chops per week. What is the price elasticity of demand for pork chops on the part of Mrs. Smith? Is her demand for pork chops price elastic or price inelastic? Will an increase in the price of pork chops result in an increase, or a decrease, in the total amount of money that she spends on pork chops?

16. Explain what is meant by the "substitution effect" and the "income effect." Can the substitution effect be positive? Can the income effect be positive?

17. **Explain the difference between normal and inferior goods. What is Giffen's paradox?**

18. **Explain the meaning of consumer's surplus.**

19. *a.* Suppose Mrs. Smith's utility function can be described by $U = Q_c Q_p$, where U is her utility, Q_c is the amount of corn she consumes, and Q_p is the amount of potatoes she consumes. Draw her indifference curve when $U = 10$.

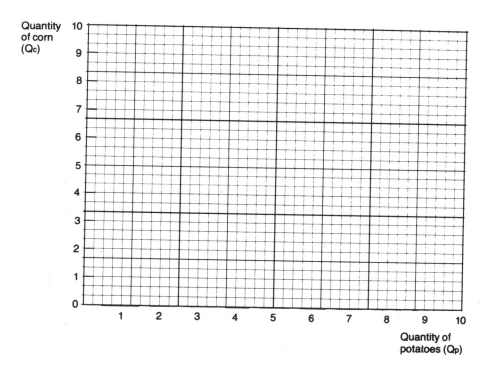

b. Suppose that the total amount of money she can spend on these two commodities is $100 and the price of corn is $1 per lb. How many potatoes will she buy if potatoes are 50 cents per lb.?

c. How much corn will she buy under these circumstances?

20. (*Advanced*) Derive a formula for Mrs. Smith's demand curve for potatoes. Let the price of potatoes be P_p and the price of corn be P_c. Let the total amount she spends on these two commodities be I. And assume that her utility function is $U = Q_c Q_p$.

21. What is the difference between a Laspeyres index and a Paasche index? How is each index useful?

22. The federal government is interested in purchasing two types of antipollution equipment. After extensive tests, government officials are convinced that two units of type A equipment are as effective as one unit of type B equipment. Assuming that the officials want to reduce pollution, draw their indifference curves for the two types of equipment.

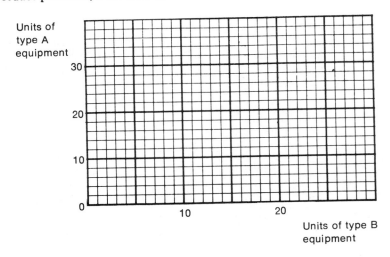

Units of type A equipment

Units of type B equipment

23. Assuming that the government has $20 million to spend on either type A equipment, type B equipment, or a combination of both, draw the relevant budget line, and indicate the optimal choice of type of equipment if a unit of type A equipment costs $1 million and a unit of type B equipment costs $4 million.

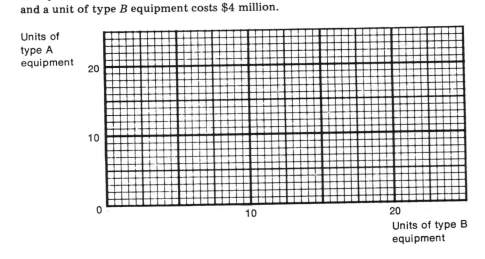

Units of type A equipment

Units of type B equipment

Completion Questions

1. If the income effect of a price change is zero, but the substitution effect is nonzero, the quantity demanded of the good must be (directly, inversely, neither directly nor inversely) _____ related to the good's price.

2. The substitution effect is always _____.

3. Cost-of-living indexes have often been closely associated with _____.

4. An Engel curve is the relationship between the _____ and _____
_____.

5. The demand for a commodity is said to be price _____ if the elasticity of demand exceeds one.

6. The demand for a commodity is said to be price _____ if the elasticity of demand is less than one.

7. The demand for a commodity is said to be of _____ if the price elasticity of demand is equal to one.

8. The total effect of a change in price is the sum of the _____ effect and the _____ effect.

9. If the consumer is in equilibrium and if the price of good X is \$2 and the price of good Y is \$1, then the marginal rate of substitution of good X for good Y must equal _____.

10. If increases in real income (with no price changes) result in increases in the consumption of a good, this good is a _____ good.

11. If you can buy a good for \$5 but you would be willing to pay as much as \$50, the consumer's surplus is \$_____.

True or False

_____ 1. If John Jones's demand curve for water is $P = 4 - Q$, where P is the price of water (in cents per gallon) and Q is the number of gallons of water demanded per day, the maximum amount that he will pay for a fourth gallon of water per day is 2 cents.

_____ 2. If a good is a Giffen good, it must be inferior.

_____ 3. The income-consumption curve is of no use in determining the Engel curve.

_____ 4. The price-consumption curve is of use in determining the individual demand curve.

_____ 5. A consumer's demand curve for a commodity generally will shift if his or her income changes.

_____ 6. A consumer's demand curve for a commodity generally will shift if the prices of other commodities change.

_____ 7. A consumer's demand curve for a commodity generally will shift if the consumer's tastes change a great deal.

_____ 8. The price elasticity of demand is measured by the slope of the demand curve.

_____ 9. If a good is price elastic, a decrease in its price will result in a decrease in the amount of money spent on it.

_____ 10. If a good is price elastic, an increase in its price will result in a decrease in the amount of money spent on it.

_____ 11. If the demand for a good is of unitary elasticity, the same amount of money is spent on it regardless of its price.

_____ 12. Giffen's paradox is a frequent occurrence.

_____ 13. Consumer's surplus can never be positive.

_____ 14. The Paasche index is a better measure of the income effect than the Laspeyres index.

Multiple Choice

1. If the price-consumption curve for a commodity is horizontal,
   a. the demand curve for the commodity is downward sloping to the right.
   b. the price elasticity of demand for the commodity is one.
   c. the amount spent on the commodity is the same, regardless of its price.
   d. all of the above.
   e. none of the above.

2. The substitution effect must always be
   a. positive.
   b. negative.
   c. zero.
   d. bigger than the income effect.
   e. none of the above.

3. The income effect
   a. must always be negative.
   b. must always be positive.
   c. can be positive or negative.
   d. must be smaller than the substitution effect.
   e. none of the above.

4. Normal goods experience an increase in consumption when
   a. real income increases.
   b. real income falls.
   c. price rises.
   d. tastes change.
   e. none of the above.

5. The Laspeyres index
   a. measures the change in the cost of the market basket purchased in the original year.
   b. measures the change in the cost of the market basket purchased in the later year.
   c. always exceeds 1.
   d. always is less than 1.
   e. none of the above.

6. The Paasche index   G NP – Deflator

   a. measures the change in the cost of the market basket purchased in the original year.

   b. measures the change in the cost of the market basket purchased in the later year.

   c. always exceeds 1.

   d. always is less than 1.

   e. none of the above.

Key Concepts for Review

Engel curves	Price elasticity of demand
Income-consumption curves	Substitution effect
Price-consumption curves	Income effect
Individual demand curves	Normal goods
Inferior goods	Laspeyres index
Real income	Paasche index
Giffen's paradox	Index numbers
Consumer's surplus	Unitary elasticity
Cost of living	

Answers

Case Study: The Benefits from a New Highway

Mr. Marshall's reasoning is fallacious because he takes no account of the effect on the number of trips he makes of the reduction in the cost of a trip. If the cost of a trip is 30 cents, he makes

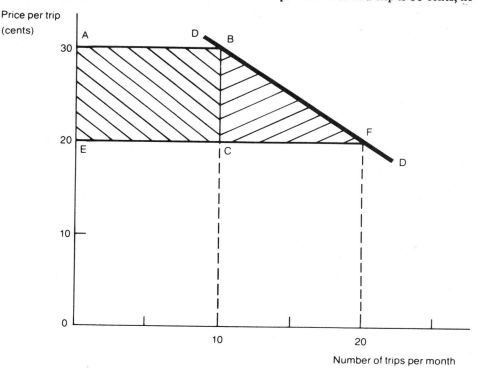

10 trips per month. The new highway reduces the cost of these trips; the saving being the area *ABCE*, which equals $1.00. In addition, however, Mr. Marshall will make 10 extra trips per month if the cost is 20 cents, and the consumer's surplus from these trips is equal to the area *BCF*. In other words, he would be willing to pay an amount equal to the area *BCF* (in addition to the amount he does pay) for the extra 10 trips. The total benefit to Mr. Marshall is the sum of the two shaded areas in the diagram above (that is, it equals *ABFE*), not *ABCE* alone. Thus, Mr. Marshall is underestimating the benefit to him from the new highway. Since the area *BCF* equals $(1/2)(10)(10)$ cents, or 50 cents, the total area *ABFE* equals $1.50. This, not $1.00, is the maximum amount he should be willing to pay per month for the new highway.

Problems and Review Questions

1. Yes. The market basket in the earlier period is specified, and its cost in the later period is compared with its cost in the earlier period.

2. *a.* When the price of good *B* is $50, the budget line is line I (since it cuts the horizontal axis at 20, which is the maximum number of units of good *B* that the consumer can buy if this is the price). If this is the budget line, she attains her highest indifference curve when she purchases 10 units of good *B*. Thus, the quantity of good *B* she consumes when its price is $50 is 10 units, which defines one point on her demand curve. When the price of good *B* is $20, the budget line is line II (since it cuts the horizontal axis at 50, the maximum number of units of good *B* that she can buy if this is the price). If this is the budget line, she attains her highest indifference curve when she purchases 30 units of good *B*. Thus, the quantity of good *B* she consumes when its price is $20 is 30 units, which defines a second point on her demand curve.

   b. Any demand curve is based on the assumption that the prices of other goods are held constant. In this case, the price of good *A* is held constant at $20 per unit. To prove that this is the case, note that each budget line intersects the vertical axis at 50 units, which means that, if she devotes her entire income to good *A*, she can purchase 50 units. Since her income is specified to be $1,000, this means that the price of good *A* must be taken as $20 per unit.

3. *a.* If $y = 5$, $U = (20)(5)x = 100x$. Since a 1-unit increase in x will increase U by 100 utils, the marginal utility of good *X* is 100 utils.

   b. Yes, because marginal utility does not depend on x in this case.

   c. No. It violates the law of diminishing marginal utility.

4.

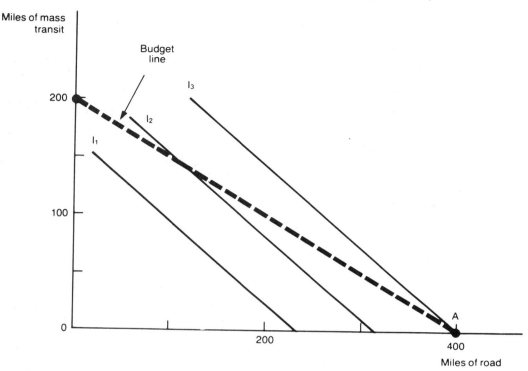

a. The budget line is the broken line in the diagram above. Since the maximum number of miles of mass transit that can be installed is $2 billion ÷ $10 million, or 200 miles, this line intersects the vertical axis at 200. Since the maximum number of miles of road that can be installed is $2 billion ÷ $5 million, or 400 miles, this line intersects the horizontal axis at 400. The point on this budget line that is on the highest indifference curve is point A, where 400 miles of road and no miles of mass transit are installed.

b. None.

c. No, because the indifference curves never have the same slope as the budget line. This is an example of a "corner" solution. More is said about such solutions in the appendix on linear programming.

5. a. Yes.

b. If all consumers are maximizing utility (and if the optimal point is a tangency point, not a corner solution), the marginal rate of substitution of telephone calls for newspapers must equal the price of a telephone call divided by the price of a newspaper.

c. Yes, it equals 10 ÷ 15, or 2/3.

6. Both part (b) and part (c) are true.

7. The Laspeyres index equals:

$$L = \frac{100 \times \$0.50 + 120 \times \$40}{100 \times \$0.30 + 120 \times \$30} = \frac{\$4,850}{\$3,630} = 1.34$$

The Paasche index equals:

$$P = \frac{140 \times \$0.50 + 130 \times \$40}{140 \times \$0.30 + 130 \times \$30} = \frac{\$5,270}{\$3,942} = 1.34$$

Thus, in this case, the results are the same.

8. Yes.
   Because the farm price and the retail price do not vary proportionately.
9. The price elasticity of demand for a particular fuel (like oil or natural gas) is probably greater in the long run than in the short run.
10. The marginal rate of substitution is the rate at which the consumer is *willing* to substitute good X for good Y, holding his total level of satisfaction constant. Thus, if the marginal rate of substitution is three, the consumer is willing to give up three units of good Y in order to get one more unit of good X.
    The ratio of the price of good X to the price of good Y is the rate at which the consumer is *able* to substitute good X for good Y. Thus, if $P_x \div P_y$ is two, he must give up two units of good Y to get one more unit of good X.
    If the consumer is in equilibrium, the rate at which the consumer is willing to substitute good X for good Y (holding satisfaction constant) must equal the rate at which he is able to substitute good X for good Y. Otherwise it is always possible to find another market basket that will increase the consumer's satisfaction.
11. The Engel curve is as follows:

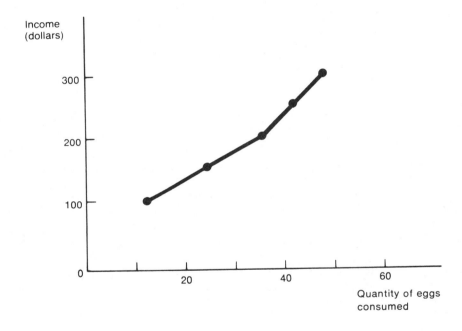

12. The shape of a consumer's Engel curve for a particular good will depend on the nature of the good, the nature of the consumer's tastes, and the level at which prices are held constant. For example, Engel curves for salt or shoelaces would generally show that the consumption of these commodities does not increase very much in response to increases in income. But goods like caviar or filet mignon might be expected to have Engel curves showing that their consumption is much more sensitive to changes in income.

13. A price-consumption curve connects the various points at which the budget line is tangent to a consumer's indifference curves, given the level of his income and the price of good Y. (Only the price of good X varies.) Reading off the amount consumed of good X at each price of good X, one can get from the price-consumption curve the basic data needed to formulate the individual demand curve.

14. The demand curve is as follows:

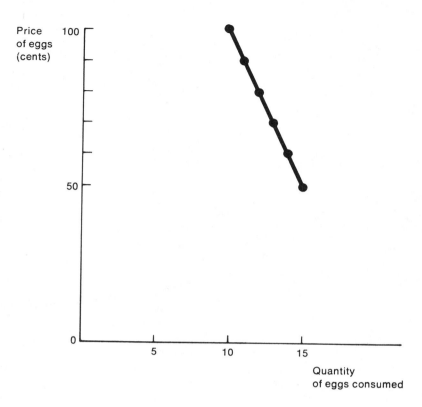

15. Three.
Price elastic.
Decrease.
16. The substitution effect is the change in quantity demanded of a good resulting from a change in its price, when the level of satisfaction, or real income, is held constant.
   The income effect is the change in quantity demanded of a good due entirely to a change in real income, all prices being held constant.
   No, the substitution effect cannot be positive.
   Yes, the income effect can be positive.
17. Normal goods are goods where increases (decreases) in real income result in increases (decreases) in consumption of the good. Inferior goods are goods where the opposite is true.
   Giffen's paradox occurs when an inferior good's income effect is powerful enough to offset the substitution effect, the result being that quantity demanded is positively related to price, at least over some range of variation of price.
18. Consumer's surplus is the difference between the maximum amount that a consumer would pay and the amount that he or she actually pays.

19. *a.* This indifference curve is:

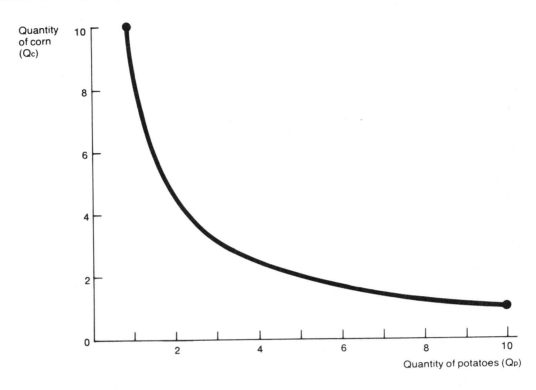

Quantity of corn (Qc) — vertical axis; Quantity of potatoes (Qp) — horizontal axis

b. The budget line is $Q_c + 0.5\,Q_p = 100$. This line is tangent to an indifference curve when $Q_p = 100$.

c. The budget line in part *b* is tangent to an indifference curve when $Q_c = 50$ (and $Q_p = 100$).

20. Since $\partial U/\partial Q_c = Q_p$ and $\partial U/\partial Q_p = Q_c$, $Q_p \div P_c = Q_c \div P_p$. Moreover, $P_c Q_c + P_p Q_p = I$. Thus $2 P_p Q_p = I$, and the demand curve is

$$P_p = I \div 2\,Q_p.$$

21. The Laspeyres index measures the change in cost of the market basket purchased by the consumer in the *original* year. The Paasche index measures the change in cost of the market basket purchased by the consumer in the *later* year.

We can be sure that the consumer's welfare has increased if the ratio of his later money income to his earlier money income is greater than the Laspeyres price index. And we can be sure that his welfare has decreased if the ratio of his later money income to his earlier money income is less than the Paasche price index.

22. The indifference curves are as follows:

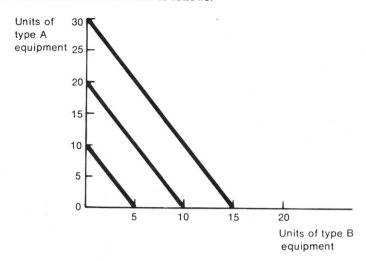

23. The budget line is the broken line.
    Given the indifference map of solid lines, the optimal point is A, where 20 units of type *A* equipment are purchased.

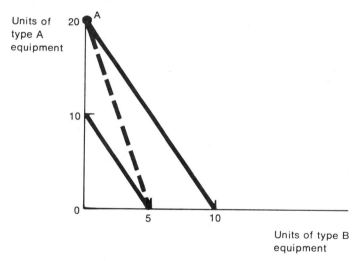

Completion Questions

1. inversely
2. negative
3. inflation
4. consumer's income; the amount of a good that he or she demands
5. elastic
6. inelastic
7. unitary elasticity

8. substitution; income
9. two
10. normal
11. $45

True or False

1. False   2. True   3. False   4. True   5. True   6. True   7. True   8. False   9. False
10. True   11. True   12. False   13. False   14. False

Multiple Choice
1. *d*   2. *b*   3. *c*   4. *a*   5. *a*   6. *b*

CHAPTER 5 Market Demand

Case Study: The Demand for Oranges

The Economic Research Service of the U.S. Department of Agriculture has reported the results of a study of the effects of the price of various types of oranges on the rate at which they were purchased.* In particular, three types of oranges were studied: (1) Florida Indian River, (2) Florida Interior, and (3) California. In nine test stores in Grand Rapids, Michigan, the researchers varied the price of each of these types of oranges for a month. The effect of a 1 percent increase in the price of each type of orange on the rate of purchase of this and each of the other types of oranges is shown in Table 1. For example, a 1 percent increase in the price of Florida Indian River oranges (holding other prices constant) seemed to result in a 3.1 percent

Table 1: Results of study

A 1 percent increase in the price of:	Results in the following percentage change in the rate of purchase of:		
	Florida Indian River	Florida Interior	California
Florida Indian River	-3.1	+1.6	+0.01
Florida Interior	+1.2	-3.0	+0.1
California	+0.2	+0.1	-2.8

decrease in the rate of purchase of Florida Indian River oranges, a 1.6 percent increase in the rate of purchase of Florida Interior oranges, and a 0.01 increase in the rate of purchase of California oranges.

a. What seems to be the price elasticity of demand for each type of orange?
b. What seems to be the cross elasticity of demand for each pair of types of oranges?
c. Which types of oranges seem to be the closest substitutes?
d. Of what use might these results be to orange producers?
e. How accurate do you think that this study was? What improvements would you make in it?

Problems and Review Questions

1. *a.* According to J. Fred Bucy, president of Texas Instruments, his firm continually makes detailed studies of the price elasticity of demand for each of its major products in order to determine how much its sales will increase if it changes its price by a particular

---

*M. Godwin, W. Chapman, and W. Manley, *Competition Between Florida and California Valencia Oranges in the Fresh Market*, Department of Agriculture, December 1965. This paper is also summarized in G. Stokes, *Managerial Economics: A Casebook*, New York: Random House, 1969. I have changed the numbers slightly.

amount.* For example, Texas Instruments has to estimate the effect of a 10 percent reduction in the price of the TI-55, a hand calculator that Texas Instruments produces, and whether such a price reduction would increase sales by a large enough amount to be profitable. What sorts of techniques does Texas Instruments use to make such estimates?

b. In the electronics industry, prices for many products have tended to drop dramatically. During the 1970s, simple four-function hand calculators declined in price from about $150 to less than $10. Other products that experienced similar price reductions were transistor radios and digital watches. Do the costs of producing such products tend to fall as larger and larger quantities of them are produced?

c. In 1982, Texas Instruments cut the price of its 99/4A home computer from $299 to $199, and its rivals followed suit. If the price elasticity of demand was greater than one, did the price cut increase the amount spent on such computers?

2. The price elasticity of good Y is 2, and marginal revenue for good Y is $2. What is the price of good Y?

3. (*Advanced*) The demand curve for screwdrivers shifts from D_1 in 1985 to D_2 in 1986. Use calculus to prove that the price elasticity of demand at any price less than $10 will be the same as it was before the shift in the demand curve.

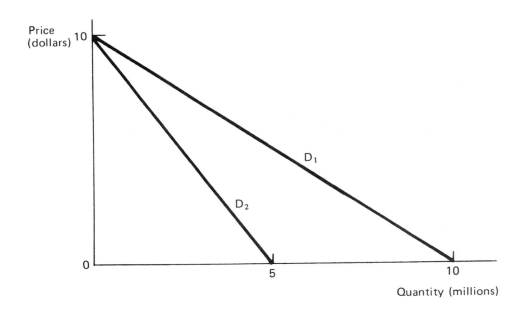

*See his paper in J. Backman and J. Czepiel, eds., *Changing Marketing Strategies in a New Economy* (Indianapolis: Bobbs Merrill, 1977). Also see "How Texas Instruments Shot Itself in the Foot," *Business Week* (June 27, 1983).

4. A colleague of yours claims that the price elasticity of demand is the same as the slope of the demand curve. You (quite correctly) argue that this is not true. To buttress your point, you draw a linear demand curve (from B to A on the grid below) and point out that, although the slope is the same at all points along the demand curve, the price elasticity of demand differs from point to point. (Thus, the slope and the price elasticity of demand cannot be the same.) Your colleague asks you to identify those points (on the demand curve you have drawn) where the demand for the product is price elastic, those points where it is price inelastic, and those points where it is of unitary elasticity. Respond to his request.

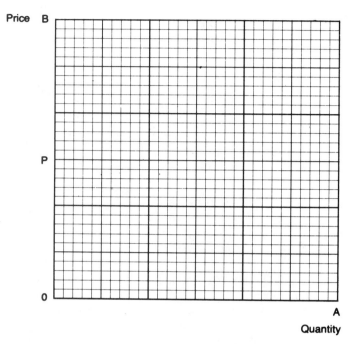

5. The XYZ Manufacturing Company believes that the demand curve for its product is

$$P = 5 - Q$$

where P is the price of its product (in dollars) and Q is the number of millions of units of its product sold per day. It is currently charging a price of $1 per unit for its product.

a. The president of the firm asks you to comment on the wisdom of its pricing policy. Write a short paragraph on this score.

b. A marketing specialist says that the price elasticity of demand for the firm's product is 1.0. Do you agree? Why or why not?

6. There are 15 people comprising the market for good X. The quantity of good X that each person demands at each price is shown below:

Price of good X (dollars per lb.)

Person	1	2	3	4	5
	pounds of good X per year				
Allen	20	18	16	14	12
Bach	15	13	11	9	7
Creamer	100	90	80	70	60
Dow	30	28	26	24	22
Easton	10	9	8	7	6
Farnsworth	5	4	3	2	1
Grettle	60	58	56	54	52
Howe	6	6	6	6	6
Irwin	18	17	14	10	6
Jarvis	12	11	10	9	8
Koch	13	13	12	12	12
Leaton	11	10	10	9	9
Martin	5	4	3	3	3
Nash	90	80	70	65	60
Otter	12	11	11	10	10

   a. Calculate the market demand curve for good X.
   b. What is the price elasticity of demand when:
      (1) the price is between $1 and $2 per pound.
      (2) the price is between $3 and $4 per pound.

7. Suppose that Jeremy Jarvis considers Geritol of supreme importance and that he spends all of his income on Geritol.
   a. To this consumer, what is the price elasticity of demand for Geritol?
   b. What is the income elasticity of demand for Geritol?
   c. What is the cross elasticity of demand between Geritol and any other good?

8. Which of the following are likely to have a positive cross elasticity of demand:
   a. automobiles and oil?
   b. wood tennis rackets and metal tennis rackets?
   c. gin and tonic?
   d. fishing poles and fishing licenses?
   e. a Harvard education and a Stanford education?

9. Show that, if the Engel curve for a good is a straight line through the origin, the income elasticity of demand for the good is one.

10. According to Richard Tennant, "The consumption of cigarettes is . . . [relatively] insensitive to changes in price. . . . In contrast, the demand for individual brands is highly elastic in its response to price. . . . In 1918, for example, Lucky Strike was sold for a short time at a higher retail price than Camel or Chesterfield and rapidly lost half its business."* Explain

*R. Tennant, "The Cigarette Industry," in W. Adams, The Structure of American Industry (New York: Macmillan, 1961), p. 371.

why the demand for a particular brand is more elastic than the demand for all cigarettes. If Lucky Strike raised its price by 1 percent in 1918, was the price elasticity of demand for its product greater than 2?

11. According to the president of Bethlehem Steel, the demand for steel is price inelastic because steel generally constitutes a very small percentage of the total cost of the product that includes it as a raw material.* If this is the case, will a price increase result in an increase or decrease in the amount of money spent on steel?

12. What is meant by a market? How can one derive the market demand curve from the demand curves of the individuals comprising the market?

13. What is the difference between the point elasticity of demand and the arc elasticity of demand?

14. Suppose that the relationship between the price of steel and the quantity of steel demanded is as follows:

Price ($)	Quantity
1	8
2	7
3	6
4	5
5	4

What is the arc elasticity of demand when price is between $1 and $2? Between $2 and $3? Between $4 and $5?

15. Suppose that the demand curve for aluminum is DD', as shown below. Provide a measure of the price elasticity of demand at price OP.

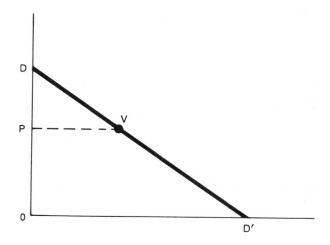

*W. Adams, "The Steel Industry," in ibid., p. 164.

16. Discuss in detail the determinants of the price elasticity of demand.

17. Define the income elasticity of demand. How does the income elasticity of demand differ between luxuries and necessities? What does Engel's law state?

18. Define the cross elasticity of demand. How does the cross elasticity of demand differ between substitutes and complements?

19. If the relationship between price and quantity is as given below, derive the marginal revenue at various quantities and plot in the graph below the table.

Price (dollars)	Quantity
10	1
9	2
8	3
7	4
6	5
5	6
4	7
3	8
2	9

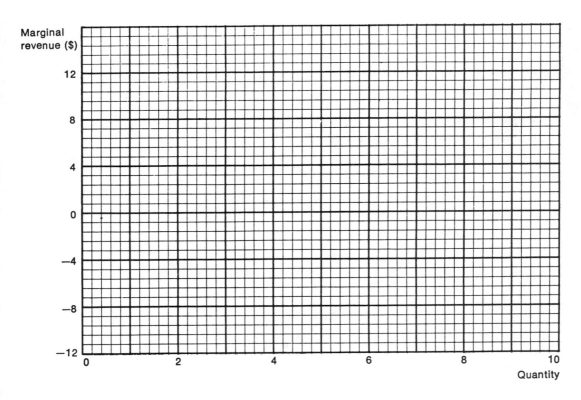

20. If the demand curve is DD' in the graph below, draw in the marginal revenue curve.

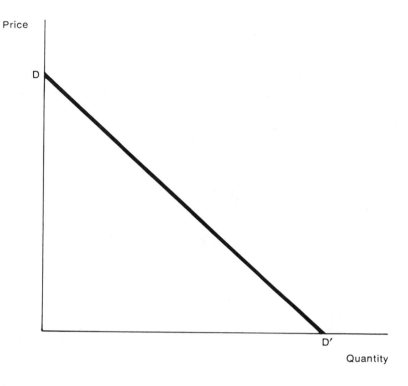

21. **What does the firm's demand curve look like under perfect competition? Why?**

22. (*Advanced*) Use calculus to derive marginal revenue as a function of price (p) and the price elasticity of demand (n).

23. **Discuss various ways that demand curves can be measured.**

24. **Suppose the Mayor of New York asked you to advise him concerning the proper fare that should be charged by the New York City subway. In what way might information concerning the price elasticity of demand be useful?**

25. **Suppose you are a business consultant and you become convinced that the U. S. steel industry underestimates the price elasticity of demand for steel. In what way might this information be useful to the steel companies? To the public?**

26. Suppose you are a trustee of a major university. At a meeting of the board of trustees, one university official argues that the demand for places at this university is completely inelastic. As evidence, he cites the fact that, although the university has doubled its tuition in the last decade, there has been no appreciable decrease in the number of students enrolled. Do you agree? Comment on his argument.

27. Studies from cross-section data indicate that the income elasticity of demand for servants in the United States exceeds 1.00. Yet the number of servants has been decreasing during the last 50 years, while incomes have risen in the United States. How can these facts be reconciled?

28. *a.* According to Gregory Chow of Princeton University, the price elasticity of demand for automobiles in the United States is 1.2, and the income elasticity of demand for automobiles is 3.0. What would be the effect of a 3 percent decline in auto prices on the quantity of autos demanded, assuming Chow's estimates are right?

    b. What would be the effect of a 2 percent increase in income?

29. According to the Swedish economist Herman Wold's estimates, the income elasticity of demand for liquor is about 1.00. If you were an executive of a liquor firm, of what use might this fact be to you in forecasting sales?

30. According to Rex Daly of the Department of Agriculture, the price elasticity of demand for coffee is about 0.25 to 0.30, and the income elasticity of demand is about 0.23. Suppose you were an economist for the coffee industry. How could you use this information to help forecast coffee sales in the United States?

31. According to Professor M. L. Burstein, the price elasticity of demand for refrigerators is between 1.00 and 2.00, and the income elasticity of demand is between 1.00 and 2.00. Compare these elasticities with those for coffee (in question 30). Why are the results for refrigerators so different from those for coffee?

32. *a.* According to S. Sackrin of the U. S. Department of Agriculture, the price elasticity of demand for cigarettes is between 0.3 and 0.4, and the income elasticity of demand is about 0.5. Suppose the federal government, influenced by findings that link cigarettes and cancer, were to impose a tax on cigarettes that tripled their price. What effect would this have on cigarette consumption?

    b. Suppose a brokerage house advised you to buy cigarette stocks because, if incomes rose by 50 percent in the next decade, cigarette sales would be bound to spurt enormously. What would be your reaction to this advice?

Completion Questions

1. If the government imposes a tax on coal of 10 cents per ton, it will obtain the most revenue from the tax if coal's price elasticity of demand equals _____. The largest burden of the tax is borne by consumers of coal if the price elasticity of demand equals _____ .

2. If the cross elasticity of demand between goods X and Y is positive, these goods are classified as _____ .

3. The income elasticity of demand is the percentage change in quantity demanded resulting from a _____ change in money income.

4. Luxury goods are generally assumed to have a _____ income elasticity of demand.

5. If a commodity has many close substitutes, its demand is likely to be _____ _____.

6. The price elasticity of demand equals _____.

7. Engel's law states that _____.

8. The demand curve for the individual firm under perfect competition is _____ _____.

9. The price elasticity of demand is generally _____ in the long run than in the short run.

10. The total amount of money spent by consumers on a commodity equals the industry's ___ _____.

11. The _____ curve shows marginal revenue at various quantities of output.

12. If the industry is not perfectly competitive, the firm's demand curve will not be _____ _____.

13. Direct experimentation can be a _____ way to obtain data concerning a firm's or product's demand curve.

True or False

_____ 1. The demand for open heart surgery is likely to be less price elastic than the demand for aspirin.

_____ 2. If a good's income elasticity exceeds one, a decrease in the price of the good will increase the total amount spent on it.

_____ 3. Summing horizontally the individual demand curves for all of the consumers in the market will produce the demand curve for the market.

_____ 4. The demand curve for an individual firm under perfect competition is downward sloping, its slope being −1.

_____ 5. The market demand curve for a product under perfect competition is horizontal.

_____ 6. The demand for salt and pepper is likely to be price elastic.

_____ 7. In general, demand is likely to be more inelastic in the long run than in the short run.

_____ 8. The income elasticity of demand for food is very high.

_____ 9. It is always true that $n_{xy} = n_{yx}$.

_____ 10. The direct approach of simply asking people how much they would buy of a particular commodity is the best way to estimate the demand curve.

_____ 11. The identification problem is the problem of identifying the person who knows what the demand curve looks like.

_____ 12. The income elasticity of demand will always have the same sign regardless of the level of income at which it is measured.

_____ 13. Marginal revenue is the ratio of the value of sales to the amount sold.

_____ 14. When the demand curve is linear, the slope of the marginal revenue curve is twice (in absolute value) the slope of the demand curve.

Multiple Choice

1. The president of a leading producer of tantalum says that an increase in the price of tantalum would have no effect on the total amount spent on tantalum. If this is true, the price elasticity of demand for tantalum is
    a. less than zero.
    b. 1.   unitary
    c. 2.
    d. more than 1.
    e. none of the above.

2. Suppose that the demand curve is GG' in the graph below:

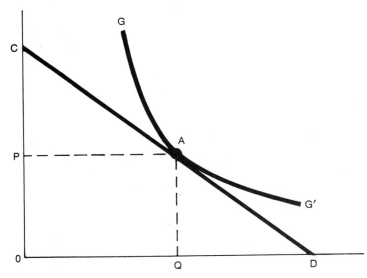

The price elasticity of demand is equal to
    a. $AD \div CA$.
    b. $AD \div AQ$.
    c. $CA \div PA$.

-70-

d. ~~OP ÷ OQ.~~
e. none of the above.

3. The demand for a good is price inelastic if
   a. the price elasticity is one.
   b. the price elasticity is less than one. — *not so much*
   c. the price elasticity is greater than one.
   d. all of the above.
   e. none of the above.

4. The relationship between marginal revenue and the price elasticity of demand is
   a. $MR = P\left(1 - \dfrac{1}{n}\right)$.
   b. $P = MR\left(1 - \dfrac{1}{n}\right)$.
   c. $P = MR(1 + n)$.
   d. $MR = P(1 + n)$.
   e. none of the above.

$$MR = P\left(1 - \frac{1}{\eta}\right)$$

$$P\left(1 - \frac{1}{|\varepsilon_D|}\right)$$

5. A demand curve with unitary elasticity at all points is
   a. a straight line.
   b. a parabola.
   c. a hyperbola.
   d. all of the above.
   e. none of the above.

6. Suppose we are concerned with the relationships between the quantity of food demanded and aggregate income. It seems most likely that this relationship will look like:
   a. curve A below.
   b. curve B below.
   c. curve C below.
   d. the vertical axis.
   e. the horizontal axis.

Q_{TD}^{F} I $NC.$

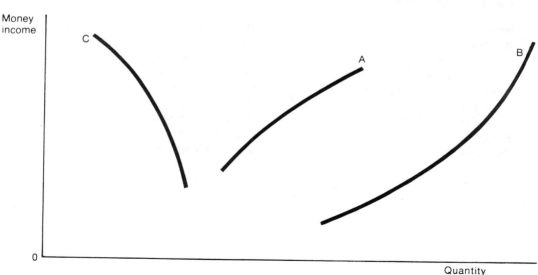

7. If goods X and Y are substitutes, the relationship between the quantity demanded of good X and the price of good Y should be like:

   a. curve A below.
   b. curve B below.
   c. the vertical axis.
   d. the horizontal axis.
   e. none of the above.

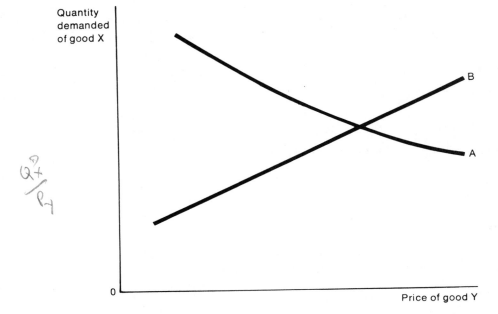

Key Concepts for Review

Market
Market demand curve
Price elasticity of demand
Total revenue
Income elasticity of demand
Engel's law
Cross elasticity of demand
Substitute
Complement

Marginal revenue
Marginal revenue curve
Industry demand curve
Firm demand curve
Perfect competition
Identification problem
Direct experimentation
Consumer clinics
Horizontal demand curve

Answers

Case Study: The Demand for Oranges

a. The price elasticity of demand for Florida Indian River oranges seems to be 3.1; the price elasticity of demand for Florida Interior oranges seems to be 3.0; and the price elasticity of demand for California oranges seems to be 2.8.

b. The cross elasticities (η_{xy}) are as follows:

	X		
Y	Florida Indian River	Florida Interior	California
Florida Indian River	—	1.6	0.01
Florida Interior	1.2	—	0.1
California	0.2	0.1	—

c. Clearly, Florida Indian River and Florida Interior oranges are closer substitutes than the Florida and California oranges.

d. The fact presented in part (c) is of obvious use to orange growers in both parts of the country.

e. The study is limited, of course, by the fact that it pertains to only one city at only one relatively short period of time.

Problems and Review Questions

1. a. Statistical and econometric analyses, as well as experiments.
   b. Yes.
   c. Yes.

2. Since $MR = P\left(1 - \dfrac{1}{\eta}\right)$, it follows that $P = MR \div \left(1 - \dfrac{1}{\eta}\right)$. In this case, $MR = \$2$ and $\eta = 2$; thus, $P = \$2 \div \left(1 - \dfrac{1}{2}\right)$, or \$4. (MR equals marginal revenue, P equals price, and η equals the price elasticity of demand.)

3. The price elasticity of demand is $-\dfrac{dQ}{dP} \cdot \dfrac{P}{Q}$. If the demand curve is D_1, $\dfrac{dQ}{dP} = -1$; thus, $-\dfrac{dQ}{dP} \cdot \dfrac{P}{Q} = \dfrac{P}{Q} = \dfrac{P}{10-P}$. If the demand curve is D_2, $\dfrac{dQ}{dP} = \dfrac{-1}{2}$; thus, $-\dfrac{dQ}{dP} \cdot \dfrac{P}{Q} = \dfrac{P}{2Q} = \dfrac{P}{10-P}$.

Since the price elasticity of demand equals $\dfrac{P}{10-P}$ in each case, it must be the same for both demand curves if the price is the same. (Note that if the demand curve is D_1, $Q = 10-P$; and if it is D_2, $Q = 5 - \dfrac{1}{2}P$. This is clear from the diagram in the question.)

4. The demand curve you have drawn is BA:

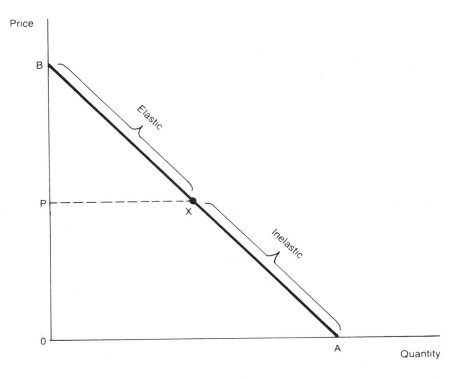

Find the point that is midway between B and A, and call this point X. Since you have chosen X so that $BX = XA$, it follows from Equation 5.1 in the text that demand must be of unitary elasticity at point X. For points on the demand curve above X, demand must be elastic because the distance from such points to A is greater than the distance to B. Thus Equation 5.1 says that demand must be price elastic at such points. For points on the demand curve below X, demand must be inelastic because the distance from such points to A is less than the distance to B. Thus Equation 5.1 says that demand must be price inelastic at such points.

5. *a.* If P equals 1, the demand for the firm's product is inelastic. To see that this is the case, note that, if $P = 1$, $Q = 5 - 1 = 4$; thus, the firm's total revenue is \$4 million per day. If $P = 2$, $Q = 5 - 2 = 3$; thus, the firm's total revenue is \$6 million per day. Since an increase in price (from \$1 to \$2) increases total revenue, demand must be price inelastic. It is unwise for a firm to operate at a point where the demand for its product is price inelastic. By increasing its price, it can increase its total revenue and (because it generally costs less to produce less output) reduce its total cost. Thus, it can increase its total profit. Thus, the XYZ Corporation should consider a price hike.

   b. Let's compute the arc elasticity of demand when price is between \$1.00 and \$1.01. When $P = 1$, $Q = 4$. If $P = 1.01$, $Q = 5 - 1.01 = 3.99$. Thus

$$\eta = -\frac{(4.00 - 3.99)}{(4.00 + 3.99)/2} \div \frac{(1.00 - 1.01)}{(1.00 + 1.01)/2} = \frac{0.01}{3.995} \div \frac{0.01}{1.005} = 0.25$$

Thus, the price elasticity of demand is about 0.25, not 1.0. The marketing specialist is wrong.

-74-

6. *a.* Summing up the quantities demanded by the individuals at each price, the market demand curve is:

Price (dollars)	Quantity
1	407
2	372
3	336
4	304
5	274

b. When the price is between $1 and $2

$$\eta = -\frac{(407-372)}{(407+372)/2} \div \frac{(1-2)}{(1+2)/2} = \frac{35}{389.5} \div \frac{1}{1.5} = 0.13.$$

When the price is between $3 and $4

$$\eta = -\frac{(336-304)}{(336+304)/2} \div \frac{(3-4)}{(3+4)/2} = \frac{32}{320} \div \frac{1}{3.5} = 0.35.$$

7. *a.* Holding his income constant, the total amount he spends on Geritol is constant too; that is

$$PQ = I$$

where P is the price of Geritol, Q is the quantity demanded by Mr. Jarvis, and I is his income. Thus

$$Q = \frac{I}{P}.$$

Since I is held constant, this demand curve is a rectangular hyperbola, and the price elasticity of demand equals 1.

b. Since $Q = I/P$, it follows that a 1 percent increase in I will result in a 1 percent increase in Q, when P is held constant. Thus the income elasticity of demand equals 1.

c. Since Q does not depend on the price of any other good, the cross elasticity of demand equals zero.

8. Substitutes have a positive cross elasticity of demand. Thus cases (*b*) and (*e*) are likely to have a positive cross elasticity of demand.

9. The Engel curve shows the relationship between money income and the amount consumed of a particular commodity. If this relationship is a straight line through the origin, it follows that the amount consumed of this commodity is *proportional* to the consumer's money income. Thus, a 1 percent increase in the consumer's money income results in a 1 percent increase in the amount consumed of this commodity. Consequently, the income elasticity of demand for this commodity equals 1.

10. Because there are lots of very close substitutes for a particular brand, but not for cigarettes as a whole.
    Yes.

11. It will result in an increase in the amount of money spent on steel.

12. A market is a group of firms and individuals that are in touch with each other in order to buy or sell some good. Basically, all markets consist primarily of buyers and sellers, although third parties like brokers and agents may be present as well.
    The market demand curve is simply the horizontal summation of the individual demand curves of all the consumers in the market.

13. If ΔP is very small, we can compute the point elasticity of demand, which is

$$\frac{\Delta Q}{Q} \div \frac{\Delta P}{P}$$

If we have data concerning only large changes in price, we can compute the arc elasticity of demand, which is $\dfrac{\Delta Q\,(P_1 + P_2)}{\Delta P\,(Q_1 + Q_2)}$.

14. $\dfrac{\Delta Q\,(P_1 + P_2)}{\Delta P\,(Q_1 + Q_2)} = \dfrac{1\,(1+2)}{1\,(8+7)} = \dfrac{3}{15} = .20$

$\dfrac{\Delta Q\,(P_1 + P_2)}{\Delta P\,(Q_1 + Q_2)} = \dfrac{1\,(2+3)}{1\,(7+6)} = \dfrac{5}{13} = .38$

$\dfrac{\Delta Q\,(P_1 + P_2)}{\Delta P\,(Q_1 + Q_2)} = \dfrac{1\,(4+5)}{1\,(5+4)} = \dfrac{9}{9} = 1.00$

15. The price elasticity of demand equals $VD' \div DV$.

16. First, and foremost, the price elasticity of demand for a commodity depends on the number and closeness of the substitutes that are available. If a commodity has many close substitutes, its demand is likely to be price elastic.

   The extent to which a commodity has close substitutes depends on how narrowly it is defined. In general, one would expect that, as the definition of the market becomes narrower and more specific, the product will have more close substitutes and its demand will become more price elastic.

   Second, it is sometimes asserted that the price elasticity of demand for a commodity is likely to depend on the importance of the commodity in consumers' budgets.

   Third, the price elasticity of demand for a commodity is likely to depend on the length of the period to which the demand curve pertains.

17. The income elasticity of demand is $\dfrac{\Delta Q}{Q} \div \dfrac{\Delta I}{I}$, where Q is quantity demanded and I is income.

   One would expect the income elasticity of demand generally to be higher for luxuries than for necessities.

   Engel's law states that better-off nations spend a smaller proportion of their incomes on food than do poorer nations, the income elasticity of demand for food being quite low.

18. The cross elasticity of demand is the percentage change in the quantity of good X resulting from a 1 percent change in the price of good Y.

   The cross elasticity of demand is positive if goods X and Y are substitutes and negative if goods X and Y are complements.

19. The following table derives marginal revenue:

Quantity	Price (dollars)	Total revenue (dollars)	Marginal revenue (dollars)
1	$10	$10	$18 – $10 = $ 8
2	9	18	24 – 18 = 6
3	8	24	28 – 24 = 4
4	7	28	30 – 28 = 2
5	6	30	30 – 30 = 0
6	5	30	28 – 30 = –2
7	4	28	24 – 28 = –4
8	3	24	18 – 24 = –6
9	2	18	

The marginal revenue curve is as follows:

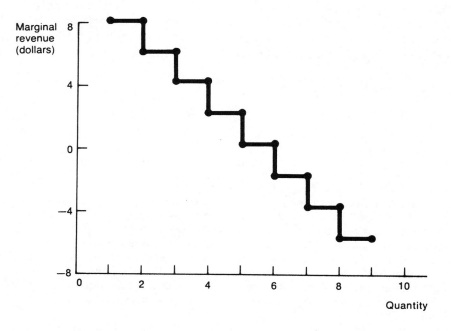

20. The marginal revenue curve is *DR* below.

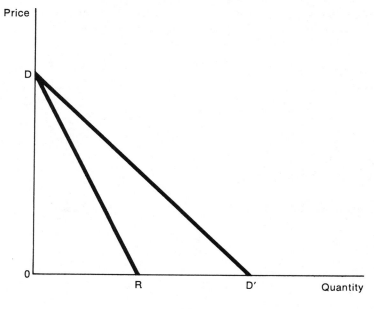

21. The firm's demand curve under perfect competition is a horizontal line. This is caused by the fact that the firm can sell all it wants without influencing the price. A very small decrease in price would result in an indefinitely large increase in the quantity it could sell, and a very small increase in its price would result in its selling nothing.

22. For students with a grasp of elementary calculus, the derivation is:

$$MR = p + q\,\frac{dp}{dq}$$

$$= p\left(1 + \frac{q}{p}\frac{dp}{dq}\right)$$

$$= p\left(1 - \frac{1}{\eta}\right)$$

23. One method is direct market experimentation; another is to interview consumers and administer questionnaires concerning buying habits; another is to use statistical methods to extract information from past market data. Each of these methods has its problems, but the difficulties, although sometimes formidable, are not insoluble.

24. It would indicate the extent to which fare increases would decrease subway travel. For example, William Vickrey's data seem to indicate that fare increases would increase total revenue since demand is price inelastic. Obviously this is an important fact.

25. It might indicate that both the companies and the public might be better off if steel prices were lowered somewhat, since the quantity demanded might expand more than heretofore expected.

26. Other factors—notably the general level of prices and incomes and the quality of the students—have not been held constant. Holding these factors—and the tuition rates at other universities—constant, it is almost surely untrue that large increases in tuition at this university would not cut down on the number of students demanding admission to the university.

27. There have been changes in the price of servants, the distribution of income, tastes, and other relevant factors. Taking these changes into account, there is no contradiction.

28. *a.* There would be a 3.6 percent increase in quantity demanded.
   b. There would be a 6-percent increase in quantity demanded.

29. All other things equal, you could expect that a 1 percent increase in income would result in about a 1 percent increase in the total quantity of liquor demanded.

Completion Questions

1. zero, zero
2. substitutes
3. 1 percent
4. high
5. price elastic
6. $-\dfrac{\Delta Q}{Q} \div \dfrac{\Delta P}{P}$
7. the income elasticity of food is low
8. horizontal
9. higher
10. total revenue
11. marginal revenue
12. horizontal
13. risky

True or False

1. True 2. False 3. True 4. False 5. False 6. False 7. False 8. False 9. False
10. False 11. False 12. False 13. False 14. True

Multiple Choice

1. *b* 2. *a* 3. *b* 4. *a* 5. *c* 6. *b* 7. *b*

Part 3   THE FIRM: ITS TECHNOLOGY AND COSTS

CHAPTER 6   The Firm and Its Technology

Case Study: Japanese Manufacturing Techniques

No topic has received more attention among policymakers in Washington and elsewhere than Japanese competition. In industries like consumer electronics, steel, and autos, the Japanese have increased their share of the American market, and, according to many experts, have achieved superior productivity and quality. An engineering comparison of a compact-car plant in Japan and the U.S. is as follows:

	U.S.	Japan
Parts stamped per hour	325	550
Manpower per press line	7–13	1
Time needed to change dies	4–6 hours	5 minutes
Average production run	10 days	2 days
Time needed per small car	59.9 hours	30.8 hours
Number of quality inspectors	1 per 7 workers	1 per 30 workers

a. One of the concepts at the core of Japanese production management is "just-in-time" production, which calls for goods being produced and delivered just in time to be sold, subassemblies to be produced and delivered just in time to be assembled into finished goods, and fabricated parts to be produced and delivered just in time to go into subassemblies. What are the advantages of this system?

b. What are the disadvantages of this system?

c. Another major Japanese production concept is "total quality control," or "quality at the source," which means that errors should be found and corrected *by the people performing the work*. In the West, inspection is performed by statistical sampling *after* a lot of goods is produced. What are the advantages of the Japanese system?

d. Does microeconomics play an important role in determining whether these production techniques should be adopted in the U.S.? If so, how?

Problems and Review Questions

1. According to data derived by Earl Heady and others on the basis of an experiment carried out at the Animal Husbandry Department of Iowa State University,* the following combinations of hay and grain consumption per lamb will result in a 25-pound gain on a lamb:

---

*See E. Heady, *Economics of Agricultural Production and Resource Use* (Englewood Cliffs, N.J.: Prentice-Hall, 1952), p. 155.

Pounds of hay	Pounds of grain
40	130.9
50	125.1
60	120.1
70	115.7
80	111.8
90	108.3
110	102.3
130	97.4
150	93.8

a. You are asked by a local farmer to estimate the marginal product of a pound of grain in producing lamb. Can you provide such an estimate on the basis of these data?

b. The local farmer is convinced that constant returns to scale prevail in lamb production. If this is true, and if hay and grain consumption per lamb are the only inputs, how much gain will accrue if the hay consumption per lamb is 100 pounds and the grain consumption per lamb is 250.2 pounds?

c. What is the marginal rate of technical substitution of hay for grain when between 40 and 50 pounds of hay (and between 130.9 and 125.1 pounds of grain) are consumed per lamb?

d. Suppose that a major advance in technology occurs which allows farmers to produce a 25-pound gain on a lamb with less hay and grain than the above table indicates. If the marginal rate of technical substitution (at each rate of consumption of each input) is the same after the technological advance as before, can you draw the new isoquant corresponding to a 25-pound gain on a lamb?

2. Suppose that an entrepreneur's utility depends on the size of her firm (as measured by its output) and its profits. In particular, the indifference curves are as follows:

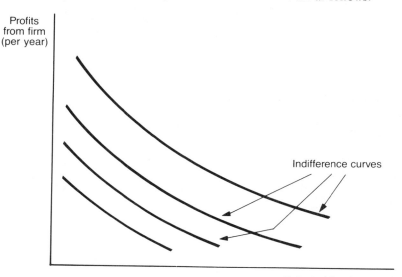

a. Will the entrepreneur maximize profit?

b. Draw a graph to indicate how one can determine the output she will choose.

3. At the Amarillo Piano Company, the average product of labor equals 5, regardless of how much labor is used.
   a. What is the marginal product of the first unit of labor?
   b. What is the marginal product of the eightieth unit of labor?
   c. By how much will output increase if labor is increased by 100 units?
   d. By how much will output fall if labor is reduced by 50 units?
   e. Does this case conform to the law of diminishing marginal returns? Why or why not?
   f. Does this case seem realistic? Why or why not?

4. Based on data obtained by the U. S. Department of Agriculture, the relationship between a cow's total output of milk and the amount of grain it is fed is as follows:

Amount of grain (pounds)	Amount of milk (pounds)
1,200	5,917
1,800	7,250
2,400	8,379
3,000	9,371

(This relationship assumes that forage input is fixed at 6,500 pounds of hay.)
   a. Calculate the average product of grain when each amount is used.
   b. Estimate the marginal product of grain when between 1,200 and 1,800 pounds are fed, when between 1,800 and 2,400 pounds are fed, and when between 2,400 and 3,000 pounds are fed.
   c. Does this production function exhibit diminishing marginal returns?

5. The Antioch Corporation, a hypothetical producer of paper napkins, claims that in 1985 it has the following production function:

$Q = 3 + 4L + 2P$

where Q is the number of paper napkins it produces per year, L is the number of hours of labor per year, and P is the number of pounds of paper used per year.
   a. Does this production function seem to include all of the relevant inputs? Explain.

   b. Does this production function seem reasonable, if it is applied to all possible values of L and P? Explain.
   c. Does this production function exhibit diminishing marginal returns?

6. Earl Heady of Iowa State University estimated a Cobb-Douglas production function for six types of farms, there being 5 inputs in the production function: (1) land, (2) labor, (3) equipment, (4) livestock and feed, and (5) other resource services. The exponent of each input was as shown on the next page:

				Exponent	
Farm type	Land	Labor	Equipment	Livestock and feed	Other resource services
Crop farms	0.24	0.07	0.08	0.53	0.02
Hog farms	0.07	0.02	0.10	0.74	0.03
Dairy farms	0.10	0.01	0.06	0.63	0.02
General farms	0.17	0.12	0.16	0.46	0.03
Large farms	0.28	0.01	0.11	0.53	0.03
Small farms	0.21	0.05	0.08	0.43	0.03

Source: E. Heady, Ibid.

a. Do there appear to be increasing returns to scale in any of these six types of farms?

b. In what type of farm does a 1 percent increase in labor have the largest percentage effect on output?

c. Based on these results, would you expect that output would increase if many of the farms included in Heady's sample were merged?

7. Fill in the blanks in the following table:

Number of units of variable input	Total output (number of units)	Marginal product* of variable input	Average product of variable input
3	— —	Unknown	30
4	— —	20	— —
5	130	— —	— —
6	— —	5	— —
7	— —	— —	19 ½

*These figures pertain to the interval between the indicated amount of the variable input and one unit less than the indicated amount of the variable input.

8. As the quantity of a variable input increases, explain why the point where *marginal* product begins to decline is encountered before the point where *average* product begins to decline. Explain too why the point where *average* product begins to decline is encountered before the point where *total* product begins to decline.

9. The following graph shows the combinations of quantities of grain and protein that must be used to produce 150 pounds of pork. Curve A assumes that no Aureomycin is added, while curve B assumes that some of it is added.

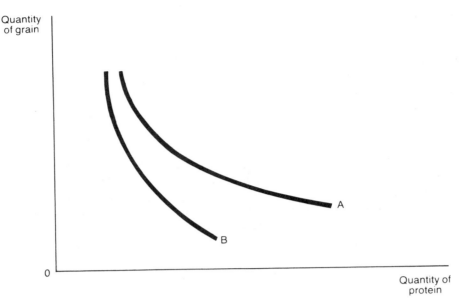

a. If Aureomycin can be obtained free, should pork producers add it?
b. Does the addition of Aureomycin affect the marginal rate of technical substitution? If so, how?

10. In the early 1880s, cigarette-rolling machinery became available. The new machines cut the cost of fabricating a cigarette in half. Assuming that capital and labor are the only inputs, what effect did this innovation have on the production function for cigarettes? Once the new machines were available, how did the optimal input combination differ from what it was before their introduction?

11. According to Joe Bain, there are important economies of scale in automobile production up to a plant size equaling about 5-10 percent of U.S. auto output. What are the implications of this fact for the number of auto companies that we are likely to find in the United States? In Chile? How would you go about obtaining data concerning economies of scale in some other industry?

12. If Q is the number of cars washed per hour and L is the number of men employed, a study of an auto laundry* found the following short-run relationship:

$$Q = -0.8 + 4.5L - 0.3L^2.$$

Do there appear to be diminishing marginal returns?

*M. Spencer and L. Siegelman, *Managerial Economics*, Homewood, Ill.: Irwin, 1959, p. 204.

13. Discuss the limitations of profit maximization as an assumption concerning the motivation of the firm. What alternative assumptions can be made? Why does profit maximization remain the principal assumption made by economists?

14. Discuss the nature of technology and the constraints it imposes on the firm's behavior. What are fixed inputs? Variable inputs?

15. Discuss the meaning of the production function. What is the short run? The long run? How does the production function in the short run differ from that in the long run?

16. *a.* Suppose the production function for a cigarette factory is as given below, there being only one input.

Amount of input (units per year)	Amount of output (units per year)
1	7
2	14.5
3	22
4	29
5	35
6	39
7	39

Plot the average product curve for the input in the graph below:

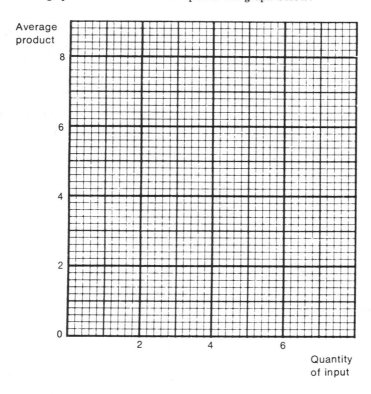

b. On the basis of the production function given in the first part of this question, plot the marginal product curve of the input.

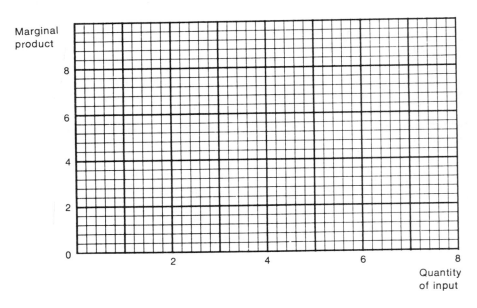

17. State the law of diminishing marginal returns. Indicate how this law is used to deduce the shape of the marginal product curve.

18. On the basis of the total product curve shown in the graph below, derive a measure of the average product and marginal product at OQ units of input by graphical techniques.

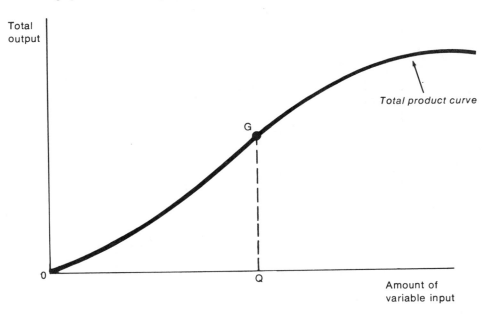

19. Describe an isoquant. Define the marginal rate of technical substitution.

20. (*Advanced*) Use calculus to show that the marginal rate of technical substitution of labor for capital is equal to the ratio of the marginal product of labor to the marginal product of capital.

21. Describe what is meant by increasing returns to scale, decreasing returns to scale, and constant returns to scale. Discuss the factors that might be responsible for increasing returns to scale. Discuss the factors that might be responsible for decreasing returns to scale.

22. Describe the principal methods used to measure production functions in particular firms and industries. What are their limitations and advantages?

23. Define Herbert Simon's concept of satisficing, and contrast it with William Baumol's theory of decision-making in the firm.

24. Econometric studies of the cotton industry in India indicate that the Cobb-Douglas production function can be applied and that the exponent of labor is 0.92 and the exponent of capital is 0.12. Suppose that both capital and labor were increased by 1 percent. By what percent would output increase?

25. In the Cobb-Douglas production function, is the exponent of labor generally larger or smaller than that of capital?

26. Suppose that in a chemical plant $Q = AL^\alpha K^\beta$ where Q is the output rate, L is the rate of labor input, and K is the rate of capital input. Statistical analysis indicates that $\alpha = 0.8$ and $\beta = 0.3$. The owner of the plant claims that there are increasing returns to scale in the plant. Is he right?

27. (*Advanced*) Suppose you are assured by the owner of an aluminum plant that his plant is subject to constant returns to scale, labor and capital being the only inputs. He claims that output per worker in his plant is a function of capital per worker only. Is he right?

Completion Questions

1. At the Tangway Corporation, the average product of labor equals $3L$, where L is the number of units of labor employed per day. The total output produced per day if 4 units of labor are employed per day is _____. The total output produced per day if 5 units of labor are employed per day is _____. The marginal product of the fifth unit of labor employed per day is _____.

2. In the _____, all inputs are variable.

3. Herbert Simon is a proponent of _____ rather than maximization of profit.

4. The _____ production function can be written $Q = AL^{\alpha_1} K^{\alpha_2} M^{\alpha_3}$.

5. A fixed input is _____.

6. A variable input is _____.

7. In both the short run and the long run, a firm's productive processes generally permit substantial _____ in the proportions in which inputs are used.

8. The average product of an input is total product divided by _____
_____.

9. The marginal product of an input is the addition to total output due to _____
_____.

10. Underlying the law of diminishing marginal returns is the assumption that technology remains _____.

11. Two isoquants can never _____.

True or False

_____ 1. If the average product of labor equals $\dfrac{10}{L}$, where L is the number of units of labor employed per day, total output is the same regardless of how much labor is used per day.

_____ 2. The law of diminishing marginal returns is inconsistent with increasing returns to scale.

_____ 3. An isoquant is analogous to the budget line in the theory of consumer demand.

_____ 4. The marginal rate of technical substitution equals minus one times the slope of the isoquant.

_____ 5. Isoquants are concave.

_____ 6. All production functions exhibit constant returns to scale.

_____ 7. Increasing returns to scale can occur because of the difficulty of coordinating a large enterprise.

_____ 8. Whether there are increasing, decreasing, or constant returns to scale in a particular case is an empirical question.

_____ 9. Statistical studies of production functions are hampered by the fact that available data do not always represent technically efficient combinations of inputs and outputs.

_____ 10. The only goal of any firm is to maximize profits.

_____ 11. The concept of profit maximization is well defined in an uncertain world.

_____ 12. The production function is not closely related to a firm's or industry's technology.

_____ 13. The law of diminishing marginal returns applies to cases where there is a proportional increase in all inputs.

Multiple Choice

1. At the La Roche Company, the average product of labor equals $5 \div \sqrt{L}$, where L is the amount of labor employed per day. Thus,
   - *a.* labor always is subject to diminishing marginal returns.
   - *b.* labor is subject to diminishing marginal returns only when L is greater than 5.
   - *c.* labor is not subject to diminishing marginal returns.
   - *d.* labor is not subject to diminishing marginal returns when L is greater than 5.
   - *e.* none of the above.

2. Suppose that the production function is as follows:

   $AP = \dfrac{TP}{Q} = \dfrac{15}{7} = 2.14$

Quantity of output per year	m_p	Quantity of input per year	AP
2	3	1	2
5	4	2	2.5
9	3	3	3
12	2	4	3
14	1	5	2.8
15	0	6	2.5
15	-1	7	2.14
14		8	1.7

   The average product of the input when 7 units of the input are used is
   - *a.* 7.
   - *b.* 15.
   - *c.* 2 1/7.
   - *d.* 7/15.
   - *e.* none of the above.

3. If the production function is as given in question 2, the marginal product of the input when between 1 and 2 units of the input is used is
   - *a.* 2.
   - *b.* 5.
   - *c.* 3.
   - *d.* 4.
   - *e.* none of the above

4. If the production function is as given in question 2, the marginal product of the input begins to decline
   a. after 3 units of input are used.
   b. after 2 units of input are used.
   c. after 4 units of input are used.
   d. after 7 units of input are used.
   e. none of the above.

5. If the production function is as given in question 2, the marginal product of the input is negative when more than
   a. 7 units of input are used.
   b. 6 units of input are used.
   c. 5 units of input are used.
   d. 4 units of input are used.
   e. none of the above.

6. The marginal product equals the average product when the latter is
   a. 1/2 of its maximum value.
   b. 1/4 of its maximum value.
   c. equal to its maximum value.
   d. 1 1/2 times its maximum value.
   e. none of the above.

7. A firm's aspiration level is
   a. its profits last year.
   b. the boundary between "satisfactory" and "unsatisfactory" outcomes.
   c. its highest previous profit level.
   d. related to the shoe size of the firm's president.
   e. none of the above.

Key Concepts for Review

Profit
Profit maximization
Technology
Input
Fixed input
Variable input
Short run
Long run
Production function
Marginal product

Average product
Law of diminishing marginal returns
Isoquants
Economic region of production
Marginal rate of technical substitution
Increasing returns to scale
Decreasing returns to scale
Constant returns to scale
Cobb-Douglas production function

Answers

Case Study: Japanese Manufacturing Techniques

a. Because of its hand-to-mouth nature, just-in-time production means that a firm holds less inventories of parts, subassemblies, and finished goods. Because it is expensive to hold inventories, this is an advantage. Also, defects tend to be discovered more quickly and their causes may be nipped in the bud.

b. If goods, subassemblies, and parts are to be produced and delivered just in time for use or sale, they must be produced in small lots, which means that the equipment used to produce them must be set up more often. Each setup is expensive; it often involves moving heavy dies into place, making adjustments, and inspecting the results until the settings are right. To overcome this disadvantage, the Japanese have worked very hard to reduce setup costs. For example, Toyota has reduced the time to set up 800-ton presses used in forming auto hoods and fenders from an hour in 1971 to about 10 minutes or less.

c. Higher quality of product, less waste of materials, a heightened awareness of the causes of defects on the part of the people doing the work, and fewer inspectors.

d. Yes. To see whether they should be adopted in the U.S., engineering principles alone do not suffice. It is essential that microeconomic concepts be applied to find out whether these techniques really would lower costs and increase efficiency.*

Problems and Review Questions

1. a. No.
    b. 50 pounds, since half of these amounts (that is, 50 pounds of hay and 125.1 pounds of grain) results in a 25-pound gain.
    c. 0.58.
    d. No, because it is impossible to tell (from the information given in the question) how much hay and grain can be used to produce a 25-pound gain after the advance in technology.

*See R. Schonberger, *Japanese Manufacturing Techniques* (New York: The Free Press, 1982); and Y. Tsurumi, "Japan's Challenge to the U.S.," *Columbia Journal of World Business* (Summer 1982).

2. *a.* No.
   b. She will choose point *A* in the graph below. Thus, output will be *Oq*. See Example 6.1 in the text.

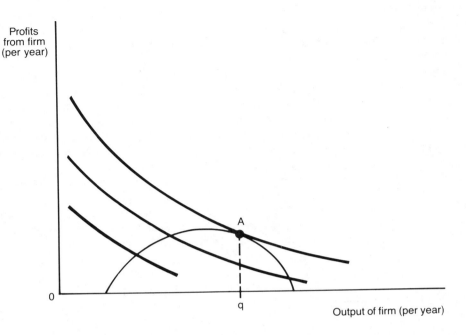

3. *a.* 5
   b. 5
   c. 500
   d. 250
   e. No.
   f. No.

4. *a.* and *b.* The average and marginal products of grain when each amount is used are calculated as follows:

Amount of grain	Average product	Marginal product
1,200	$5{,}917 \div 1{,}200 = 4.93$	$\dfrac{7{,}250 - 5{,}917}{1{,}800 - 1{,}200} = 2.22$
1,800	$7{,}250 \div 1{,}800 = 4.03$	$\dfrac{8{,}379 - 7{,}250}{2{,}400 - 1{,}800} = 1.88$
2,400	$8{,}379 \div 2{,}400 = 3.49$	$\dfrac{9{,}371 - 8{,}379}{3{,}000 - 2{,}400} = 1.65$
3,000	$9{,}371 \div 3{,}000 = 3.12$	

   c. Yes. The marginal product of grain decreases as more of it is used.

5. *a.* No. It seems likely that some capital and land are used.
   b. No. It says that an extra ¼ hour of labor, or an extra ½ pound of paper, will result in an extra paper napkin, regardless of the number of paper napkins produced. Beyond some output level, one would expect the marginal product of labor and of paper to fall.
   c. No.
6. *a.* No.
   b. General farms.
   c. No.
7. The complete table is:

Number of units of variable input	Total output	Marginal product	Average product
3	90	Unknown	30
4	110	20	27 ½
5	130	20	26
6	135	5	22 ½
7	136 ½	1 ½	19 ½

8. Because of the law of diminishing marginal returns, the marginal product begins to decline at some point. If the marginal product exceeds the average product at that point, the marginal product can fall to some extent without reducing the average product. Only when it falls below the average product will the average product begin to decrease. The marginal product can continue to fall without reducing the total product. Only when it falls below zero will the total product begin to decrease.
9. *a.* Yes, since it seems to reduce the amount of grain and protein that must be used to produce 150 pounds of pork. However, this assumes that it has no negative effect on the quality of the pork and that it does not increase the amount of other inputs that must be used.
   b. At each quantity of protein, curve *B* is steeper than curve *A*. In other words, the absolute value of its slope is greater. Thus, the marginal rate of technical substitution of protein for grain is greater when Aureomycin is added than when it is not.
10. It resulted in more output being obtainable from a fixed amount of capital and labor than before. Once the new machines were available, the optimal input combination was one where the capital-labor ratio was higher than before.
11. It is clear that we are unlikely to find more than about 10–20 auto firms in the United States. Since Chile produces far fewer autos, we would expect to find far fewer auto firms than this number. Engineering estimates and statistical analysis of costs are some important techniques to estimate economies of scale.
12. Yes. The marginal product of labor equals the slope of this relationship. If you plot the relationship, you will find that the slope decreases as *L* increases.
13. First, the making of profits generally requires time and energy, and, if the owners of the firm are the managers as well, they may decide that it is preferable to sacrifice profits for leisure. Second, in an uncertain world, the concept of maximum profit is not clearly defined. Third, it is often claimed that firms pursue other objectives than profits: e.g., better social conditions, a good image, higher market share, and so forth.

   Alternative assumptions are as follows: We can assume that firms maximize utility, not profit. We can assume that they maximize some function of expected profit and the variance of profits. We can assume that they "satisfice." Or we can assume that they maximize sales subject to a profit constraint.

   Profit maximization remains the standard assumption in microeconomics because it is a close enough approximation for many important purposes, because alternative theories sometimes require unavailable data, and because it provides rules of rational behavior for firms that do want to maximize profits.

14. Technology is the sum total of society's pool of knowledge concerning the industrial and agricultural arts. How much can be produced with a given set of inputs depends upon the level of technology.

    A fixed input is an input whose quantity cannot be changed during the period of time under consideration.

    A variable input is an input whose quantity can be changed during the relevant period.

15. The production function is the relationship between the quantities of various inputs used per period of time and the maximum quantity of the output that can be produced per period of time.

    The short run is that period of time in which some of the firms's inputs are fixed.

    The long run is that period of time in which all inputs are variable.

    In the short run, certain inputs are fixed in quantity, whereas this is not the case in the long run.

16. *a.* The average product curve is as follows:

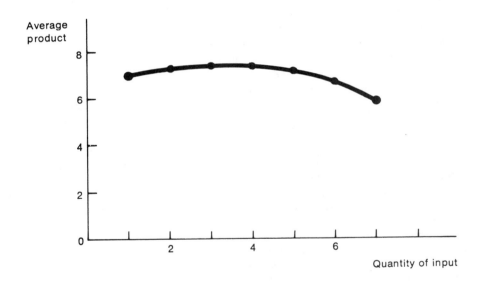

b. The marginal product curve is as follows:

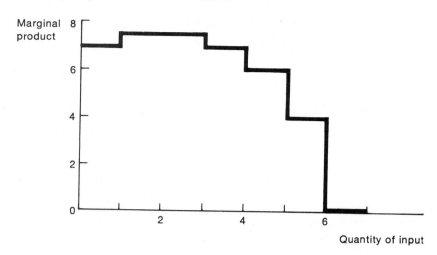

17. The law of diminishing marginal returns states that, if equal increments of an input are added, the quantities of other inputs being held constant, the resulting increments in product will decrease beyond some point.

Since marginal product decreases beyond some point, the marginal product curve must turn down beyond some point.

18. The average product of *OQ* units of input equals the slope of *OG*, a straight line that connects *O* and *G*. The marginal product at *OQ* units of input equals the slope of *VV'*, the tangent at *G*.

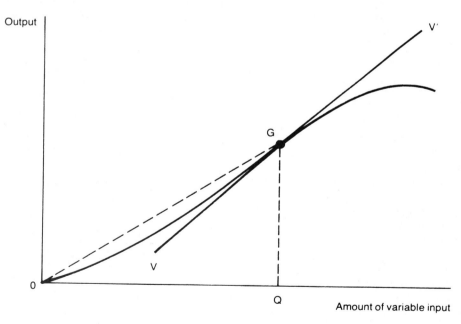

19. An isoquant is a curve showing all possible (efficient) combinations of inputs that can produce a certain quantity of output.

   The marginal rate of technical substitution is the rate at which one input can be substituted for another to maintain a constant output rate.

20. Letting Q be output, x_1 be the amount of labor, and x_2 be the amount of capital,

$$dQ = \frac{\partial f}{\partial x_1} dx_1 + \frac{\partial f}{\partial x_2} dx_2 \; ,$$

where f is the production function. Since $dQ = 0$, the marginal rate of technical substitution is

$$\frac{-dx_2}{dx_1} = \frac{\partial f}{\partial x_1} \div \frac{\partial f}{\partial x_2}$$

21. If all inputs are increased by a certain percentage, with the result that output increases by
more than this percentage, this is a case of increasing returns to scale.

   If all inputs are increased by a certain percentage, with the result that output increases
by less than this percentage, this is a case of decreasing returns to scale.

   If all inputs are increased by a certain percentage, with the result that output increases
by the same percentage, this is a case of constant returns to scale.

   Increasing returns to scale may be due to indivisibilities, various geometrical relations,
greater specialization, probabilistic considerations, and so forth.

   Decreasing returns to scale may result from the difficulties of managing a large enterprise.

22. The three principal methods have been time-series analysis, cross-section studies, and
methods based on information supplied by engineers or agricultural scientists. One problem is that the data may not pertain to efficient combinations of inputs. Another problem is the difficulty of measuring capital. Despite these and many other problems, the resulting estimates have been of considerable interest and use.

23. According to Simon, firms aim at a "satisfactory" level of profit rather than maximum
profit. According to Baumol, firms maximize sales, subject to the constraint that a certain
minimum profit level is attained.

24. 1.04 percent.

25. It is generally larger than the coefficient of capital.

26. Yes.

27. Yes.

Completion Questions

1. 48, 75, 27
2. long run
3. "satisficing"
4. Cobb-Douglas
5. fixed in quantity
6. variable in quantity
7. variation
8. the quantity of the input
9. an extra unit of the input
10. constant
11. intersect

True or False

1. True   2. False   3. False   4. True   5. False   6. False   7. False   8. True   9. True
10. False   11. False   12. False   13. False

Multiple Choice

1. *a*   2. *c*   3. *c*   4. *a*   5. *a*   6. *c*   7. *b*

CHAPTER 7 Optimal Input Combinations and Cost Functions

Case Study: Cost Functions in the Railroad Industry

Edwin Mansfield and Harold Wein estimated the relationship between total cost and output in a railroad freight yard. *All yards contain sets of tracks. In large yards, the tracks are generally of three types: receiving tracks where incoming freight cars are stored, classification tracks where cars are switched, and outbound tracks where cars that were situated on a classification track are stored until a locomotive hauls them away as a train. Freight yards switch cars; that is, they sort incoming cars by putting them on the appropriate classification tracks, and in this way they break up incoming trains to form new trains. Most yards also deliver and pick up cars. Engines are assigned to deliver cars to industrial sidings and other yards and to pick them up there.

For the particular yard studied by these authors, the relationship between total cost and output is

$$C = 4{,}914 + 0.42S + 2.44D$$

where C is daily cost (in dollars), S is the number of cuts switched per day, and D is the number of cars delivered per day. A "cut" is a group of cars that rolls as a unit on to the same classification track; it is often used as a measure of switching output.

  a. If this yard delivers no cars and switches 1,000 cuts on a given day, what is the average total cost of switching each cut?

  b. If this yard switches no cuts and delivers 1,000 cars on a given day, what is the average total cost of delivering a car?

  c. What is the marginal cost of switching a cut? Based on the above equation, does the marginal cost of switching a cut depend on the number of cars delivered?

  d. What is the marginal cost of delivering a car? Based on the above equation, does the marginal cost of delivering a car depend on the number of cuts switched?

  e. Do you think that the above equation holds for any value of S or D, no matter how large? Explain.

Problems and Review Questions

1. Elizabeth Winter's farm is a profit maximizing, perfectly competitive producer of tomatoes. It produces tomatoes using one acre of land (price = $2,000) and varying amounts of labor (price = $500 per man-month). The production function is as follows:

*E. Mansfield and H. Wein,"A Regression Control Chart for Costs," *Applied Statistics* (March 1958).

Number of man-months (per month)	Output of tomatoes per month (in truckloads)
0	0
1	1
3	2
7	3
12	4
18	5
25	6

Show that Ms. Winter's farm is subject to increasing marginal cost as output increases.

2. John Merriwether, vice-president of sales of a textile firm, is 47 years old, makes $50,000 a year, and is an executive on the rise. Besides his accomplishments in business, Mr. Merriwether is an artist with some talent but no training. He talks wistfully of spending a year or two at an art school but concludes ruefully that "It would cost too much." Mrs. Merriwether, who has never had a job, also has some artistic talent and enrolls at a local art school when her youngest child enters college.
  a. Why, if Mr. Merriwether feels that a year or two of art school would cost too much, is he willing to let his wife enroll?
  b. Is the cost the same to Mrs. Merriwether as to her husband?
  c. What is the cost to her husband of a year at art school?
  d. Indicate how this case helps to explain why the young, rather than the middle-aged, go to college.

3. According to data published by the U. S. Department of Agriculture, 8,500 pounds of milk can be produced by a cow fed the following combinations of hay and grain:

Quantity of hay (pounds)	Quantity of grain (pounds)
5,000	6 154
5,500	5,454
6,000	4,892
6,500	4,423
7,000	4,029
7,500	3,694

  a. A cost-minimizing farmer has a cow producing 8,500 pounds of milk, and he is feeding the cow 7,000 pounds of hay and 4,029 pounds of grain. What is the lowest possible value for the ratio of the price of grain to the price of hay? Why?
  b. Under the conditions described in part (a), what is the highest possible value of this ratio? Why?
  c. If the price of a pound of hay equals one-half the price of a pound of grain (which equals P), what is the cost of each input combination?
  d. Under the conditions described in part (c), what is the minimum-cost input combination (of those shown above)?

4. The Miracle Manufacturing Company's short-run average cost function in 1985 is

$$AC = 3 + 4Q$$

where AC is the firm's average cost (in dollars per pound of the product), and Q is its output rate.

  a. Obtain an equation for the firm's short-run total cost function.
  b. Does the firm have any fixed costs? Explain.
  c. If the price of the Miracle Manufacturing Company's product (per pound) is $2, is the firm making profits or losses? Explain.

5. Fill in the blanks in the table below:

Output	Total cost	Total fixed cost	Total variable cost	Average fixed cost	Average variable cost
0	50	____	____	____	____
1	70	____	____	____	____
2	100	____	____	____	____
3	120	____	____	____	____
4	135	____	____	____	____
5	150	____	____	____	____
6	160	____	____	____	____
7	165	____	____	____	____

6. In recent years, there has been considerable pressure from consumer advocates and other groups for more and better safety devices in automobiles. What effect do you think the adoption of these devices has on the total cost function of an automobile manufacturer? Does it affect total fixed costs? Marginal costs? If so, how?

7. Based on results obtained by Harold Cohen, the total cost of operating a hospital can be approximated by $4,700,000 + .00013X^2$, where X is the number of patient days (a crude measure of output).[*] Derive an expression for the relationship between the cost per patient day and the number of patient days. How big must a hospital be (in terms of patient days) to minimize the cost per patient day?

8. J. A. Nordin[†] found the following relationship between an electric light and power plant's fuel costs (C) and its eight-hour output as a percent of capacity (Q):

$$C = 16.68 + 0.125\ Q + 0.00439Q^2$$

When Q increases from 50 to 51, what is the increase in the cost of fuel for this electric plant? Of what use might this result be to the plant's managers?

9. Show that a firm will maximize output—for a given outlay—by distributing its expenditures among various inputs in such a way that the marginal product of a dollar's worth of any input is equal to the marginal product of a dollar's worth of any other input that is used.

[*]H. Cohen, "Hospital Cost Curves with Emphasis on Measuring Patient Care Output." in H. Klarman. *Empirical Studies in Health Economics* (Baltimore, Md.: Johns Hopkins University Press, 1970).

[†]J. A. Nordin, *Econometrica* (July 1947).

10. Suppose that capital and labor are the only inputs used by a printing plant and that capital costs $1 a unit and labor costs $2 a unit. Draw the isocost curves corresponding to an outlay of $200 and $300.

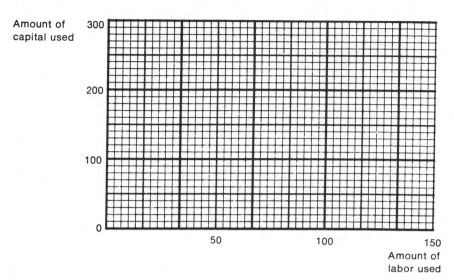

11. Discuss the reasons why the firm, if it is to minimize the cost of producing a given output, must equate the marginal rate of technical substitution and the input-price ratio.

12. Discuss the nature and importance of the opportunity cost or alternative cost doctrine.

13. What are the differences between private and social costs? Illustrate your answer with cases of environmental pollution.

14. What are the differences between explicit and implicit costs? Why do economists bother with implicit costs?

15. What is the difference between the short run and the long run? What is the difference between fixed inputs and variable inputs?

16. *a.* Suppose that a steel firm's costs are as shown below:

Units of output	Total fixed cost (dollars)	Total variable cost (dollars)
0	$500	0
1	500	50
2	500	90
3	500	140
4	500	200
5	500	270
6	500	350
7	500	450
8	500	600

Draw the firm's total fixed cost function below:

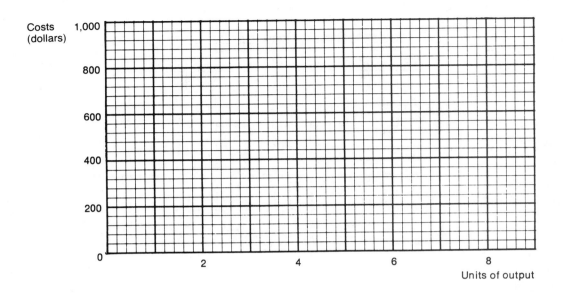

Costs (dollars) / Units of output

b. **Draw the firm's total variable cost function below:**

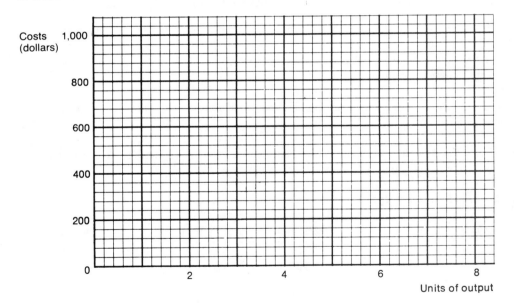

Costs (dollars) / Units of output

c. Draw the firm's total cost function below:

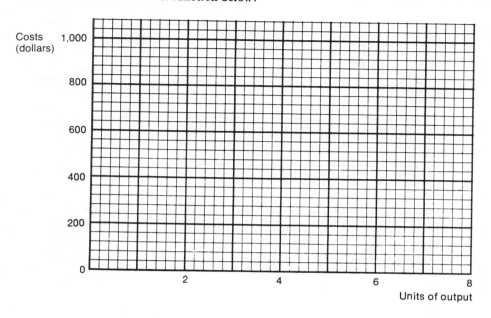

d. Draw the firm's average fixed cost function below:

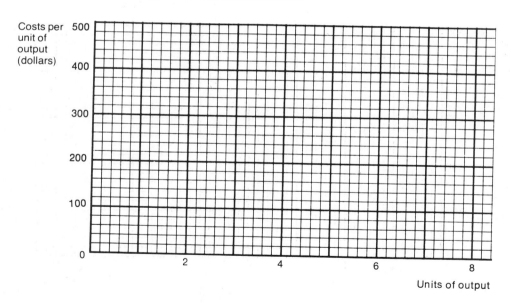

e. Draw the firm's average variable cost function below:

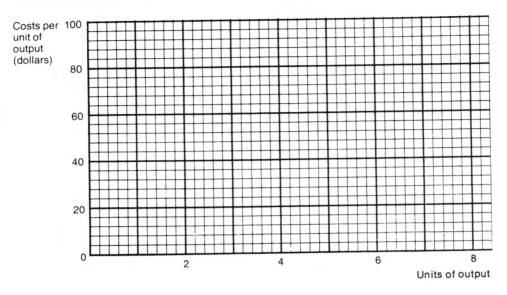

f. Draw the firm's average total cost function below:

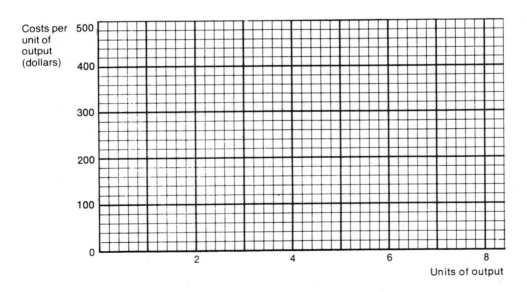

g. Draw the firm's marginal cost function below:

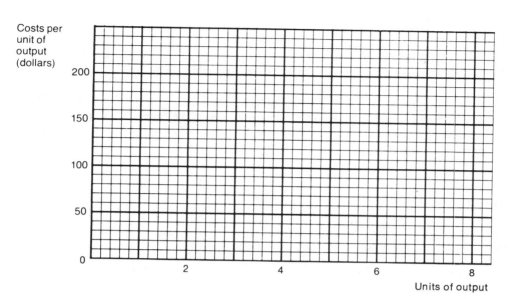

17. Suppose that you are a consultant to a firm that publishes books. Suppose that the firm is about to publish a book that will sell for $10 a copy. The fixed costs of publishing the books are $5,000; the variable cost is $5 a copy. What is the break-even point for this book?

18. If the price were $8 rather than $10 in the previous problem, what would be the break-even point?

19. *a.* Suppose that a steel plant's production function is $Q = 5L\,K$, where Q is its output rate, L is the amount of labor it uses per period of time, and K is the amount of capital it uses per period of time. Suppose that the price of labor is $1 a unit and the price of capital is $2 a unit. The firm's vice-president for manufacturing hires you to figure out what combination of inputs the plant should use to produce 20 units of output per period. What advice would you give him?

b. Suppose that the price of labor increases to $2 per unit. What effect will this have on output per unit of labor?

20. *a.* According to Joel Dean's classic study of a hosiery mill, total cost equaled $2,936 + 1.998 Q, where Q is output. How does marginal cost behave, according to this finding?

b. How does average cost behave, according to this finding?

c. What factor could account for Dean's finding that marginal cost does not increase as output rises?

21. According to Frederick Moore, engineers sometimes rely on the so-called "0.6 rule" which

states that the increase in cost is given by the increase in capacity raised to the 0.6 power; that is,

$$C_2 = C_1 (X_2/X_1)^{0.6}$$

where C_1 and C_2 are the costs of two pieces of equipment and X_1 and X_2 are their respective capacities. Does the 0.6 rule imply economies of scale?

22. According to many econometric studies of long-run average cost in various industries, the long-run average cost curve tends to be L-shaped. For example, this is one of the conclusions reached by A. A. Walters in his well-known review article. Does this mean that there are constant returns to scale at all levels of output?

Completion Questions

1. If the average fixed cost of producing 10 units of output at the Rothschild Manufacturing Company is $10, the average fixed cost of producing 20 units is _____. If the marginal cost of each of the first 20 units of output is $5, the average variable cost of producing 20 units is _____. And the average total cost of producing 20 units is _____.

2. If it minimizes cost, a firm will produce at a point where the isocost curve is _____ _____ to the isoquant.

3. Plant and equipment of a firm are _____ in the short run.

4. Total cost equals _____ plus variable cost.

5. Average cost must equal marginal cost at the point where average cost is a _____.

6. The long-run total cost equals output times _____.

7. _____ include opportunity costs of resources owned and used by the firm's owner.

8. An important criticism of cross-section studies of cost functions is that they sometimes are subject to the _____.

9. The determinants of the shape of the long-run average cost curve are _____ _____.

10. The total variable cost curve turns up beyond some output level because of the _____ _____.

11. The marginal cost curve turns up beyond some output level because of the _____ _____.

12. Average variable cost equals the price of the variable input divided by _____ _____, if the price of the variable input is constant.

13. Marginal cost equals the price of the variable input divided by _____

_____, if the price of the variable input is constant.

True or False

_____ 1. If average variable cost always equals $20 when output is less than 100 units, marginal cost is less than $20 when output is in this range.

_____ 2. Long-run marginal cost can never exceed short-run marginal cost.

_____ 3. A firm always can vary the quantity of labor inputs in the short run.

_____ 4. Costs that have already been incurred are important factors in making production decisions.

_____ 5. The opportunity cost doctrine says that the production of one good may reduce the cost of another good.

_____ 6. The marginal rate of technical substitution of labor for capital is the marginal product of capital divided by the marginal product of labor.

_____ 7. When the firm has constructed the scale of plant that is optimal for producing a given level of output, long-run marginal cost will equal short-run marginal cost at that output.

_____ 8. The shape of the long-run average cost function is due primarily to the law of diminishing marginal returns.

_____ 9. Average cost must exceed marginal cost at the point where average cost is a minimum.

_____ 10. The break-even point lies well above the output level that must be reached if the firm is to avoid losses.

_____ 11. Whether or not an industry is a natural monopoly depends on the long-run average cost curve and the industry demand curve.

_____ 12. Empirical studies often indicate the short-run average cost curve is S-shaped.

Multiple Choice

1. Firm X's average total cost per month equals $5 × Q$, where Q is the number of units of output produced per month. The marginal cost of the third unit of output produced per month is
   a. $15.
   b. $20.
   c. $25.
   d. $30.
   e. none of the above.

2. The curve in the graph below has the shape of
   a. marginal cost curve.
   b. average variable cost curve.
   c. average fixed cost curve.
   d. all of the above.
   e. none of the above.

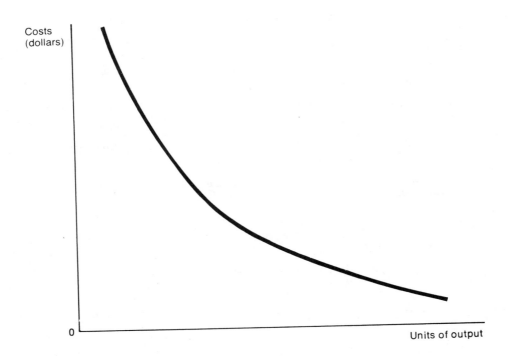

$5.$ t

3. The firm's cost functions are determined by
   a. the price of its product.
   b. its assets.
   c. its production function.
   d. the age of the firm.
   e. none of the above.

4. The following industry often is a natural monopoly:
   a. cigarette industry.
   b. publishing industry.
   c. drug industry.
   d. electric power industry.
   e. none of the above.

5. The curve shown below is
   a. an isoquant.
   b. an isocost curve.
   c. an average cost curve.
   d. a marginal cost curve.
   e. all of the above.

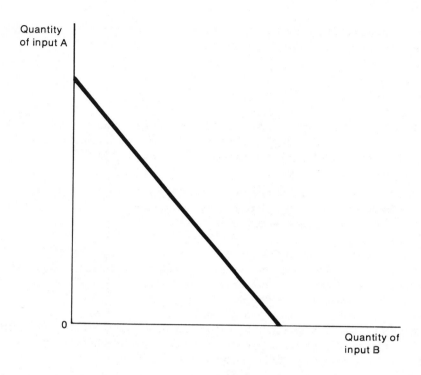

Key Concepts for Review

Isocost curve
Alternative cost
Opportunity cost
Social cost
Private cost
Explicit cost
Implicit cost
Cost function
Total fixed cost
Total variable cost

Total cost
Average fixed cost
Average variable cost
Average cost
Marginal cost
Break-even chart
Long-run average cost curve
Long-run marginal cost curve
Statistical cost functions

Answers

a. Total cost equals $4,914.00 + $420.00 = $5,334.00, so average cost equals about $5.33.
b. Total cost equals $4,914.00 + $2,440.00 = $7,354.00, so average cost equals about $7.35.
c. 42 cents. No.
d. $2.44. No.
e. No. Eventually, as more cuts are switched, the marginal cost of switching a cut is bound to rise. Eventually, as more cars are delivered, the marginal cost of delivering a car is bound to rise.

Problems and Review Questions

1. The *extra* labor needed to produce the first, second, third, fourth, fifth, and sixth truck-loads of tomatoes are 1, 2, 4, 5, 6, and 7 man-months. Thus, the marginal cost of the first, second, third, fourth, fifth, and sixth truckloads of tomatoes are $500, $1,000, $2,000, $2,500, $3,000, and $3,500.

2. a. One important reason is that the cost of Mrs. Merriwether's going to art school is likely to be much less than the cost of his going, if the cost is measured correctly. This cost includes not only the amount spent on tuition and books, but also the alternative cost of the time it takes.
   b. No, because the alternative cost of her time is less than the alternative cost of his time. If he spends a year at art school, they will lose $50,000 in forgone earnings (and perhaps more, because it may jeopardize his income in future years), whereas if she spends a year at art school, their earnings will not decline.
   c. The cost is the amount spent on tuition and books (and whatever other expenses are associated with attendance at art school) plus the alternative cost of his time. The alternative cost of his time is the amount he could have earned if he had not gone to school.
   d. The costs of going to school tend to be much higher for the middle-aged than for the young, because the alternative cost of a middle-aged person's time tends to be higher than that of a young person (because the middle-aged tend to earn more per hour than the young). In addition, of course, the benefits from going to school may be less for the middle-aged than for the young because there are fewer years ahead to reap such rewards.

3. a. If P_G is the price of a pound of grain and P_H is the price of a pound of hay

$$7,000 P_H + 4,029 P_G < 7,500 P_H + 3,694 P_G$$

$$7,000 P_H + 4,029 P_G < 6,500 P_H + 4,423 P_G$$

These inequalities hold because the chosen input combination is known to have lower cost than any of the others. Thus

$$(4,029 - 3,694) P_G < (7,500 - 7,000) P_H$$

or

$$\frac{4,029 - 3,694}{7,500 - 7,000} = \frac{335}{500} = 0.67 < \frac{P_H}{P_G}$$

and

$$(7,000 - 6,500) P_H < (4,423 - 4,029) P_G$$

-110-

or

$$\frac{7,000 - 6,500}{4,423 - 4,029} = \frac{500}{394} = 1.269 < \frac{P_G}{P_H}$$

Thus, the lowest possible ratio of the price of grain to the price of hay is 1.269.

b. In part (a), we showed that $P_H/P_G > \frac{335}{500}$. Thus

$$P_G/P_H < \frac{500}{335} = 1.492.$$

Consequently, the highest possible ratio of the price of grain to the price of hay is 1.492.

c. The cost of each input combination (in the order they appear in the table in the question) is:

$$8,654 \, P$$
$$8,204 \, P$$
$$7,892 \, P$$
$$7,673 \, P$$
$$7,529 \, P$$
$$7,444 \, P$$

d. The minimum-cost combination (of those considered here) is 7,500 pounds of hay and 3,694 pounds of grain.

4. a. Since total cost equals average cost times output, the firm's total cost function is

$$C = AC \times Q = 3Q + 4Q^2$$

b. No, since total cost equals zero when $Q = 0$.

c. If the price is $2, total revenue ($R$) equals $2Q$. Thus, the firm's profit equals

$$\pi = R - C = 2Q - (3Q + 4Q^2) = -Q - 4Q^2$$

If Q is greater than zero, π must be negative, and the firm is incurring losses. If the firm is producing nothing, it is incurring neither profits nor losses. Thus, the firm is better off to produce nothing.

5. The table is as follows:

Total fixed cost	Total variable cost	Average fixed cost	Average variable cost
50	0	—	—
50	20	50	20
50	50	25	25
50	70	$16\,^2/_3$	$23\,^1/_3$
50	85	$12\,^1/_2$	$21\,^1/_4$
50	100	10	20
50	110	$8\,^1/_3$	$18\,^1/_3$
50	115	$7\,^1/_7$	$16\,^3/_7$

6. It will probably shift the total cost function upward; that is, the total cost of producing a particular number of automobiles will increase. To the extent that automobile manufacturers must increase their plant and equipment to produce and assemble such safety devices, fixed costs will rise. Marginal cost will probably increase because the addition of the safety devices may increase the cost of producing an extra car.

7. Cost per patient day is:

$$\frac{4,700,000}{X} + .00013X$$

which is a minimum when X is approximately equal to 190,000 patient days.

8. When $Q = 50$, $C = 16.68 + (0.125)(50) + (0.00439)(2500)$, which equals 33.905. When $Q = 51$, $C = 16.68 + (0.125)(51) + (0.00439)(2601)$, which equals 34.473. Thus, the increase in fuel cost is 0.568.

This result might be of use to the managers in determining whether it would be profitable to increase output.

9. Draw the firm's isoquants, as shown below. Also draw the isocost curve corresponding to the given outlay. Clearly, point P is the input combination that maximizes output for this outlay. Since the firm's isoquant is tangent to the isocost curve at point P, the slope of the

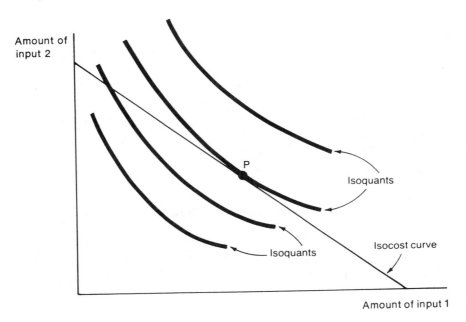

isocost curve (which equals minus one times the price of input 1 ÷ price of input 2) must equal the slope of the isoquant (which equals minus one times the marginal product of input 1 ÷ marginal product of input 2). Thus, at point P, the ratio of the marginal product to the price of each input must be the same.

10. The isocost curves are as follows:

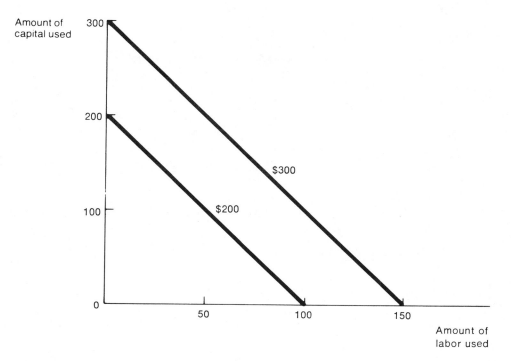

11. If the firm minimizes the cost of producing a certain output, it picks a point on the isoquant (corresponding to this output) that is on the lowest isocost curve. This means that the optimal point is a point of tangency between this isoquant and an isocost curve. But if it is a point of tangency, the slope of the isoquant must equal the slope of the isocost curve at this point. Since the slope of the isoquant is minus one times the marginal rate of technical substitution and the slope of the isocost curve is minus one times the input price ratio, it follows that the marginal rate of technical substitution must equal the input price ratio at this point.

12. According to the opportunity or alternative cost doctrine, the cost of producing a certain product is the value of the other products that the resources used in its production could have produced instead. This doctrine lies at the heart of economic analysis and is important for proper managerial decision-making as well as for the formulation of public policy.

13. Private costs are costs to individual producers. Social costs are the total costs to society. When a firm dumps wastes into the water or the air, the private costs to the firm may be nil, but the costs to other parts of society—drinkers of the water, fishermen, people who enjoy boating, etc.—may be very great.

14. Explicit costs are the ordinary expenses that accountants include as the firm's expenses. Implicit costs are the opportunity costs of the labor and capital owned and used by the firm's owners. Unless implicit costs are considered, the firm cannot determine whether or not it is making an economic profit.

15. In the short run, some inputs, particularly the firm's plant and equipment, are fixed. In the long run, no inputs are fixed. A fixed input is one that is fixed in quantity. A variable input is one that is not fixed in quantity.

16. *a.*

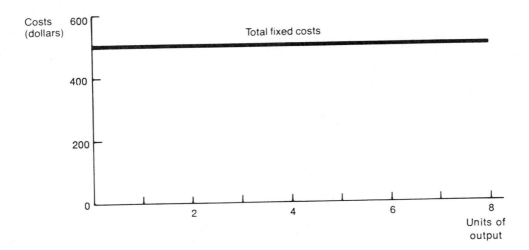

b.

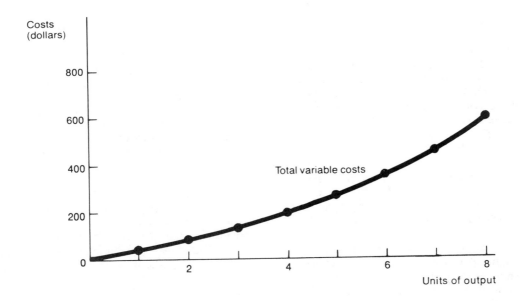

c.

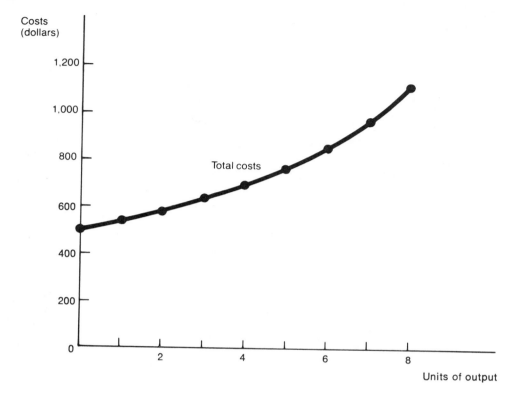

d.

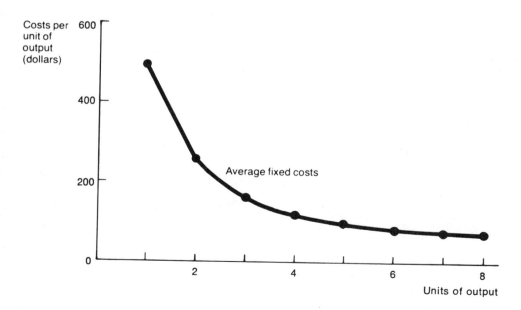

e.

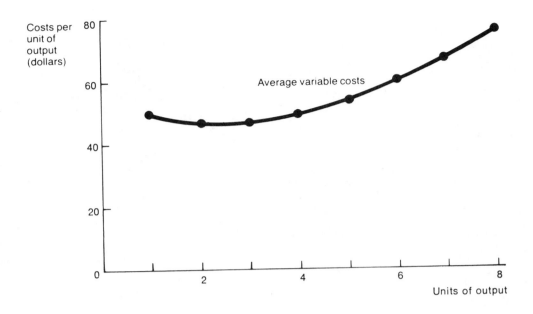

Costs per unit of output (dollars)

Average variable costs

Units of output

f.

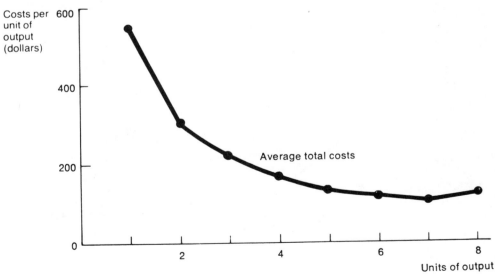

Costs per unit of output (dollars)

Average total costs

Units of output

g.

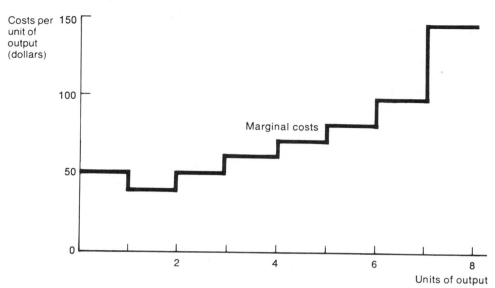

17. 1000 copies sold.
18. 1667 copies sold.
19. *a.* The isocost curve is: Cost = $1 \cdot L + 2 \cdot K$, or L = cost − $2K$. The relevant isoquant is $20 = 5L \cdot K$, or $L = 4 \div K$. The point on this isoquant that is on the lowest isocost curve is $K = \sqrt{2}$ and $L = 2\sqrt{2}$.
    b. If the price of labor is \$2 per unit, the optimal value of K is 2 and the optimal value of L is 2. Thus, output per unit of labor is $20 \div 2$, or 10, whereas it formerly was $20 \div 2\sqrt{2}$, or $10 \div \sqrt{2}$. Thus output per unit of labor has risen.
20. *a.* It is constant: \$1.998.
    b. It declines as Q increases. Specifically, it equals $1.998 + \dfrac{2936}{Q}$.
    c. The data do not cover the range of output near and at the plant's capacity.
21. Yes.
22. No.

Completion Questions

1. \$5, \$5, \$10
2. tangent
3. fixed
4. fixed cost
5. minimum
6. long-run average cost
7. implicit costs
8. regression fallacy
9. economies and diseconomies of scale
10. law of diminishing marginal returns
11. law of diminishing marginal returns
12. average variable product
13. marginal product

True or False

1. False   2. False   3. False   4. False   5. False   6. False   7. True   8. False   9. False
10. False   11. True   12. False

Multiple Choice

1. *c*   2. *c*   3. *c*   4. *d*   5. *b*

Part 4 MARKET STRUCTURE, PRICE AND OUTPUT

CHAPTER 8 Price and Output under Perfect Competition

Case Study: The Widget Industry

In 1985, the widget industry is perfectly competitive. The lowest point on the long-run average cost curve of each of the identical widget producers is $4, and this minimum point occurs at an output of 1,000 widgets per month. When the optimal scale of a firm's plant is operated to produce 1,150 widgets per month, the short-run average cost of each firm is $5. The market demand curve for widgets is

$$Q_D = 140,000 - 10,000\,P$$

where P is the price of a widget and Q_D is the quantity of widgets demanded per month. The market supply curve for widgets is

$$Q_S = 80,000 + 5,000\,P$$

where Q_S is the quantity of widgets supplied per month. (P is expressed in dollars per widget.)

a. What is the equilibrium price of a widget? Is this the long-run equilibrium price?

b. How many firms are in this industry when it is in long-run equilibrium?

c. If the market demand curve shifts to

$$Q_D = 150,000 - 5,000\,P$$

what is the new equilibrium price and output in the short run, for both the industry and each firm?

d. In the situation described in part (c), are firms making profits or losses? (Assume that the number of firms in the industry equals the number that would exist in long-run equilibrium.)

Problems and Review Questions

1. According to a study by Henry Steele, if crude oil were produced in the United States under perfectly competitive conditions, its short-run supply curve in 1965 would have been as shown on the next page.

   a. If annual production had been 2.0 billion barrels in 1965, what would have been the marginal cost of a barrel of oil, according to Steele?

   b. If crude oil were produced under perfectly competitive conditions, and its supply curve was as shown on the next page, what would have been its short-run equilibrium price if the demand for crude oil was 3 billion barrels per year, regardless of price?

   c. In fact, in 1965, there was prorationing in the oil industry, an arrangement which limited the amount that could be produced by low-cost wells. Given the existence of prorationing, was the short-run supply curve to the left or right of the one in the graph on the next page? Why?

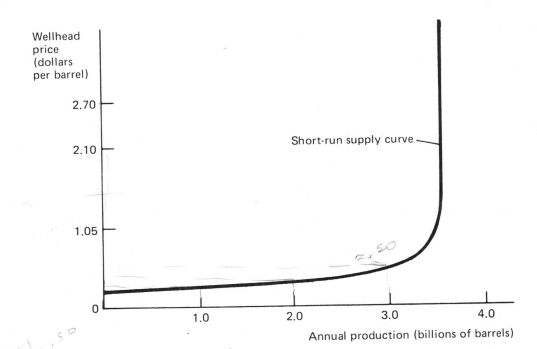

Wellhead price (dollars per barrel)

Short-run supply curve

2.70
2.10
1.05
0

1.0   2.0   3.0   4.0

Annual production (billions of barrels)

2. Suppose that a perfectly competitive firm has the short-run total cost function shown below:

Output	Total cost (dollars)
0	10
1	12
2	16
3	22
4	30
5	40

There are 1,000 firms in this industry, and the market demand curve is as follows:

Price (dollars)	Quantity demanded
3	3,000
5	2,000
7	1,500
9	1,000

a. What is the equilibrium price of the product? (Assume that the price must be $3, $5, $7, or $9.)

b. What will be the output of each firm?

c. In the long run, will firms tend to enter or leave this industry?

3. From time immemorial, moralists have been fond of counseling that "anything worth doing is worth doing well."

-120-

a. Indicate how the theory of the firm can be adapted to shed light on whether this counsel is correct.

b. Consider cleanliness, which some say is second only to Godliness. Use your answer to part (a) to explain why people settle for a lower level of cleanliness in garages than in operating rooms.

4. The long-run supply curve for a good is a horizontal line at a price of $3 per unit of the good. The demand curve for the good is

$$Q_D = 50 - 2P$$

where Q_D is the quantity of the good demanded (in millions of units per year) and P is the price per unit (in dollars).

a. What is the equilibrium output of the good?

b. If a tax of $1.00 is imposed on the good, what is the equilibrium output of the good?

c. After the tax is imposed, a friend of yours buys a unit of the good for $3.75. Is this the long-run equilibrium price?

5. (Advanced*) A firm's total cost function (where C is total cost in dollars and Q is quantity) is

$$C = 200 + 4Q + 2Q^2$$

a. If the firm is perfectly competitive and if the price of its product is $24, what is its optimal output rate?

b. At this output rate, what are its profits?

c. Derive the firm's short-run supply curve.

6. If the textile industry is a constant-cost industry and the demand curve for textiles shifts upward, describe the process by which a perfectly competitive market generates an increased quantity of textiles. What happens if the government will not allow the price of textiles to rise?

7. A perfectly competitive firm has the following total cost function:

Total output	Total cost (dollars)
0	20
1	30
2	42
3	55
4	69
5	84
6	100
7	117

How much will the firm produce, if the price is:

a. $13?

b. $14?

c. $15?

d. $16?

e. $17?

*This problem involves the use of some elementary calculus.

-121-

8. Suppose that there are 100 firms producing the good in question 7 and that each firm has the total cost function shown there. If input prices remain constant, draw the industry supply curve in the graph below (when the price is between $13 and $17).

9. An economist estimates that, in the short run, the quantity of widgets supplied at each price is as follows:

Price (dollars)	Quantity supplied per year (millions)
1	5
2	6
3	7
4	8

Calculate the arc elasticity of supply when the price is between $3 and $4 per widget. (Review Chapter 2 if you do not recall the definition of the arc elasticity of supply. Note that this supply curve is quite different from that which was given in the case study at the beginning of this chapter, perhaps because they pertain to different time periods or markets.)

10. The Besser Manufacturing Company had only 465 employees in 1951 and sales of less than $15 million. Given that it is a small firm, can we be reasonably sure that it will have little or no control over the price of its product (concrete block machinery)?

11. In late 1962, Karl Fox* estimated that, based on a fairly typical farm situation in northeast Iowa, the most profitable number of dairy cows a farm operator should keep (at various expected prices of farm-separated cream) was as follows:

$$MP_c = \frac{Q}{C}$$

Expected price of cream (cents per pound)	Number of cows
60	2
80	4
100	6
120	11

$$\frac{6-4}{6+4} \qquad = \frac{2}{10} = \frac{1}{5} \cdot \frac{9}{}$$
$$\frac{100-80}{100+80} \qquad = \frac{20}{180} \qquad 1.8$$
$$(\varepsilon_D / > 1$$

If each cow yields the same amount of cream, what is the price elasticity of supply of cream for this farm when the expected price of cream is between 80 and 100 cents per pound?

12. Describe the four basic conditions that define perfect competition. How often are they encountered in the real world? *homo. largest.*

13. Describe how equilibrium price is determined in a perfectly competitive market in the market period. *homog. summation*

14. Suppose that the supply of a certain kind of paintings is fixed at 8 units and that the demand curve for these paintings is as shown below. What is the equilibrium price for these paintings?

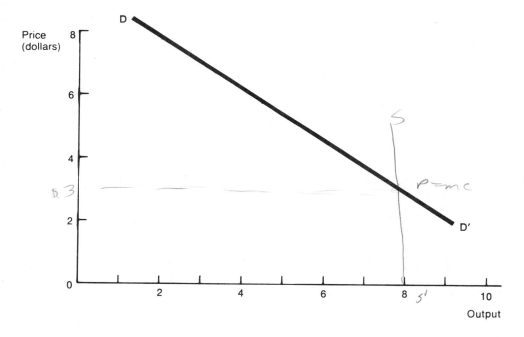

Farming, Farmers, and Markets for Farm Goods, Committee for Economic Development, 1962, p. 68.

15. Show that the perfectly competitive firm's supply curve in the short run is its marginal cost curve.

16. If the supplies of inputs to the industry as a whole are perfectly elastic, show that the industry supply curve in the short run is the horizontal summation of the firm supply curves.

17. *a.* If the coal industry's demand and supply curves are as shown below, what are the equilibrium price and output?

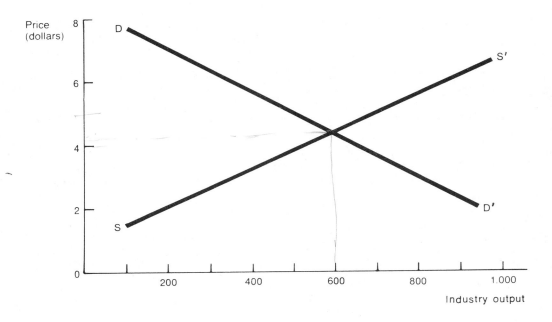

    b. Why can't a price of $6 prevail in this market? Why can't a price of $2 prevail?

18. Describe the forces that determine whether there will be a net in-migration or out-migration of firms from a particular industry.

19. Describe the equilibrium conditions for the perfectly competitive firm in the long run.

20. Describe what is meant by constant-cost industries.

21. Describe what is meant by increasing-cost industries.

22. Describe what is meant by decreasing-cost industries.

23. Given that price is currently at *OP*, show how price and output will move in succeeding periods, according to the cobweb theorem. (*DD'* is the demand curve; *SS'* is the supply curve.)

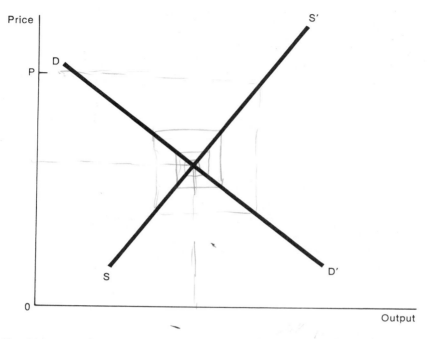

24. To what extent does the cotton textile industry conform to the assumptions of perfect competition?

25. Explain why, if we correct for changes in the price level resulting from over-all inflation, there was a declining trend in farm prices up to 1973.

26. Explain why farm prices vary between good times and bad to a much greater extent than nonfarm prices.

27. According to the U. S. Census Bureau, the largest four producers of rubber products accounted for about 50 percent of the industry's value added. Do you think that the perfectly competitive model will work as well in rubber products as in cotton textiles? Why or why not?

28. According to Marc Nerlove and W. Addison, the long-run elasticity of the supply of green peas is about 4.40. Of what use might this fact be to the Department of Agriculture?

29. According to Arthur Harlow of the Bonneville Power Administration, there is an important cycle in hog production. "Price preceded pig crop by one year, and slaughter followed the pig crop by a year. Prices were high when slaughter was low and vice versa." Is this sort of behavior consistent with the cobweb theorem?

30. According to D. Suits and S. Koizumi, the supply function for onions in the United States is log q = 0.134 + 0.0123 t + 0.324 log P − 0.512 log C, where q is the quantity supplied in a particular year, t is the year (less 1924), P is the price last season, and C is the cost index last season. Suppose that price is estimated by one forecaster to be 10 cents this season, whereas another says that it will be 11 cents. How much difference will this make in the quantity supplied next season?

31. The Alliance Delivery Company operates under perfectly competitive conditions, its only variable input being labor. In the short run, its production function is as follows:

Quantity of labor (people hired per day)	Quantity of output (pounds per day)
0	0
1	50
2	75
3	95
4	110

In 1985, the daily wage of a worker is $40.

a. Plot the Alliance Delivery Company's total variable cost function in the graph below.

b. Plot the Alliance Delivery Company's marginal cost function in the graph below.

c. What is the optimal output of the firm if the price of a pound of output is $2?   *95*

d. Would the answers to the previous questions be the same if the firm could hire fractional numbers of workers per day?

e. In fact, is it possible for a firm to hire a fractional number of workers per day? Explain.

32. The Miller Company is a perfectly competitive firm. Its output is 50 units per month, its total revenue is $35,000 per month, its average total cost is $700, and its average variable cost is $500. It is operating at the output where average total cost is a minimum. What is each of the following?

a. Price.

b. Total cost.

c. Total fixed cost.

d. Total profit.

e. Marginal cost.

700 $=TFC$ $\overset{LR}{=TVC}$

$TC = FC + VC$ = $10000 + 25000 = 35000$

$TFC =$ → $T.C - TVC$

$\pi = TR - TC$ $= 35000 - 25000 = 10000$

$\doteq 0$ in LR

$= \dfrac{\Delta TC}{\Delta Q} = \dfrac{35000}{50} = 700$

$P = ATC$

$AVC = \dfrac{TVC}{q}$

$500 \quad \dfrac{TVC}{50}$

$25000 = TVC$

33. The Milton Corporation's marginal cost curve is

$$MC = 4 + 3Q \quad = P$$

where MC is the cost (in dollars) of producing the Qth unit of its product and Q is the number of units of its product produced per day. The price of a unit of its product is $3. A student at a local business school who works for the firm during the summer argues that, based on this evidence, the firm would make more money by shutting down than by continuing to operate. Do you agree? Explain.

$MC = 4 + 3(1) = 7$

$VC = $ cost of each add. unit

$P = 3

$MC < P$

P not cover VC

34. The Zoroaster Company's average cost curve is

$$AC = \frac{400}{Q} + 3Q$$

[handwritten: $=142.3$ $AC = \frac{400}{3} + (3)(3)$ $142.3(3)=TC$ $426.9 = TC$ $AC = \frac{TC}{Q}$ $mc = 220.9$]

where AC is its average cost (in dollars) and Q is the number of units of its product that is produced per day. The price of a unit of its product is $3.

a. If the firm produces more than one unit per day, is it making profits or losses? Explain.

b. Is the firm better off to shut down or operate? Explain.

[handwritten: $AC = \frac{400}{2} + 3(2) = 206 = AC$ $AC = \frac{TC}{Q}$ $206 = \frac{TC}{2}$ $TC = 412$]

35. Suppose that a firm's marginal cost curve is a horizontal line at $3 per unit of output, if output is less than or equal to 100 units per month. If the price of the product is $4 per unit, should the firm produce at least 100 units per month? Why or why not?

36. Suppose that you own a car wash and that its total cost function is

$$C = 20 + 2Q + 0.3Q^2$$

[handwritten: $mc = 2 + .6Q = 0$]

where C is total cost (in dollars) per hour and Q is number of cars washed per hour. Suppose that you receive $5 for each car that is washed. What is the optimal number of cars to wash per hour? What is the maximum profit that you can obtain?

[handwritten: $TR = P \cdot Q = 5 \cdot 0$]

37. Suppose once again that you are the owner of the car wash described in the previous problem. If the price you receive for each car wash falls from $5 to $2, will you continue to stay in operation? Why or why not?

38. *a.* Suppose that a perfectly competitive firm's total costs are as follows:

[handwritten left: MC: 0, 5, 5, 5, 5, 5 TR: 0, 5, 10, 15, 20, 25 $P \cdot Q$ P: 5]

Output rate	P	Total cost (dollars)	*MC*
0	5	10	> 10
1		12	> 2
2		15	> 3
3		19	> 4
4		24	> 5
5		30	> 6

If the price of the product is $5, how many units of output should the firm produce?

*[handwritten: 37) $TR = P \cdot Q = 2Q$
$TR - TC = \Pi = 2Q - (20 + 2Q + 0.3Q^2)$
$= -20 - 0.3Q^2$
$\Pi =$
$\Pi' = -0.6Q = 0$
$Q = 0$
NO]*

b. Draw the firm's total costs and total revenues in the graph below:

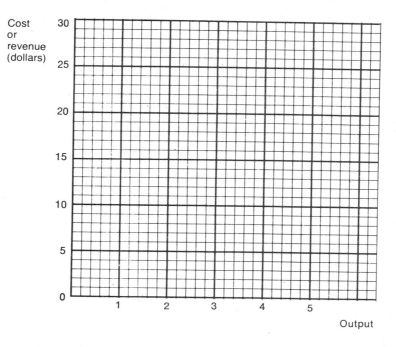

c. Draw the firm's marginal cost curve in the graph below, and find the output where price equals marginal cost.

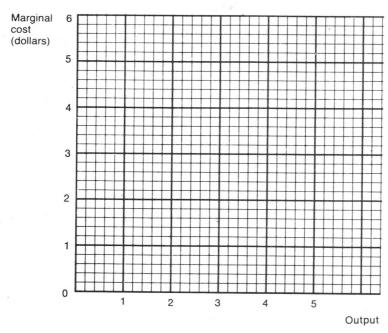

39. Show why the firm will continue to produce so long as price exceeds average variable cost, even if it is smaller than average total cost.

*40. Discuss what is meant by the product transformation curve and how this curve can help to show how much of each product a firm should produce.

*41. If the price of product 1 is $2 and the price of product 2 is $3, draw in the graph below the isorevenue line corresponding to a revenue of $200.

Completion Questions

1. If a firm's revenues cover its variable costs, but not its total costs, its economic profit is (zero, positive, negative) _____ , which means that its resources could yield (more, less, the same) _____ elsewhere.

2. In the market period, quantity is set by _____ alone.

3. In the market period, price is set by _____ alone, given a fixed quantity.

*This material pertains to chapter Appendix.

4. In the long run, a perfectly competitive firm's equilibrium position is at the place where its long-run average cost equals _____ .

5. A decreasing cost industry has a _____ long-run supply curve.

6. An increasing cost industry has an _____ long-run supply curve.

7. A constant cost industry has a _____ long-run supply curve.

8. The supply curve in the market period is _____ .

9. At the optimal level of production, profit maximization requires that long-run marginal cost equals short-run _____ equals price.

10. If the supply curve is steeper than the demand curve, price tends to _____ _____ , if the cobweb theorem holds.

11. Short-run supply elasticities tend to be _____ than long-run supply elasticities in American agriculture.

12. External economies may result in _____ that occur when the industry expands.

13. Increasing-cost and constant cost industries are more _____ than decreasing cost industries.

*14. If one were to draw a product transformation curve where the *same* product was on both the vertical and horizontal axes, this curve (would, would not) _____ be a straight line, and its slope would equal _____ .

15. Suppose that a cotton textile firm's total costs and total revenue are as follows:

Total output	Total cost (dollars)	Total revenue (dollars)
0	$30	0
1	33	$10
2	37	20
3	42	30
4	50	40
5	60	50
6	90	60

This firm's marginal cost between 2 and 3 units of output is _____ .

16. On the basis of the figures in question 15, this firm will produce_____units of output.

17. This firm will make a loss of _____ .

*This material pertains to chapter Appendix

18. If the firm shut down completely, it would make a loss of _____ .

19. The price of this firm's product is _____ .

20. At an output of between 4 and 5 units, the firm's marginal cost is _____ .

21. If price is less than marginal cost, decreases in output will _____ profit.

22. For a firm in a perfectly competitive market, if price is more than marginal cost, increases in output will _____ profit.

*23. The negative of the slope of the product transformation curve is _____ _____ .

True or False

_____ 1. If a firm's price is fixed, then increases in output will have little effect on the firm's profits.

_____ 2. If all firms are identical with respect to technology and managerial ability, the industry supply curve under perfect competition is horizontal.

_____ 3. An industry with increasing returns to scale must be a decreasing-cost industry.

_____ 4. In the short run, equilibrium price under perfect competition may be above or below average total cost.

_____ 5. In the long run, equilibrium price under perfect competition may be above or below average total cost.

_____ 6. The supply curve is a horizontal line in the market period.

_____ 7. The quantity demanded of a good is fixed in the market period.

_____ 8. Under perfect competition, one producer can produce a somewhat different good from other producers in his industry.

_____ 9. Under perfect competition, each firm must be careful not to produce too much and spoil the market.

_____ 10. One can derive the firm's supply curve in the short run by simply tracing out its average cost curve.

_____ 11. One can always derive the industry's supply curve by summing up the firm's marginal cost curves.

_____ 12. At the equilibrium price, price will equal marginal cost (for all firms that choose to produce) under perfect competition.

*This material pertains to chapter Appendix.

_____ 13. Under perfect competition, marginal cost is the same for all producers of a particular product in equilibrium.

_____ 14. Firms that appear to have lower average costs than others often have superior resources or managements.

_____ 15. The Brannan plan may cost the Treasury more than the previous price supports and production controls.

Multiple Choice

1. The market demand curve for a particular kind of desk chair is as follows:

Price (dollars)	Quantity demanded
30	200
20	300
10	400
5	600
3	800

The industry producing this kind of chair is a constant cost industry, and each firm has the following long-run total cost curve:

Output	Total cost (dollars)
1	10
2	12
3	15
4	30

$$A \quad C = \frac{TC}{Q}$$

$$1 \quad 0$$
$$6$$
$$5$$
$$7.5$$

(Each firm can produce only integer numbers of units of output.)

In the long run, the total number of firms in this industry will be about:
a. 100.
b. 200.
c. 300.
d. 400.
e. 500.

$$3\overline{)600} \qquad ?$$

2. The long-run average cost curve of a perfectly competitive firm is given below. Given that this curve does not shift, the long-run equilibrium output of the firm will be

a. 4 units.   d. 7 units.
b. 5 units.   e. 8 units.
c. 6 units.

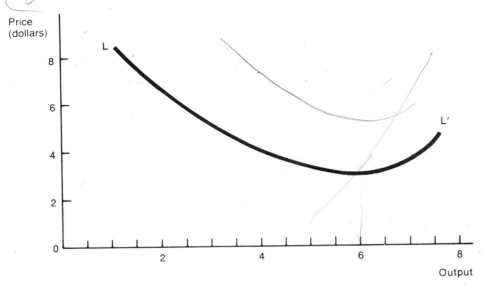

3. According to the cobweb theorem, the amount supplied of a commodity depends on
   a. this period's price.
   b. price in the previous period.
   c. expectations of future price.
   d. expectations of future demand.
   e. none of the above.

4. If the demand curve shifts to the right (and if the supply curve is upward sloping), equilibrium price will
   a. decrease.
   b. increase.
   c. stay the same.
   d. all of the above.
   e. none of the above.

5. Recognizing that the assumptions of perfect competition never hold at all precisely, the perfectly competitive model is
   a. interesting mainly for academic studies.
   b. outmoded and seldom used even by academic economists.
   c. of considerable use to industrial economists, as well as academic economists.
   d. all of the above.
   e. none of the above.

6. Under perfect competition, rivalry is
   a. impersonal.
   b. very personal and direct, advertising being important.
   c. nonexistent since the firms cooperate and collude.
   d. all of the above.
   e. none of the above.

7. If average total cost is less than marginal cost at its profit-maximizing output, a perfectly competitive firm $ATC < mc$
   a. will make positive profits.
   b. will operate at a point to the right of the minimum point on the average total cost curve.
   c. will not discontinue production.
   d. all of the above.
   e. none of the above.

8. The following graph shows the total cost and total revenue of a perfectly competitive firm.

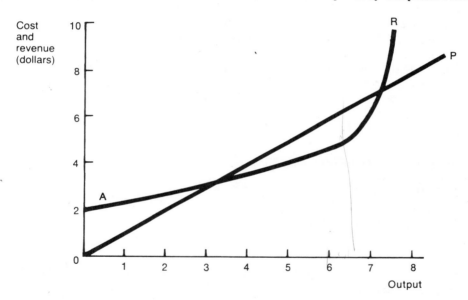

The line *OP* is
   a. the total cost curve.
   b. the total revenue curve.
   c. the relationship between price and output.
   d. all of the above.
   e. none of the above.

9. The curve *AR* is
   a. the total cost curve.
   b. the total revenue curve.
   c. the relationship between price and output.
   d. all of the above.
   e. none of the above.

10. The optimal output of the firm
    a. is less than 5.
    b. is more than 7.
    c. is between 5 and 7.
    d. all of the above.
    e. none of the above.

Key Concepts for Review

Market structure
Perfect competition
Market period
Supply curve in the short run
Equilibrium price
Equilibrium output
Economic profit
Entry of firms
Exit of firms
Long-run equilibrium of the firm
Isorevenue line*

Constant cost industries
Increasing cost industries
Decreasing cost industries
External economies
Path to equilibrium
Cobweb theorem
Support price
Production quota
Brannan plan
Product transformation curve*
Marginal rate of product transformation*

Answers

Case Study: The Widget Industry

a. If we set $Q_D = Q_S$

$$140{,}000 - 10{,}000\,P = 80{,}000 + 5{,}000\,P$$
$$140{,}000 - 80{,}000 = (5{,}000 + 10{,}000)\,P$$
$$P = \frac{60{,}000}{15{,}000} = 4$$

Thus, the equilibrium price equals $4. Since the long-run equilibrium price equals the mini-
mum point on the firms' long-run average cost curves (that is, it equals $4), this is the long-
run equilibrium price.

b. When $P = 4$, $Q = 140{,}000 - (10{,}000)(4) = 100{,}000$. Thus, since industry output is 100,000
and the minimum point on each firm's long-run average cost curve occurs at an output of
1,000, there are 100 firms in the industry when each firm operates at the minimum point on
its long-run average cost curve.

c. Setting $Q_D = Q_S$, we have

$$150{,}000 - 5{,}000\,P = 80{,}000 + 5{,}000\,P$$
$$150{,}000 - 80{,}000 = (5{,}000 + 5{,}000)\,P$$
$$P = \frac{70{,}000}{10{,}000} = 7$$
$$Q = 150{,}000 - 5{,}000\,(7) = 115{,}000$$

Thus, price equals $7 and output equals 115,000.

*This material pertains to chapter Appendix.

d. If the industry output is 115,000, if there are 100 firms, and if each firm produces the same amount, the output of each firm is 1,150 widgets per month. It is stated at the outset that a firm producing this amount has a short-run average cost of $5. Since price equals $7, each firm is making profits.

Problems and Review Questions

1. a. Based on the graph, it appears that the marginal cost would have been about 30 cents, since this is the price corresponding on the supply curve to an annual production of 2 billion barrels.
   b. The equilibrium price would have been about 42 cents per barrel, since, if the demand curve were a vertical line at an annual production of 3 billion barrels, it would intersect the supply curve at 42 cents.
   c. It was to the left of the one in the graph, because less could be supplied at each price.*

2. a. $5.
   b. 2 units.
   c. They will tend to leave this industry.

3. a. A person should increase the quality of the job he or she is carrying out so long as the marginal benefit from an extra unit of quality exceeds the marginal cost from this extra unit. Thus, to maximize his or her satisfaction, the quality of the job should be set at Ou units of quality in the case shown below:

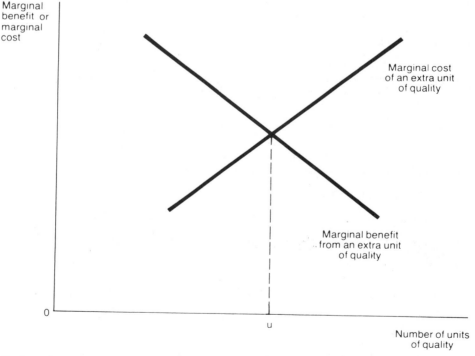

*For further discussion, see H. Steele's testimony in Senate Subcommittee on Antitrust and Monopoly, *Hearings on Governmental Intervention in the Market Mechanism* (Washington, D.C.: U.S. Government Printing Office, 1969); and J. Blair, *The Control of Oil* (New York: Pantheon Books, 1976).

Obviously, the optimal quality level may be quite *low* if the marginal benefit from an extra unit of quality is small and/or the marginal cost of an extra unit of quality is high. This graph is analogous to Figure 8.3 in the text, which shows the marginal cost and marginal revenue of a competitive firm. Just as a firm should produce no more output when it reaches the point where the marginal cost exceeds the marginal revenue, so a person should add no more quality to a job when the marginal cost of an extra unit of quality exceeds the marginal benefit from an extra unit of quality.

b. All other things equal, the marginal benefit from an extra unit of cleanliness (that is, one less unit of dirt) tends to be higher in an operating room than in a garage. An extra unit of cleanliness may save a life in an operating room whereas it may have little effect in a garage. Thus the marginal-benefit curve in the graph above will tend to be higher in an operating room, and the optimal quality level—that is, the optimal level of cleanliness—will tend to be higher there than in a garage.

4. *a.* Since the equation for the supply curve is $P = 3$, the long-run equilibrium output can be determined by finding the value of Q_D if $P = 3$. (This is the value where the supply and demand curves intersect.) Thus, since $Q_D = 50 - 2P$, the equilibrium output is $50 - (2)(3)$, or 44 million units per year.

   b. As we know from Chapter 2 of the text, a tax of $1 will raise the supply curve by $1, which means that its equation will be $P = 4$. Thus the long-run equilibrium output can be determined by finding the value of Q_D if $P = 4$. (This is the value where the demand curve intersects the new supply curve.) Thus, since $Q_D = 50 - 2P$, the equilibrium output is $50 - (2)(4)$, or 42 million units per year.

   c. No. The long-run equilibrium price after the imposition of the tax is $4.

5. *a.* Marginal cost equals the following:

$$MC = \frac{dC}{dQ} = 4 + 4Q$$

Setting marginal cost equal to price, we have

$$4 + 4Q = 24$$
$$4Q = 20$$
$$Q = 5$$

Thus the optimal output rate is 5.

   b. Profit equals total revenue minus total cost. Since total revenue equals $24Q$, profit equals

$$\pi = 24Q - 200 - 4Q - 2Q^2 = -200 + 20Q - 2Q^2$$

Because $Q = 5$,

$$\pi = -200 + (20)(5) - (2)(5)^2 = -200 + 100 - 50 = -150$$

Thus the firm loses $150.

   c. The firm's short-run supply curve is its marginal cost curve, $4 + 4Q$, so long as price exceeds average variable cost. Total variable cost equals $4Q + 2Q^2$, so average variable cost equals

$$4 + 2Q$$

and its minimum value is $4. Thus, so long as price (P) exceeds $4, the firm's short-run supply curve is

$$P = 4 + 4Q$$

-138-

6. The shift in the demand curve will cause the price of textiles to rise, with the result that textile firms will increase production and will earn economic profits. The profits will attract entrants, with the result that the supply curve for textiles will shift to the right. Eventually the price of textiles will go back to its original level, but the output of textiles will be higher because of the entrants. If the government does not allow the price of textiles to rise, this process is nipped in the bud. There is no incentive for existing firms to increase production or for firms to enter the industry.

7. The firm's marginal cost curve is

Output	Marginal cost (dollars)
0 to 1	10
1 to 2	12
2 to 3	13
3 to 4	14
4 to 5	15
5 to 6	16
6 to 7	17

    a. If the price is $13, the firm will produce 2 or 3 units.
    b. 3 or 4 units.
    c. 4 or 5 units.
    d. 5 or 6 units.
    e. 6 or 7 units.

8. The industry supply curve is shown below:

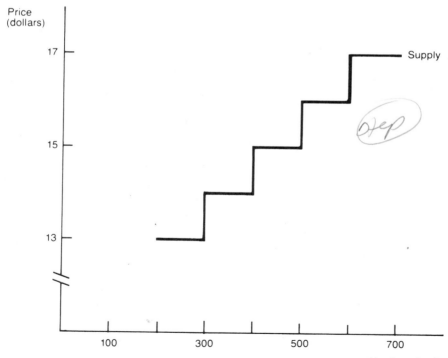

Number of units = # Total output x no. of firms

-139-

9. $\eta_S = \dfrac{(8-7)}{(8+7)/2} \div \dfrac{(4-3)}{(4+3)/2} = \dfrac{1}{7.5} \div \dfrac{1}{3.5} = 0.47.$

10. No. In fact, Besser was found guilty of illegally monopolizing the industry in 1951 (F. M. Scherer, *Industrial Market Structure and Economic Performance* [Skokie, Ill.: Rand McNally, 1970], p. 11).

11. The arc elasticity of supply is $\dfrac{6-4}{5} \div \dfrac{100-80}{90} = 1.8$.

12. First, perfect competition requires that the product of any one seller be the same as the product of any other seller.

    Second, perfect competition requires each participant in the market, whether buyer or seller, to be so small, in relation to the entire market, that he cannot affect the product's price.

    Third, perfect competition requires that all resources be completely mobile.

    Fourth, perfect competition requires that consumers, firms, and resource owners have perfect knowledge of all relevant economic and technological data.

    No industry meets all of these characteristics, but some, like particular agricultural markets, may be reasonably close.

13. In the market period, supply is fixed, as shown in the following graph. Equilibrium price is determined by the intersection of the demand curve (DD') and the supply curve (SS'); that is, it is OP.

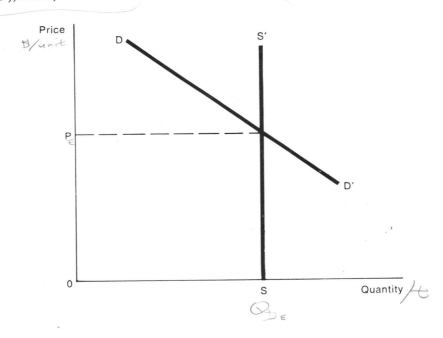

14. $3, as shown below:

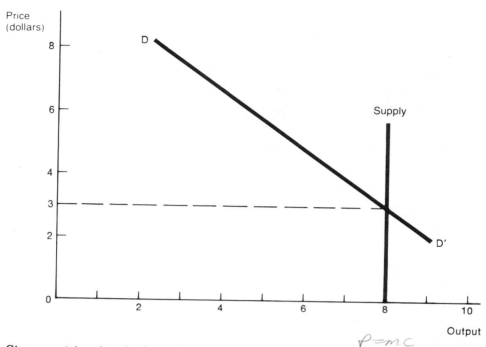

15. Given a certain price, the firm will produce an amount such that price equals marginal cost. $P = mc$
    Thus, if we vary the price, the amount that the firm will produce at each price will be given
    by the marginal cost curve (as long as price exceeds average variable cost). $P > AVC$
16. If the level of the industry output does not affect the cost curves of the individual firms,
    the industry supply at a given price can be determined by summing up the amount supplied
    by each of the firms, as indicated by their marginal cost curves.
17. *a.* Equilibrium output is 600 units. Equilibrium price is $4 1/3.
    b. If price were $6, the amount demanded would be less than the amount supplied. If
        price were $2, the amount supplied would be less than the amount demanded.
18. If there are economic profits, new firms will tend to enter an industry. If there are eco-
    nomic losses, there will tend to be an out-migration of firms from the industry.
19. In the long run, firms operate where long-run marginal cost equals short-run marginal cost
    equals long-run average cost equals short-run average cost equals price. This means that
    firms operate at the minimum point of the long-run average cost curve.
20. A constant cost industry is an industry where expansion of the industry does not result in a
    change in input prices and firms' costs. The long-run supply curve of the industry is hori-
    zontal.
21. An increasing cost industry is an industry where expansion of the industry results in an in-
    crease in firms' costs. The long-run supply curve of the industry is upward-sloping.
22. A decreasing cost industry is an industry where expansion of the industry results in a de-
    crease in firms' costs. The long-run supply curve of the industry is downward-sloping.

23.

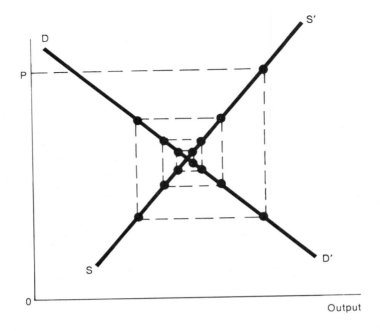

24. It is fairly close. The product is reasonably homogeneous. There is a large number of buyers and sellers. Entry is not difficult. But it does not conform to all of the assumptions of perfect competition. ~~mobile units?, perfect knowledge?~~
25. The supply function has been shifting rapidly to the right because of rapid technological change. This more than offset the slower movements to the right of the demand curve stemming from increases in population and income.
26. Because both the demand curve and the supply curve of agricultural commodities are quite price-inelastic.
27. No.
28. It would indicate the long-run effect on quantity supplied of changes in price. Apparently, a 1 percent increase in price would result in a 4.4 percent increase in quantity supplied.
29. Yes. ~~QS always try to catch up w/ QD at a certain (given) P~~
30. A difference of about 3.24 percent.

31. a. The firm's total variable cost function is:

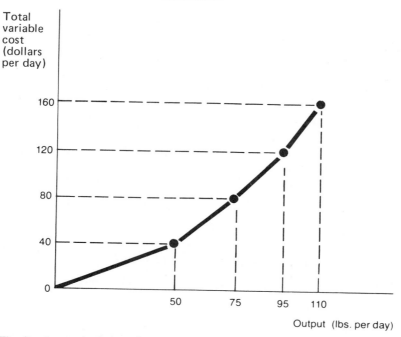

b. The firm's marginal cost function is:

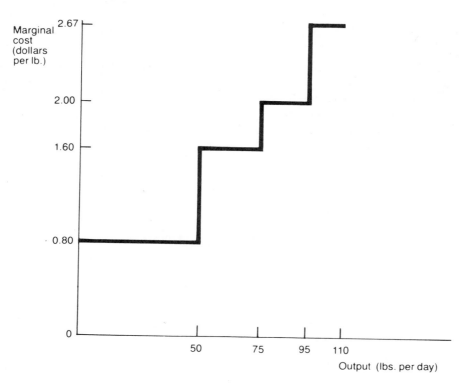

c. 75 or 95 pounds per day.

d. No.

e. Yes. For example, 1½ workers per day can be hired by having one worker work every day and one worker work every other day.

32. a. $700.

b. $35,000.

c. $10,000.

d. zero.

e. $700.

33. According to this evidence, the marginal cost of the first unit of output is $4 + (3)(1) = \$7$, and the marginal cost of each additional unit of output is higher than $7. Clearly, if the price of a unit of the product is $3, the firm loses money on each unit it sells. Indeed it does not even cover its variable costs. Thus, the student is right; the firm should produce nothing.

34. a. The firm's total cost function is:

$$C = AC \times Q = (\frac{400}{Q} + 3Q)Q = 400 + 3Q^2$$

TR = Q·P

The firm's total revenue equals $R = 3Q$. Thus, its profit equals

$$\pi = R - C = 3Q - 400 - 3Q^2 = -400 - 3(Q^2 - Q) = -400 - 3Q(Q - 1)$$

If $Q > 1$, the firm incurs losses because $\pi = -400 - 3Q(Q - 1)$ is negative.

b. Since $\pi = -400 - 3Q(Q - 1)$, the maximum value of π is not achieved at $Q = 0$. For example, if $Q = 1/2$, $\pi = -400 - 3(1/2)(-1/2) = -399¼$. This is a higher value of π than -400, which is the value of π when $Q = 0$. Thus, assuming that the firm can produce fractional units of output per day, it is better off to operate than to shut down.

35. Yes, because each additional unit produced (up to and including 100) brings in $1 more than it costs.

36. Profit $= 5Q - 20 - 2Q - 0.3Q^2 = -20 + 3Q - 0.3Q^2$. If you plot profit against Q, you will find that it is a maximum at $Q = 5$. At $Q = 5$, profit equals $-\$12.50$ per hour. This is the best you can do under these circumstances.

37. If the price is $2, profit $= 2Q - 20 - 2Q - 0.3Q^2 = -20 - 0.3Q^2$. If you plot profit against Q, you will find that it is a maximum at $Q = 0$. Thus, you will shut down.

$\pi' = 3 - 0.6Q = 0$

$3 = Q$

$.6 = 5$

38. *a.* 3 or 4 units of output.
    b.

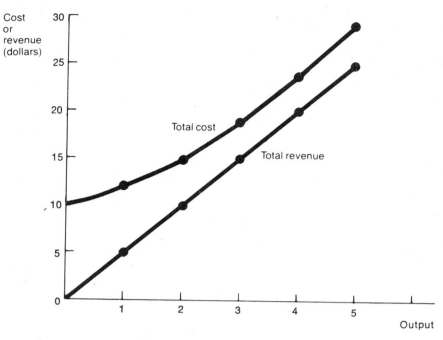

c. Price equals marginal cost between 3 and 4 units of output.

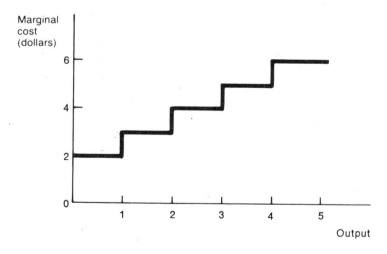

39. It will lose less money than if it shuts down completely. As long as price (P) exceeds average variable costs (AVC),

$$ATC - AFC < P$$

where ATC is average total cost and AFC is average fixed cost. The loss is $Q\,(ATC - P)$, which must be less than $Q \times AFC$, since

$$ATC - P < AFC$$

40. The product transformation curve shows the maximum amount of a particular good that can be produced, given various output levels for another good. Given a series of isorevenue lines that show the firm's revenue from various output combinations, one can find the output combination that maximizes profits. This combination is represented by the point on the product transformation curve that is on the highest isorevenue line.

41. The isorevenue line is as follows:

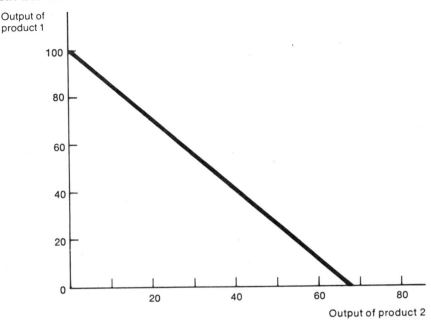

Completion Questions

1. negative, more
2. supply
3. demand
4. price
5. downward-sloping
6. upward-sloping
7. horizontal
8. vertical
9. marginal cost (also average cost)
10. converge
11. less
12. cost reductions

13. common
14. would, minus one
15. $5
16. 4 or 5
17. $10
18. $30
19. $10
20. $10
21. increase
22. increase
23. the marginal rate of product transformation

True or False

1. False   2. False   3. False   4. True   5. False   6. False   7. False   8. False   9. False
10. False   11. False   12. True   13. True   14. True   15. True

Multiple Choice

1. *b*   2. *c*   3. *b*   4. *b*   5. *c*   6. *a*   7. *d*   8. *b*   9. *a*   10. *c*

CHAPTER 9

Price and Output Under Pure Monopoly

Case Study: Subway Fares

The problems of the New York subway are by no means new. In the early 1950s, it was felt by many responsible citizens that the burden on the city budget due to the subway deficit was perhaps the single most important factor in New York City's financial problem. The increased operating cost resulting from the adoption of the forty-hour week, together with higher prices of materials, was expected to cause an operating deficit for 1951–52 of almost $30 million for the city's transit system.

In response to this problem, the question was raised of whether or not subway fares should be increased. William Vickrey of Columbia University was asked by the Mayor's Committee on Management Survey of the City of New York to make a study of this question. Vickrey made four estimates of the demand curve, each based on a different assumption regarding its form. In Case *A*, he assumed that equal absolute changes in fare result in equal absolute changes in traffic. In Case *B*, he assumed that equal absolute changes in fare result in equal percentage changes in traffic. In Case *C*, he assumed that equal percentage changes in fare result in equal absolute changes in traffic. And in Case *D*, he assumed that equal percentage changes in fare result in equal percentage changes in traffic.* His results are shown below.

Suppose that you were a member of the Mayor's Committee on Management Survey and that you were presented the data below. How would these data be useful in deciding whether or not to raise the subway fare from the then-prevailing level of 10 cents? What additional data would you need in order to come to a conclusion on this score? Do you think that data of this sort would be as useful now as in the early 1950s?

Alternative estimates of demand schedule for subway travel, New York, 1952

Fare (cents)	Case A Passengers	Total revenue (dollars)	Case B Passengers	Total revenue (dollars)	Case C Passengers	Total revenue (dollars)	Case D Passengers	Total revenue (dollars)
			(passengers and revenues in millions per year)					
5	1945	$ 97.2	1945	$ 97.2	1945	$ 97.2	1945	$ 97.2
10	1683	168.3	1683	168.3	1683	168.3	1683	168.3
15	1421	213.2	1458	218.7	1530	229.5	1547	232.0
20	1159	231.8	1262	252.4	1421	284.2	1457	291.5
25	897	224.2	1092	273.0	1347	336.8	1390	348.2
30	635	190.5	945	283.5	1278	383.4	1340	402.0

Source: W. S. Vickrey.

*This very brief sketch cannot do justice to Vickrey's study, which was concerned with many other important aspects of the problem. See W. Vickrey, *The Revision of the Rapid Transit Fare Structure of the City of New York*, Technical Monograph No. 3, Finance Project, Mayor's Committee on Management Survey of the City of New York, 1952.

Problems and Review Questions

1. Firm X has a complete monopoly over the production of nutmeg. The following information is given:

   Marginal revenue = 1,000 – 20Q
   Total revenue = 1,000Q – 10Q²
   Marginal cost = 100 + 10Q,

   [handwritten: $1000 - 20Q = 100 + 10Q$, $900 = 30Q$, $30 = Q$, $AC = \frac{TC}{Q} =$]

   where Q equals the output of nutmeg per unit of time. How much nutmeg would be sold and at what price if *[handwritten: $MC = AC$]*
   a. the firm sets price as a monopoly?
   b. the industry (firm) behaves perfectly competitively?

2. A garbage collector in an Ohio community is a monopolist. The community imposes a *lump sum tax* of $20,000 per year on the garbage collector. Can the garbage collector shift the burden of the tax to consumers?

3. A firm has 2 plants with the following marginal cost functions:

   $MC_1 = 20 + 2Q_1$
   $MC_2 = 10 + 5Q_2$

   where MC_1 is marginal cost in the first plant, MC_2 is marginal cost in the second plant, Q_1 is output in the first plant, and Q_2 is output in the second plant. If the firm is minimizing its costs and if it is producing 5 units of output in the first plant, how many units of output is it producing in the second plant? Explain.

4. The QXR Corporation has bought exclusive rights to sell hot dogs in a local sports arena. The fee it paid for this concession was $200. The variable cost of obtaining and marketing each hot dog is 10 cents. The demand schedule for hot dogs in this arena is as follows:

   [handwritten: $\frac{\Delta TR}{\Delta Q} =)$, $= TR$, $P \cdot Q$]

Price per hot dog (cents)	Thousands of hot dogs sold per game		
20	10		
25	9		
30	8		
35	7		
40	6		
45	5		
50	4		

   [handwritten annotations around table: "1 time MC", "cost 1500", "-100", "-150", "-100", "VC = .10", "-150", "MC = MR -100", "-100", TC column: 1000 (X·10), 900, 850, 700, 600, 500, 400; and: 2000, 2250, 2400, 2450, 2400, 2250, 2000; MR column: 2000, 250, 150, 50, -50, -150, -250]

   It is assumed that prices must be multiples of a nickel.
   a. What price should the QXR Corporation charge for a hot dog?
   b. What is the maximum amount that the QXR Corporation should pay for this concession for a single game?

5. A monopolist has the following total cost function and demand curve:

-148-

P·Q
∨
TR
40
42
42
40
36
30

Price (dollars)	Output	Total cost (dollars)	TR−TC / π
8	5	20	20
7	6	21	21
6	7	22	20
5	8	23	17
4	9	24	12
3	10	30	0

What price should it charge?

greatest (π = TR−TC)

6. Authors receive a royalty that is a fixed percentage of the price of the book. For this reason, economists have pointed out that an author has an interest in a book's price being lower than the price which maximizes the publisher's profits. Prove that this is true.

7. According to Spencer, Seo, and Simkin, the makers of methyl methacrylate used to sell it at 85 cents per pound for commercial purposes.* However, for denture purposes, it was sold to the dental profession for $45 per pound. Assuming that there was no difference in quality, why would the producers of methyl methacrylate, DuPont and Rohm and Haas, find it profitable to charge different prices? In which of these markets (the commercial market or the dental market) do you think that the price elasticity of demand was lower?

8. According to Meyer, Peck, Stenason, and Zwick, trucks "have a comparative long-run marginal cost advantage over rails only on hauls of less than roughly 100 miles. Yet 97 percent of all manufactured goods ton-miles transported by common motor carriers in the early 1950s were on hauls of more than 100 miles."† What are the implications for resource allocation in transportation? What policies of the ICC help to account for this fact?

9. Define pure monopoly. Is a monopolist subject to any kind of competition?

10. What are some of the most important factors that give rise to monopoly?

11. How does the monopolist's demand curve differ from that of a perfectly competitive firm? How do his costs differ from those of a competitive firm?

12. *a.* Suppose that a monopolist's demand curve and total cost curve are as follows:

Output	Price (dollars)	Total cost (dollars)
1	10	20
2	9	21
3	8	22
4	7	23
5	6	24
6	5	26
7	4	29
8	3	32

*M. Spencer, K. Seo, and M. Simkin, *Managerial Economics* (Homewood, Ill.: Irwin, 1975), p. 384.

†F. M. Scherer, *Industrial Market Structure and Economic Performance* (Chicago, Ill.: Rand McNally, 1970), pp. 539–40.

Plot the monopolist's total revenue and total cost curves in the graph below:

b. Plot the monopolist's marginal revenue and marginal cost curves in the graph below:

c. What output will maximize the monopolist's profit? Is this output the one where marginal cost equals marginal revenue? What price should the monopolist charge?

13. Show why a monopolist will always set his output at the point where marginal revenue equals marginal cost, if he maximizes profit and if price exceeds average variable cost.

14. Suppose that a monopolist has more than one plant. If he minimizes costs, how will he allocate production among the plants? Why?

15. Compare the long-run equilibrium of monopoly with that of perfect competition. How does output compare? How do costs compare? How does price compare?

16. Describe how, according to some economists, the welfare loss to society due to monopoly can be measured by the so-called "welfare triangle."

17. Are price and output determined exactly by the theory of bilateral monopoly? Where might this theory be of some relevance?

18. What is price discrimination? Under what circumstances is it feasible for a firm to practice discrimination? Under what circumstances is it profitable for the firm to practice price discrimination?

19. Under price discrimination, how does a monopolist decide how much to produce? How does he decide how to allocate this output among markets?

20. According to C. Emery Troxel, a general rate case is the common sort of regulatory "contest" in the Michigan telephone industry. What sorts of concepts and methods are used by these commissions in such cases?

21. *a.* Suppose that you are the owner of a metals-producing firm that is an unregulated monopoly. After considerable experimentation and research you find that your marginal cost curve can be approximated by a straight line, $MC = 60 + 2Q$, where MC is marginal cost (in dollars) and Q is your output. Moreover, suppose that the demand curve for your product is $P = 100 - Q$, where P is the product price (in dollars) and Q is your output. If you want to maximize profit, what output should you choose?

    b. What price should you charge?

22. *a.* Suppose that you are hired as a consultant to a firm producing ball bearings. This firm is a monopolist which sells in two distinct markets, one of which is completely sealed off from the other. The demand curve for the firm's output in the one market is $P_1 = 160 - 8Q_1$, where P_1 is the price of the product and Q_1 is the amount sold in the first market. The demand curve for the firm's output in the second market is $P_2 = 80 - 2Q_2$, where P_2 is the price of the product and Q_2 is the amount sold in the second market. The firm's marginal cost curve is $5 + Q$, where Q is the firm's entire output (destined for either market). The firm asks you to suggest what its pricing policy should be. How many units of output should it sell in the second market?

    b. How many units of output should it sell in the first market?

23. Many industries—for example, the steel industry—claim that the demand for their product is price-inelastic. Suppose that you were able to bring together all of the firms in an industry and form a monopoly. Would you operate at a point on the demand curve where demand is price inelastic.

24. According to Milton Friedman of the Hoover Institution at Stanford University, it is preferable in cases of natural monopoly for society to tolerate private unregulated monopoly rather than to attempt to regulate natural monopolies. Do you agree? Why or why not?

25. The Aluminum Company of America (Alcoa) was the sole manufacturer of virgin aluminum ingot in the United States from its inception in the late nineteenth century until World War II. Suppose that in the 1920s you had had the power to break up Alcoa into several smaller firms. Would you have done so? Why?

26. According to Sir John Hicks,"The best of all monopoly profits is a quiet life." If so, how would this affect the theory of pure monopoly?

27. According to Henry C. Simons, "The great enemy of democracy is monopoly in all of its forms." Do you agree? Why or why not?

Completion Questions

1. A monopolist can sell 12 units of output when it charges $8 a unit, 11 units of output when it charges $9 a unit, and 10 units of output when it charges $10 a unit. The marginal revenue from the eleventh unit of output equals _____. The marginal revenue from the twelfth unit of output equals _____.

2. The threat of potential competition often acts as a _____ on the policies of a monopolist.

3. A monopolist's demand curve is the same as the industry _____.

4. For a monopolist, marginal revenue is _____ than price.

5. Under monopoly, there is not always a _____ relationship between price and output.

6. In the long run, a monopolistic firm will _____ incur losses, but it may make _____.

7. Under multiplant monopoly, the monopolist will equalize the _____ of the output of each plant if it minimizes cost.

8. If the demand curve for the product shifts to the right, the monopolist _____ _____ increase price.

9. Price will be _____ under monopoly than under perfect competition.

10. Output will be _____ under monopoly than under perfect competition.

11. Average cost will be _____ under monopoly than under perfect competition.

12. Bilateral monopoly occurs when a monopolistic seller is confronted with _____

_____ .

13. Under bilateral monopoly, price and output are _____ .

True or False

_____ 1. A profit-maximizing monopolist will always choose an output in the short run where average total cost is less than average revenue.

_____ 2. If the government sets a price ceiling below the equilibrium price, a perfectly competitive firm will reduce output, but a monopolist may increase output.

_____ 3. If a monopolist sells in two markets, each of which has a linear demand curve, and the demand curves have equal slopes, the monopolist will charge the same price in both markets.

_____ 4. At the point where total revenue is maximized, the price elasticity of demand equals 1.

_____ 5. A monopolist always produces an output such that the price elasticity of demand equals 1.

_____ 6. Price discrimination cannot occur unless consumers can be segregated into classes and the commodity cannot be transferred from one class to another.

_____ 7. Price discrimination always occurs when differences in price exist among roughly similar products, even when their costs are not the same.

_____ 8. Price discrimination is profitable even when the price elasticity of demand is the same among each class of consumer in the total market.

_____ 9. If a monopolist practices price discrimination, he does not set marginal revenue equal to marginal cost.

_____ 10. First-degree price discrimination occurs frequently, particularly in the auto industry.

_____ 11. Sometimes a commodity cannot be produced without price discrimination, for the industry would have to produce at a loss otherwise.

Multiple Choice

1. A monopolist's total cost equals $100 + 3Q$, where Q is the number of units of output it produces per month. Its demand curve is $P = 200 - Q$, where P is the price of the product. The marginal revenue from the twentieth unit of output per month equals
   a. $3,600.
   b. $3,439.
   c. $180.
   d. $140.
   e. none of the above.

-153-

2. Monopolies can arise as a consequence of
   a. patents.
   b. control over the supply of a basic input.
   c. franchises.
   d. the shape of the long-run average cost curve.
   e. all of the above.

3. A monopolistic firm will expand its output when
   a. marginal revenue exceeds marginal cost.
   b. marginal cost exceeds marginal revenue.
   c. marginal cost equals marginal revenue.
   d. marginal revenue is negative.
   e. none of the above.

4. A monopolist will never produce at a point where
   a. demand is price-inelastic.
   b. demand is price-elastic.
   c. marginal cost is positive.
   d. marginal cost is increasing.
   e. none of the above.

5. A profit-maximizing monopolist, if he owns a number of plants, will always:
   a. produce some of his output at each plant.
   b. transfer output from plants with high marginal cost to those with low marginal cost.
   c. transfer output from plants with low marginal cost to those with high marginal cost.
   d. produce all of his output at a single plant and shut down the rest.
   e. none of the above.

6. Suppose that the monopolist's marginal cost is constant in the relevant range and that his demand curve is downward-sloping and linear. Suppose that an excise tax is imposed on the monopolist's product. If he maximizes profit, he will increase his price by
   a. an amount less than the tax.
   b. an amount equal to the tax.
   c. an amount more than the tax.
   d. no amount at all.
   e. none of the above.

7. To determine how a discriminating monopolist will allocate output between two classes of consumers, one must
   a. compare the marginal revenues in the classes.
   b. compare the prices in the classes.
   c. compare the slopes of the demand curves in the classes.
   d. compare the heights of the demand curves in the classes.
   e. none of the above.

$MR = P\left(1 - \dfrac{1}{|\varepsilon_D|}\right)$

-154-

Key Concepts for Review

Monopoly

Natural monopoly

Patents

Market franchise

Multiplant monopoly

Bilateral monopoly

Price discrimination

First-degree price discrimination

Second-degree price discrimination

Third-degree price discrimination

Fair rate of return

Regulatory commissions

Value of plant

Answers

Case Study: Subway Fares

Regardless of which case (A, B, C, or D) you choose, the demand for subway travel is shown by the table to be price inelastic at the then-prevailing fare of 10 cents. This means that increases in the fare would increase total revenues. Also, they would reduce the deficit because fewer passengers would mean lower costs (or at least no higher costs). But this is not the only consideration. You would probably want to investigate how such a fare increase would affect various parts of the population—the poor, the rich, rush-hour traffic, non-rush-hour traffic, and so on. Data of this sort would be just as relevant now as in the early 1950s.

Problems and Review Questions

1. *a.* Since marginal revenue would equal marginal cost, $1000 - 20Q = 100 + 10Q$. Thus, $Q = 30$. Because $PQ = 1,000Q - 10Q^2$, it follows that $P = 1,000 - 10Q$. Thus, price equals 700.
    b. Since the demand curve is $P = 1000 - 10Q$, and the supply curve is $P = 100 + 10Q$, they intersect at $Q = 45$ and $P = 550$.
2. No. The lump sum tax adds to the garbage collector's fixed costs but does not affect his marginal costs. Thus, since both the marginal revenue curve and marginal cost curve are unaffected by the tax, the profit-maximizing output is the same, with or without the tax, and the price too must be the same. Because the price is unaffected, none of the tax burden is shifted to consumers.
3. If the firm is producing 5 units in the first plant, the marginal cost in the first plant equals $20 + (2)(5)$, or 30. Thus, if the firm is minimizing costs, marginal cost in the second plant must also equal 30, which means that

$$10 + 5Q_2 = 30$$
$$5Q_2 = 20$$
$$Q_2 = 4$$

Consequently, the second plant must be producing 4 units of output.

4. *a.* Since total cost (excluding the fee) is 10 cents times the number of hot dogs sold, the QXR Corporation's total profit per game is shown below, under various assumptions concerning the price.

Thousands of hot dogs	Price (cents)	Total revenue (dollars)	Total cost (dollars) (excluding fee)	Total profit (dollars)
10	20	2,000	1,000	1,000
9	25	2,250	900	1,350
8	30	2,400	800	1,600
7	35	2,450	700	1,750
6	40	2,400	600	1,800
5	45	2,250	500	1,750
4	50	2,000	400	1,600

Thus the QXR Corporation will maximize profit if it sets a price of 40 cents.

b. $1,800, since this is the maximum amount it could make per game.

5. The monopolist's total revenue, total cost, and total profit at each level of output are as follows:

Output	Total revenue (dollars)	Total cost (dollars)	Total profit (dollars)
5	40	20	20
6	42	21	21
7	42	22	20
8	40	23	17
9	36	24	12
10	30	30	0

Thus, the optimal output is 6, which means that price should be $7.

6. Since the author's royalty is a fixed percentage of the price of the book, the total royalties per year earned by the author are proportional to the total revenue per year from the book. Consequently, the author would like to maximize total revenue, since this maximizes his or her royalties. To maximize total revenue, marginal revenue should be set equal to zero. On the other hand, the publisher would like to maximize profit, which means that marginal revenue should be set equal to marginal cost. Thus, the author would like to set marginal revenue equal to a lower value than would the publisher. Holding constant the price elasticity of demand, marginal revenue decreases as price is lowered. Thus, the author tends to prefer a lower price than does the publisher.

7. Because the price elasticity of demand was different in the two markets.
The dental market.

8. Apparently, trucks are carrying a great deal of traffic that could be carried more cheaply by railroads. In the past, the ICC often has not allowed railroads to cut their rates in order to take some of this business away from the trucks.

9. Monopoly occurs when there is one, and only one, seller in a market. The monopolist is not completely insulated from the effects of actions taken in the rest of the economy. He is affected by indirect and potential forms of competition.

10. First, a single firm may control the entire supply of a basic input that is required to make a product.
Second, a firm may become monopolistic because the average cost of producing the product reaches a minimum at an output rate that is big enough to satisfy the entire market at a price that is profitable.

Third, a firm may acquire a monopoly over the production of a good by having patents on the product or on certain basic processes that are used in its production.

Fourth, a firm may become monopolistic because it is awarded a franchise by a government agency.

11. The monopolist's demand curve is the industry demand curve. Thus it is downward-sloping, whereas a perfectly competitive firm has a horizontal demand curve.

If the monopolist is a perfect competitor in the market for inputs, the theory of cost is the same for a perfect competitor or a monopolist. Chapter 13 takes up the case where the firm is not a perfect competitor in the market for inputs.

12. *a.*

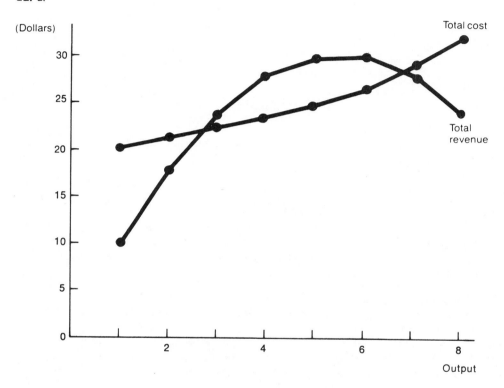

b.

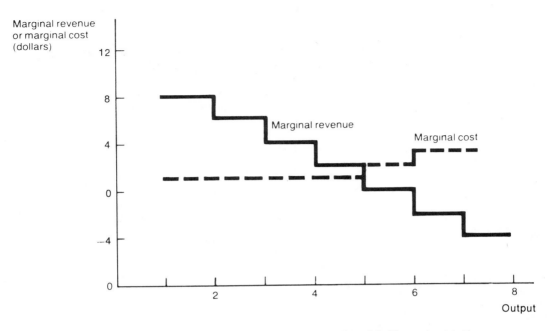

c. Five units of output will be produced, and the price will be $6. The output is the one where marginal cost equals marginal revenue.

13. If marginal revenue exceeds marginal cost, profit can be increased by increasing output. If marginal revenue is less than marginal cost, profit can be increased by decreasing output. Profit will be a maximum when marginal revenue equals marginal cost (as long as price exceeds average variable cost).

14. He will allocate output so that the marginal costs are the same at each plant. Why? Because this is a condition for cost minimization.

15. Output is less, average costs are higher, and price is higher under monopoly than under perfect competition.

16. Basically, the idea is that the value to society of the extra output resulting from perfect competition is equal to $Q_1 C A Q_0$ (in the graph on the next page), whereas the cost to society of the extra output is equal to $Q_1 B A Q_0$. Thus the net loss due to the smaller output under monopoly is equal to the triangle ABC.

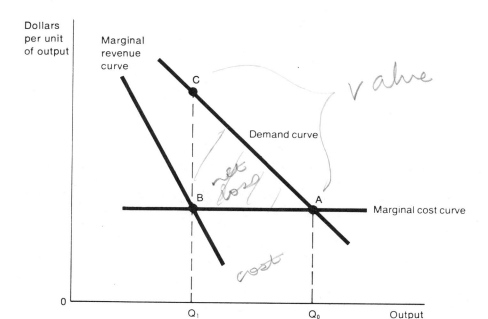

17. No.

Perhaps in the labor markets where a single firm and a single union face one another.

18. Price discrimination occurs when the same commodity is sold for more than one price. For price discrimination to be feasible, it must be possible for the seller to segregate buyers into classes and the buyers must be unable to transfer the good from low-price classes to high-price classes. For price discrimination to be profitable, the price elasticity of demand must vary among classes.

19. The monopolist will set marginal revenue in the various classes equal, and the common value of marginal revenue will be set equal to marginal cost.

20. The commissions try to establish a reasonable return on a firm's existing plant. There are many difficult questions involved in determining what is "reasonable" and what is the "value" of a firm's existing plant.

21. *a.* Marginal revenue = $100 - 2Q$.

Marginal cost = $60 + 2Q$.

Consequently, $100 - 2Q = 60 + 2Q$

$$40 = 4Q$$
$$10 = Q$$

That is, you should choose an output of 10 units.

   b. Since $P = 100 - Q$, if Q equals 10, P must equal 90. So you should charge a price of $90.

22. *a.* $MR_1 = 160 - 16Q_1$

$MR_2 = 80 - 4Q_2$

$MC = 5 + (Q_1 + Q_2)$

Therefore $160 - 16Q_1 = 5 + Q_1 + Q_2$

$\quad\quad\quad\quad 80 - 4Q_2 = 5 + Q_1 + Q_2$

Or $\quad\quad 155 - 17Q_1 = Q_2$

$\quad\quad\quad\quad 75 - 5Q_2 = Q_1$

Thus $\quad\quad 155 - 17[75 - 5Q_2] = Q_2$

$\quad\quad\quad 155 - 1275 + 85Q_2 = Q_2$

$\quad\quad\quad 84Q_2 = 1120$

$\quad\quad\quad\quad Q_2 = 1120/84$

It should sell $\dfrac{1120}{84}$ units in the second market.

b. $Q_1 = 75 - 5Q_2$

$= 75 - 5(1120/84)$

$= 75 - \dfrac{5600}{84}$

$= 75 - 66\,^2/_3$

$= 8\,^1/_3$

It should sell $8\,^1/_3$ units in the first market.

23. No. At such a point marginal revenue would be negative. Thus you could increase revenue—and consequently profit—by reducing output.

26. It would have meant that monopolists would probably worry less about maximizing profits.

Completion Questions

1. minus $1, minus $3
2. brake
3. demand curve
4. less
5. unique
6. not; profits
7. marginal cost
8. may or may not
9. higher
10. lower
11. higher
12. a single buyer
13. indeterminate

True or False

1. False   2. True   3. False   4. True   5. False   6. True   7. False   8. False   9. False
10. False   11. True

Multiple Choice

1. *e*   2. *e*   3. *a*   4. *a*   5. *b*   6. *a*   7. *a*

CHAPTER 10   Price and Output under Monopolistic Competition

Case Study: The Beer Industry

In 1974, there were 58 companies producing beer in the United States. The available evidence seems to indicate that the long-run average cost curve falls sharply until a plant size of 1.25 million barrels per year is reached. Then it declines gradually until a capacity of about 4 million barrels per year is reached, beyond which there is no further decline. According to economists who have studied the industry, there are "moderate" barriers to entry. Beer manufacturers try, of course, to differentiate their products by advertising and by other means. In recent years, there has been a reduction in the number of beer producers; in 1947, there were 404; in 1963, 150; and in 1974, 58. The rate of return, after taxes, on owner's equity in this industry was usually below 8 percent in the post–World War II period, but it increased to 9.1 percent in 1967, 10.1 percent in 1969, and 8.8 percent in 1971. For all manufacturing, the comparable rate of return in 1967, 1969, and 1971 was 11.7, 11.5, and 9.7 percent, respectively.

a. Would you characterize the beer industry in the United States as monopolistically competitive? Why or why not?

b. With regard to product differentiation, does it have the characteristics of a monopolistically competitive industry?

c. Is its profit performance similar to what would be expected in a monopolistically competitive industry?

d. Do you think that it is becoming closer to monopolistic competition than it used to be? Why or why not?

e. In 1889, Adolphus Busch, a leading brewer of the day, sent a letter to another leading brewer, Captain Pabst, in which he complained that brewers, "instead of combining their efforts and securing their own interest, . . . are fighting each other and running the profits down, so that the pleasures of managing a brewery have been diminished a good deal."* Would this attitude be likely to characterize a monopolistically competitive industry? Why or why not?

f. If brewing were a monopolistically competitive industry, would you expect the typical brewery to produce less than 4 million barrels per year? Why or why not?

Problems and Review Questions

1. The Chrome Corporation is a monopolistically competitive firm. In the short run, its marginal revenue equals $4, its total revenue equals $21, and its marginal revenue curve is $10 - 2Q$. Its average total cost is at its minimum value. If it is maximizing profit, what does each of the following equal?

   a. The firm's price. $10 - 2Q = 4$ $-2Q = -6$ $Q = 3$ $21 / \frac{7}{3}$

*This quotation, like the other factual material in this case, comes from K. G. Elzinga, "The Beer Industry," in W. Adams, ed., *The Structure of American Industry* (New York: Macmillan, 1977).

b. The firm's output. 3

c. The firm's total cost. $= mR \cdot Q = 4 \cdot 3$

d. The firm's average total cost. $12/3 = mR/Q$

e. The firm's marginal cost. $= 4 = mR$

2. For a particular monopolistically competitive firm, the DD' demand curve intersects the dd' demand curve at a price of \$10. Can the equilibrium price of the firm's product be \$12. Why or why not?

3. Explain why the extent of the excess capacity in a particular monopolistically competitive firm is inversely related to the price elasticity of demand of its product.

4. The situation facing a particular monopolistically competitive firm is the following:

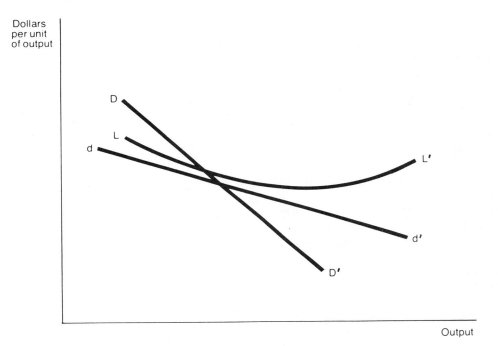

Is this situation a long-run equilibrium? Will entry occur in the industry? Will exit occur in the industry? (LL' is the long-run average cost curve, DD' is the DD' demand curve, and dd' is the dd' demand curve.)

5. According to Mann, Henning, and Meehan, there is a fairly substantial positive correlation between the ratio of advertising expenditure to sales in an industry and the percentage of the industry's sales accounted for by the four largest firms. * What factors may account for such a correlation?

*Journal of Industrial Economics, 1967.

6. According to one estimate, perhaps a fourth of the 1963 sales of drug stores, liquor stores, and gasoline stations were made by firms whose costs were 10 percent higher than the optimum, the resulting annual cost being $775 million, or 0.13 percent of GNP.* Why do such inefficiencies come about and persist?

7. What sorts of dissatisfaction with the theory of perfect competition and monopoly led to the theory of monopolistic competition? Who were the principal founders of the theory of monopolistic competition? When did their theories first appear?

8. Describe the basic assumptions underlying Chamberlin's theory of monopolistic competition.

9. Describe the two basic types of demand curves that play a fundamental role in the theory of monopolistic competition.

10. Describe the equilibrium conditions for price and output under monopolistic competition in the short run.

11. Describe the equilibrium conditions for price and output under monopolistic competition in the long run.

12. Describe how, according to Chamberlin's theory, firms determine the characteristics of their products. Describe too how they decide how much to spend on selling expenses.

13. What is meant by ideal output and ideal plant? Describe the reasoning leading to the conclusion that there will tend to be excess capacity under monopolistic competition.

14. Compare the long-run equilibrium of a monopolistically competitive industry with the long-run equilibria of perfectly competitive and monopolistic industries.

15. Describe and discuss some major criticisms of Chamberlin's theory of monopolistic competition. How important do you think these criticisms are?

16. Give five real-world examples of industries in which there is product differentiation.

17. According to some economists, there are too many gas stations and grocery stores. Is this in keeping with the theory of monopolistic competition?

Completion Questions

1. A monopolistically competitive firm is in long-run equilibrium. Its marginal revenue equals $10. If its marginal revenue plus its economic profit equal one-half of its price, its price equals _____, and its marginal cost equals _____.

$$P = mR$$
$$mR + \pi = \tfrac{1}{2}P \qquad 10 + 0 = \tfrac{1}{2}P$$
$$20 = P$$

* F. M. Scherer, *Industrial Market Structure and Economic Performance*, Skokie Ill.: Rand McNally, 1970, pp. 406–7.

2. Chamberlin's theory assumes that there are a _____ of firms and a _____ product.

3. The dd' demand curve assumes that other firms _____ their prices.

4. The DD' demand curve assumes that other firms make _____ changes in their price as the representative firm does.

5. Under monopolistic competition, the theory claims that _____ will be produced at a _____ price than under pure monopoly.

6. Under monopolistic competition, the theory suggests that _____ will be produced at a _____ price than under perfect competition.

7. It is difficult to compare perfect competition with monopolistic competition because the product is _____ under perfect competition but _____ under monopolistic competition.

8. In monopolistic competition, each firm expects its actions to have _____ on its competitors.

9. In short-run equilibrium in monopolistic competition, the dd' demand curve intersects the _____ at the output where marginal revenue equals marginal cost.

10. In long-run equilibrium in monopolistic competition, the long-run average cost curve is tangent to the _____ .

11. Excess capacity under monopolistic competition may be fairly small if the demand curve facing the monopolistically competitive firm is _____ .

True or False

_____ 1. A monopolistically competitive firm's short-run demand and cost curves are as follows:

F

TR−TC

TR = Q·P   π

Price (dollars)	Quantity demanded	Output	Total cost (dollars)		
8	1	1	5	8	3
7	2	2	7	14	7
6	3	3	9	18	9
4	4	4	11	16	5
3	5	5	20	15	−5

This firm, if it maximizes profit, will choose an output rate of 5.

_____ 2. Because monopolistically competitive firms cannot earn monopoly profits, monopolistic competition does not result in economic inefficiency.

F → does discuss excess capacity

_____ 3. Monopolistic competition is likely to result in more brands than perfect competition.

T

_____ T _____ 4. Under monopolistic competition, firms can vary the characteristics of their products.

_____ T _____ 5. Chamberlin assumes that firms in the same product group under monopolistic competition have the same cost and demand curves.

_____ F _____ 6. The dd' demand curve is less elastic than the DD' demand curve.

_____ T _____ 7. Long-run equilibrium under monopolistic competition will be achieved when economic profits are zero.

_____ T X _____ 8. Entry and exit under monopolistic competition are as free as they are under perfect competition.

_____ T _____ 9. Entry and exit have an influence on the DD' demand curve.

_____ T _____ 10. Critics have charged that Chamberlin's definition of the group of firms in the product group is very ambiguous.

_____ F _____ 11. It is obvious that product differentiation is a waste and that all industries should standardize their products.

Multiple Choice

1. One major assumption of Chamberlin's theory of monopolistic competition is that:
   a. demand curves will be the same for each firm but cost curves will be different.
   b. each firm's product is a fairly close substitute for the others in the group.
   c. there are just a few firms in each group.
   d. each firm expects its actions to influence those of its rivals.
   e. all of the above.

2. The graph on the next page contains the dd' demand curve and the DD' demand curve. The dd' demand curve is:
   a. AA'.
   b. BB'.
   c. CC'.
   d. the vertical axis.
   e. the horizontal axis.

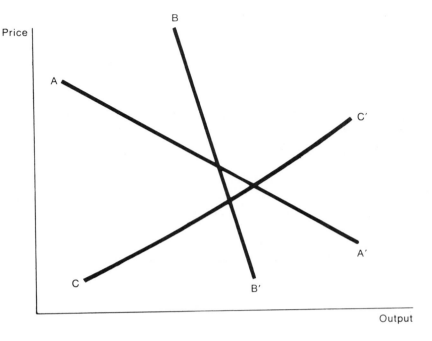

Price

B

A

C'

A'

C

B'

Output

3. In the previous question, the DD' demand curve is:
   a. AA'.
   b. BB'.
   c. CC'.
   d. the vertical axis.
   e. the horizontal axis.

4. Under monopolistic competition, a firm can use selling expenses to increase its profits. We know that such expenses are   adv.
   a. a social waste.
   b. entirely socially productive.
   c. large in many industries, but we are able to say little with confidence about their social productivity.
   d. all of the above.
   e. none of the above.

5. Given that a firm is in short-run equilibrium and UU' (shown on the next page) is the dd' demand curve, the equilibrium price is
   a. OP_0.
   b. OP_1.
   c. OP_2.
   d. zero.
   e. none of the above.

-166-

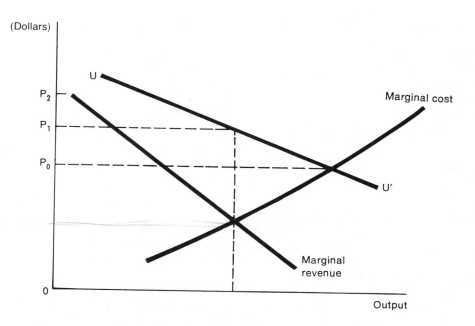

6. Suppose that a firm is in short-run equilibrium and WW' is the DD' demand curve, but the marginal revenue curve shown below is the marginal revenue curve based on the dd' demand curve. The equilibrium price would now be

a. OP_3.
b. OP_4.
c. OP_5.
d. zero.
e. none of the above.

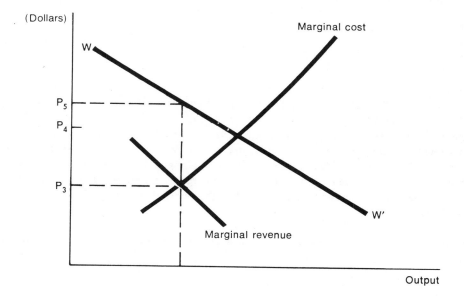

Key Concepts

Monopolistic competition
Product differentiation
Product group
dd' demand curve
DD' demand curve
Representative firm

Product variation
Selling expenses
Ideal output
Ideal plant
Excess capacity

Answers

Case Study: The Beer Industry

 a. The beer industry has some characteristics of monopolistic competition, but it departs from it in other respects. In a particular geographical market, there may be a limited number of beers that are distributed. In contrast, monopolistic competition occurs where there are a great many sellers. Also, the barriers to entry in the beer industry are not inconsiderable, whereas monopolistic competition assumes free entry.
 b. Yes, the beer industry is characterized by product differentiation.
 c. Its profits have not been above-average. In this respect, at least, its profit performance is similar to a monopolistically competitive industry.
 d. No, because the number of breweries has declined, and it seems to be increasingly oligopolistic.
 e. Monopolistic competition is characterized by rivalry and the absence of collusion, the characteristic Busch complains of. At the same time, the number of firms is so big that each firm expects its actions to go unheeded by its rivals and to be unimpeded by any retaliatory actions on their part.
 f. Yes, because a monopolistically competitive firm tends to operate a plant of smaller size than the one that would minimize long-run average cost.

Problems and Review Questions

1. *a.* $7.
  b. 3.
  c. $12.
  d. $4.
  e. $4.
2. No, because equilibrium can occur only at the point where the DD' demand curve intersects the dd' demand curve.
3. If the demand for the product is very price elastic, the demand curve will be tangent to the firm's long-run average cost curve at a point that is close to its minimum. Thus, the extent of the excess capacity will be relatively small. On the other hand, if the demand curve is not very price elastic, it will be tangent to the firm's long-run average cost curve at a point that is relatively far away from the minimum point, with the result that the extent of the excess capacity will be relatively great.
4. No.
  Exit will occur, because at every output average cost exceeds price (based on the dd' demand curve).

5. One would expect relatively tightly held oligopolies to spend more on advertising than more competitive industries. Also, the line of causation may run the other way: to some extent, the high level of concentration may be due to the fact that an industry is one where advertising is an important commercial weapon.

6. Because of resale price maintenance and other techniques used by manufacturers to keep retail prices high, as well as because of the tendency for excess capacity to occur under monopolistic competition. (In 1975, Congress passed a bill nullifying resale price maintenance agreements.)

7. Perfect competition and pure monopoly are two polar extremes. There was a feeling that more attention should be devoted to the important "middle ground" between them. Edward Chamberlin and Joan Robinson were the principal founders of the theory of monopolistic competition. Their books appeared in 1933.

8. First, he assumes that the product is differentiated and that it is produced by a large number of firms, each firm's product being a fairly close substitute for the products of the other firms in the product group.

   Second, he assumes that the number of firms in the product group is sufficiently large so that each firm expects its actions to go unheeded by its rivals and to be unimpeded by any retaliatory measures on their part.

   Third, he assumes that both demand and cost curves are the same for all of the firms in the group.

9. One demand curve—the dd' demand curve—shows how much the firm will sell if it varies its price from the going level and if other firms maintain their existing prices. A second demand curve—the DD' demand curve—shows how much the firm will sell if it varies its price from the going level and if other firms follow suit.

10. In short-run equilibrium, the marginal revenue based on the dd' demand curve equals marginal cost at the output level where the DD' demand curve intersects the dd' demand curve.

11. The long-run equilibrium is at a point where (1) the long-run average cost curve is tangent to the dd' demand curve, and where (2) the DD' demand curve intersects the dd' demand curve and the long-run average cost curve at the tangency point.

12. For each variant of the firm's product, the firm calculates the maximum profit it can attain. Then it picks the variant of its product where the maximum profit is highest. Similarly, the firm chooses its selling expenses in an attempt to maximize profit.

13. The ideal output of a firm is the output where long-run average cost is a minimum. The ideal plant is the plant with a short-run average cost curve that is tangent to the long-run average cost curve at the ideal output.

    In long-run equilibrium under monopolistic competition, the firm will produce that quantity of output at which the dd' demand curve is tangent to the long-run average cost curve. Since the dd' demand curve slopes downward, this means that the equilibrium point must be to the left of the ideal output. In other words, there is excess capacity.

14. It is difficult to make this comparison because the product is homogeneous under perfect competition or pure monopoly but differentiated under monopolistic competition. But it seems likely that price will be higher under monopolistic competition than under perfect competition, but lower than under monopoly. Output is likely to be lower under monopolistic competition than under perfect competition, but higher than under monopoly. There is likely to be some excess capacity under monopolistic competition, but not under perfect competition.

15. George Stigler attacks the concept of the group and the basic structure of Chamberlin's argument. Sir Roy Harrod questions the conclusions concerning excess capacity. The criticisms have a considerable amount of merit.

16. Automobiles, furniture, cigarettes, tires, razor blades, and many others.

17. Yes. It is quite in keeping with the excess capacity theorem.

Completion Questions

1. $20, $10
2. large number; differentiated
3. maintain
4. the same
5. more; lower
6. less; higher
7. homogeneous; differentiated
8. no effect
9. *DD'* demand curve
10. *dd'* demand curve
11. highly elastic

True or False

1. False   2. False   3. True   4. True   5. True   6. False   7. True   8. True   9. True
10. True   11. False

Multiple Choice

1. *b*   2. *a*   3. *b*   4. *c*   5. *b*   6. *c*

CHAPTER 11   Price and Output under Oligopoly

Case Study: The Pricing of American Small Cars

The major U.S. automobile manufacturers were not very enthusiastic about producing small cars during much of the period since World War II, due in part to the fact that they made a larger profit on a large car than a small one. But the explosion of gasoline prices and the press of foreign competition during the 1970s led the American producers to introduce new lines of smaller, fuel-efficient cars in the fall of 1980. The prices at which they and their Japanese competitors were offered were as follows:

Chevrolet Citation	$6,337	Subaru wagon	$5,612
GM "J" Cars	6,300	Datsun 310	5,439
Ford Escort	6,009	Subaru hatchback	5,212
Dodge Omni	5,713	Mazda GLC	4,755

a. According to some observers, "Detroit . . . priced these cars relatively high to replenish its depleted coffers as soon as possible." Is it always true that this is the effect of charging relatively high prices?

b. Some auto executives stated that the U.S. demand for smaller cars would be so great in the early 1980s that Detroit would be able to sell all such cars that it could produce. What implicit assumptions were they making?

c. In 1979, the International Trade Commission decided not to recommend curbing the imports of Japanese cars into the United States. In terms of promoting the vitality and efficiency of the U.S. automobile industry, what arguments could be made in favor of this decision?

d. Were imports of Japanese cars into the United States subsequently curbed?

Problems and Review Questions

1. Suppose that there are ten identical producers of spring water, that each of these firms has zero costs of production, so long as it produces less than (or equal to) 10 gallons of water per hour, and that it is impossible for each to produce more than 10 gallons per hour. Suppose that the market demand curve for this water is as follows:

Price (dollars per gallon)	Number of gallons demanded per hour		Price (dollars per gallon)	Number of gallons demanded per hour	
		Q·P TR			*Q·P TR*
11	0	0	5	60	300
10	10	100	4	70	280
9	20	180	3	80	240
8	30	240	2	90	180
7	40	280	1	100	100
6	50	300	1/2	105	52.5

10 x 10

a. If the firms take the price of water as given (as in the case of perfect competition), what will be the price and output of each firm?

b. If the firms form a completely effective cartel, what will be the price and output of each firm?

c. How much money will each firm be willing to pay to achieve and enforce the collusive agreement described in part *b*?

d. Suppose that one of the firms secretly breaks the terms of the agreement and shades price. What effect will this have on its profits?

2. The can industry is composed of two firms. Suppose that the demand curve for cans is:

$$P = 100 - Q, = 2 q$$

where *P* is the price of a can (in cents) and *Q* is the quantity demanded of cans (in millions per month). Suppose that the total cost function of each firm is:

$$C = 1,000,000 + 15q, \quad = TC$$

where *C* is total cost per month (in cents) and *q* is the quantity produced (in millions per month) by the firm.

a. What are the profit-maximizing price and output if the firms are Cournot duopolists?

b. What are the profit-maximizing price and output if the firms collude and act like a monopolist? (Elementary calculus is useful for the problem.)

3. An oligopolistic industry selling a homogeneous product is composed of two firms. The two firms set the same price and share the total market equally. The demand curve confronting each firm (assuming that the other firm sets the same price as this firm) is shown below. Also, each firm's total cost function is shown below.

Price (dollars)	Quantity demanded	Output	Total cost (dollars)
10	5	5	45
9	6	6	47
8	7	7	50
7	8	8	55
6	9	9	65

a. Assuming that each firm is correct in believing that the other firm will charge the same price as it does, what is the price that each should charge?

b. Under the assumptions in part *a*, what output rate should each firm set?

4. Game theory can be useful in situations other than interfirm rivalry. For example, suppose that Bonnie and Clyde are arrested for holding up a bank. The district attorney talks *separately* to each one, saying, "We've got lots of evidence indicating you robbed the bank, so you'd better confess. If you do, I'll give you a break. If you *alone* confess, I'll see to it you get only 6 months in jail. If you *both* confess, I'll see to it you get 10 years. But if you don't confess, and your partner *does*, I'll see to it you get 20 years." Both Bonnie and Clyde are sure that, if neither confesses, they will get 2 years.

a. In this situation, what is the payoff matrix?

b. What strategy will each choose, given that each tries to save his or her own skin?

5. The International Air Transport Association (IATA) has been composed of 108 American and European airlines that fly transatlantic routes. For many years, IATA acted as a cartel: it fixed and enforced uniform prices. If IATA wanted to maximize the total profit of all member airlines, what uniform price would it charge? How would the total amount of traffic be allocated among the member airlines?

6. Suppose that two firms are producers of spring water, which can be obtained at zero cost. The marginal revenue curve for their combined output is

$$MR = 10 - 2Q$$

where MR is marginal revenue and Q is the number of gallons of spring water sold by both together per hour. If the two producers act in accord with Chamberlin's oligopoly model, how much will be their combined output? Why?

7. Suppose that a cartel is formed by three firms. Their total cost functions are as follows:

Units of output	Total cost (dollars)		
	Firm 1	Firm 2	Firm 3
0	20	25	15
1	25	35	22
2	35	50	32
3	50	80	47
4	80	120	77
5	120	160	117

If the cartel decides to produce 11 units of output, how should the output be distributed among the three firms, if they want to minimize cost?

8. A firm estimates its average total cost to be $10 per unit of output when it produces 10,000 units, which it regards are 80 percent of capacity. Its goal is to earn 20 percent on its total investment, which is $250,000. If it uses cost-plus pricing, what price should it set? Can it be sure of selling 10,000 units if it sets this price?

9. In its 1932 annual report, Aluminium, Ltd. of Canada noted that "World stocks of aluminum are not excessively large. They are in firm hands and do not weight unduly upon the world market."* What did it mean by "firm hands?" Do you think that this phenomenon was at all related to the firmness of world aluminum prices during this period? Under perfect competition, do you think that aluminum prices would have remained fairly constant in the face of sharp reductions in sales during the Great Depression?

10. According to F. M. Scherer, Reynolds and American have shared price leadership in cigarettes, U.S. Steel has often been the price leader in steel, Alcoa has led most frequently in virgin aluminum, American Viscose in rayon, and DuPont in nylon and polyester fibers.† What characteristics tend to distinguish price leaders from other firms? If you had to predict which of a number of firms in an industry was the price leader, what variables would you use to make the forecast?

*F. M. Scherer, *Industrial Market Structure and Economic Performance* (Chicago:Rand McNally, 1970), p. 156. Also see the second edition of Scherer's book (Chicago: Rand McNally, 1980).
†Ibid., p. 167.

11. What is meant by oligopoly? How does oligopoly arise? What is the difference between pure oligopoly and differentiated oligopoly?

12. Describe the Cournot model. Comment on the reasonableness of its assumptions.

13. Describe the Edgeworth model. Comment on the reasonableness of its assumptions.

14. Describe the Chamberlin model. In what respect is this model more reasonable than Cournot's or Edgeworth's?

15. What is meant by the kinked oligopoly demand curve? Does this theory explain the level of price? What does it help to explain?

16. Describe the elements of game theory. To what extent are two-person zero-sum games representative of actual market conditions?

17. Suppose the payoff matrix is as given below. What strategy will firm I choose? What strategy will firm II choose?

Possible strategies for firm I	Possible strategies for firm II		
	1	2	3
	[Profits for firm I, or losses for firm II (dollars)]		
A	$10	$9	$11
B	8	8.5	10

least profits

18. What are some of the criticisms of game theory? How important do these criticisms seem to be?

19. What is a cartel? How will a perfect cartel determine its price and output? Is it likely that a cartel will allocate output among its members so as to minimize total cost? *MC*

20. Why are cartels and collusive agreements inherently unstable? Document your answer with evidence from the electrical equipment conspiracy in the United States in the 1950s.

21. Describe the dominant-firm model of price leadership. How does it differ from the barometric-firm model?

22. What is meant by cost-plus pricing? Is the cost-plus model a complete model?

23. What are some important barriers to entry?

24. Describe the effects of an oligopolistic market structure on price, output, and profits.

25. *a.* Suppose that you are on the board of directors of an oil firm which is the dominant firm in the industry; that is, it lets all of the other firms, which are much smaller, sell all they want at the existing price. In other words, the smaller firms act as perfect com-

petitors. Your firm, on the other hand, sets the price, which the other firms accept. The demand curve for your industry's product is $P = 300 - Q$, where P is the price of oil and Q is the total quantity demanded. The total amount supplied by the other firms is equal to Q_r, where $Q_r = 49P$. If your firm's marginal cost curve is $2.96 Q_b$, where Q_b is the output of your firm, at what output level should you operate to maximize profit? (P is measured in dollars per barrel; Q, Q_r, and Q_b are measured in millions of barrels per week.)

b. What price should you charge?

c. How much will the industry as a whole produce at this price?

26. According to Franklin Fisher, Zvi Griliches, and Carl Kaysen, automobile model changes during the 1950s cost about $5 billion a year. Were these expenditures socially worthwhile? How can one tell?

27. According to the Senate Subcommittee on Antitrust and Monopoly, the ethical drug industry has had much higher profit rates, as a percent of net worth, than most other industries. Is this consistent with the predictions of the theory of oligopoly?

28. According to Milton Friedman, "Few trends could so thoroughly undermine the very foundations of our free society as the acceptance by corporate officials of a social responsibility other than to make as much money for their stockholders as possible." Do you agree? Why or why not?

29. In the early 1960s, a major aluminum firm raised its price for sheet by a penny a pound. Almost a month later, the increase was rescinded because the other aluminum producers did not go along with the increase. Is this consistent with the kinked oligopoly demand curve?

30. Joe Bain has estimated that the output of an efficient-sized fresh-meat-packing plant is at most 1 percent of industry sales. He has also estimated that the output of an efficient tractor-manufacturing plant is equal to 10 to 15 percent of industry sales. Discuss the relevance of these facts for the market structure of these industries.

31. According to the Federal Trade Commission, there was collusion among the leading bakers and food outlets in the state of Washington in the late 1950s and early 1960s. Prior to the conspiracy, bread prices in Seattle were about equal to the U. S. average. During the period of the conspiracy, bread prices in Seattle were 15 to 20 percent above the U. S. average. Is this consistent with the theory of collusive behavior? Why do you think that bread prices in Seattle were not double or triple the U. S. average during the conspiracy?

32. According to John Stuart Mill, "Where competitors are so few, they always agree not to compete. They may run a race of cheapness to ruin a new candidate, but as soon as he has established his footing, they come to terms with him." Do you agree or not? Why?

33. The following table shows, for food manufacturing, the relationship between the percentage of the industry output accounted for by the top four firms and the net profit on stockholder equity of firms in the industry.

Percentage held by top four firms	Net profit on stockholder equity (percentage)
31–40	6.2
41–49	9.2
50–59	12.9
60–69	14.6
70–90	16.3

↑ % as go down

Are these results what you would expect from the theory of oligopoly? Why or why not? (The data come from the Federal Trade Commission.)

Completion Questions

1. All firms in an industry have marginal cost curves that are horizontal lines at $10 per unit of output. If they combine to form a cartel, the cartel's marginal cost (will, will not) _____ be $10 per unit of output. If the cartel maximizes profit, its marginal revenue will be (greater than, smaller than, equal to) _____ $10 per unit. Its price will be (greater than, smaller than, equal to) _____ $10 per unit of output.

2. Under oligopoly, each firm is aware that its actions are likely to elicit _____ in the policies of its competitors.

3. A good example of oligopoly in the United States is the _____ industry.

4. If an oligopoly produces a homogeneous product, it is called a _____ oligopoly.

5. The Cournot model assumes that each firm thinks that the other will hold its output constant at _____.

6. The Edgeworth model assumes that each firm thinks that the other will hold its price _____.

7. According to the Chamberlin model, the firms tacitly accept the _____ solution.

8. According to the kinked oligopoly demand curve, firms think that, if they raise their price, their rivals will _____.

9. According to the kinked oligopoly demand curve, firms think that, if they lower their price, their rivals will _____.

10. If a game is strictly determined, there is a _____ of each player.

11. Von Neumann and Morgenstern proved that a pair of optimal mixed strategies _____ in a two-person zero-sum game.

True or False

_____ 1. Collusion is often difficult to achieve and maintain because an oligopoly contains an unwieldly number of firms, or because the product is quite heterogeneous.

_____ 2. If a perfectly competitive industry is operating along the elastic portion of its demand curve, there is no point in trying to cartelize the industry.

_____ 3. Because a cartel maximizes profit, there is no incentive for a member to violate the rules of the cartel.

_____ 4. Cartels have been common and legally acceptable in Europe.

_____ 5. Cartels tend to be unstable because the demand curve facing a "cheater" is highly inelastic.

_____ 6. According to the dominant-firm model, the dominant firm allows the smaller firms to sell all they want at the price it sets.

_____ 7. Cost-plus pricing takes explicit account of the extent and elasticity of demand, as well as of marginal costs.

_____ 8. Whether or not an industry remains oligopolistic in the face of relatively easy entry depends on the size of the market for the product relative to the optimal size of firm.

_____ 9. A limit price is a price that is the maximum price the oligopolists can charge without courting the possibility of government antitrust action.

_____ 10. The basic purpose of advertising is to make the demand curve for the product more elastic.

_____ 11. Joe Bain has found that firms in industries in which the few largest firms had a high proportion of total sales tended to have higher profits than firms in industries in which the few largest firms had a small proportion of total sales.

Multiple Choice

$$MR = P\left(1 - \frac{1}{|\varepsilon_D|}\right)$$

1. Firm A's demand curve, given below, is kinked.

Price (dollars)	Quantity demanded
3	100
4	80
5	60
6	55
7	50

If the price must be an integer number of dollars, at what price is the kink?
a. $3.
b. $4.
c. $5.
d. $6.
e. $7.

-177-

2. If DD' is the industry demand curve and marginal costs are zero, the Chamberlin model predicts that price will be

$MC = 0$

a. OP_0.

b. OP_1.

c. OP_2.

d. zero.

e. none of the
   above.

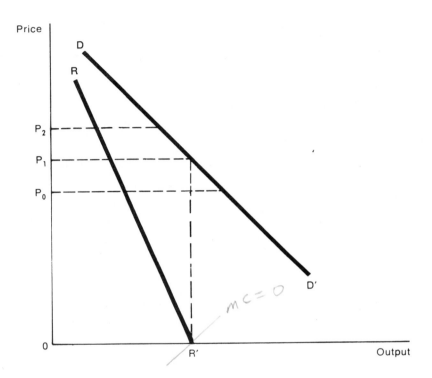

3. In the previous question, the RR' curve is

a. the marginal revenue curve.

b. the marginal cost curve.

c. the reaction curve.

d. all of the above.

e. none of the above.

4. A mixed strategy is a strategy where

a. probabilities are assigned to pure strategies.

b. a second-best approach is used.

c. pure strategies are mixed with impure strategies.

d. all of the above.

e. none of the above.

5. In the following graph, which of the curves is a kinked oligopoly demand curve?
   a. AA'.
   b. BB'.
   c. CC'.
   d. all of the above.
   e. none of the above.

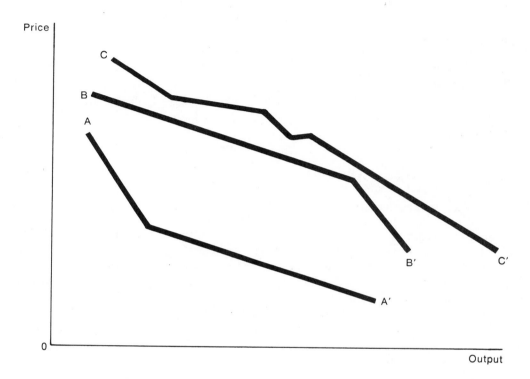

6. In the dominant-firm model, the dominant firm finds the demand curve for its output by
   a. using the unadjusted industry demand curve.
   b. adding up the small firms' demand curves.
   c. subtracting the small firms' supply from the industry demand curve.
   d. all of the above.
   e. none of the above.

Key Concepts for Review

Oligopoly

Pure oligopoly

Differentiated oligopoly

Collusion

Duopoly

Cournot model

Edgeworth model

Chamberlin Model

Kinked oligopoly demand curve

Nonprice competition

Theory of games

Player

Strategy

Payoff matrix

Minimax strategy

Mixed strategy

Cartel

Price leadership

Dominant firm

Barometric firm

Cost-plus pricing

Limit pricing

Answers

Case Study: The Pricing of American Small Cars

a. No. If a firm charges relatively high prices, it may sell relatively few units of its product, the result being that its profits are lower than if its price was somewhat lower.

b. They were assuming that U.S. consumers would not buy imported smaller cars (instead of U.S. smaller cars) in such numbers that Detroit would be unable to sell all it could produce.

c. American auto producers would have to reduce their costs and change the features of their cars to meet foreign competition, rather than rely on the government to protect them from such competition.

d. In 1981, the Japanese agreed to "voluntary" restraint on exports of cars to the United States.

Problems and Review Questions

1. a. The industry supply curve would be as shown on the opposite page. This is the horizontal sum of the firm's marginal cost curves. Since this supply curve intersects the demand curve at a price of $1, this is the equilibrium price. Since the supply and demand curves intersect at an output of 100 gallons, this is the industry output. Each firm produces one-tenth of this output, or 10 gallons.

The industry supply curve:

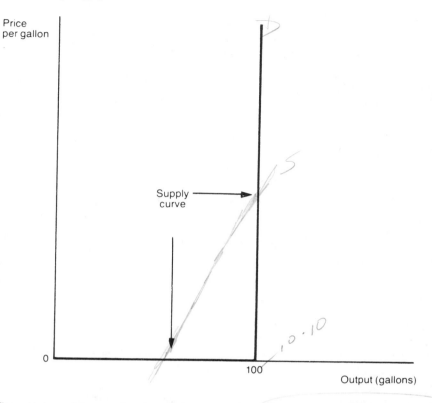

b. The cartel would expand output only so long as marginal revenue exceeds marginal cost. Since marginal cost is zero, this means that the cartel would expand output only so long as marginal revenue is positive. Marginal revenue is shown below:

Output	Total revenue (dollars)	Marginal revenue (dollars)
0	0	
10	100	10
20	180	8
30	240	6
40	280	4
50	300	2
60	300	0
70	280	−2
80	240	−4
90	180	−6
100	100	−8

Marginal revenue $= \dfrac{\Delta TR}{\Delta Q}$

$MR = (+)$

Clearly, the cartel would restrict output to 50 gallons and charge $6 per gallon. (Alternatively, it could set output at 60 gallons, and charge $5 per gallon. The profit would be the same.)

-181-

c. If the alternative to the cartel is the arrangement described in part (a), each firm would be willing to pay up to $20 per hour to achieve and enforce the cartel. With the cartel, each firm makes $30 per hour, since each produces 5 gallons per hour, and charges $6 per gallon. Under the arrangement in part (a), each firm makes $10 per hour, since each produces 10 gallons per hour and charges $1 per gallon. Thus, each firm's profit per hour is $20 higher under the cartel.

d. If the cartel sets a price of $6 per gallon, this firm can increase its profits by selling an additional 5 gallons per hour at a price per gallon of $5. But if a substantial number of firms begin to act in this way, the cartel will break apart.

2. a. For the first firm, its profit equals

$$\pi_1 = Pq_1 - 1{,}000{,}000 - 15q_1$$
$$= (100 - q_1 - q_2)q_1 - 1{,}000{,}000 - 15q_1,$$

where q_1 equals the first firm's output, q_2 equals the second firm's output, and P equals price.

$$\frac{\partial \pi_1}{\partial q_1} = 100 - 2q_1 - q_2 - 15 = 0$$

Thus,

$$85 - 2q_1 - q_2 = 0$$

Similarly,

$$\frac{\partial \pi_2}{\partial q_2} = 85 - 2q_2 - q_1 = 0$$

Solving the last two equations simultaneously, we find that $q_1 = q_2 = 85/3$ units, and price equals $100 - \dfrac{170}{3} = 43\text{-}1/3$.

b. Let Q be the combined output of the two firms, and π be their combined profit.

$$\pi = PQ - 2{,}000{,}000 - 15Q$$
$$= (100 - Q)Q - 2{,}000{,}000 - 15Q$$
$$\frac{\partial \pi}{\partial Q} = 100 - 2Q - 15 = 0$$

Thus, Q equals 42.5, and price equals $100 - 57.5 = 42.5$. If they share the output equally, each will produce 21.25 units.

3. a. $9.
   b. 6.

4. a. The payoff matrix is as follows for each person:

Possible strategies for Clyde	Bonnie's payoff matrix		Clyde's payoff matrix	
	Possible strategies for Bonnie		Possible strategies for Bonnie	
	Confess	Not confess	Confess	Not confess
	(Years of imprisonment for Bonnie)		(Years of imprisonment for Clyde)	
Confess	10	20	10	½
Not confess	½	2	20	2

-182-

b. Bonnie's payoff matrix shows that, if Clyde confesses, she is better off to confess than not to confess. If he does not confess, she is also better off to confess than not to confess. Thus, her optimal strategy is to confess. Similarly, Clyde's payoff matrix shows that he is better off to confess if Bonnie confesses and that he is also better off to confess if she does not confess. Thus, his optimal strategy too is to confess. A game of this sort is called the *Prisoner's Dilemma.* Note that, in this situation, each will do better by being altruistic than by selfishly trying to minimize his or her own stay behind bars.

5. To find the profit-maximizing price, the IATA should construct the marginal cost curve for the cartel as a whole. Then, as shown in Figure 11.5 of the text, it should determine the amount of traffic (which is the output of this industry) where marginal revenue equals marginal cost. The price that will elicit this amount of traffic is the profit-maximizing price. If IATA wants to maximize profit, it will allocate this traffic among the airlines in such a way that the marginal cost of all airlines is equal. (However, for reasons discussed in the text, it may not want to maximize profit.)

6. The two producers will choose the monopoly output, where marginal revenue equals marginal cost. Since marginal cost equals zero, this means that

$$MR = 10 - 2Q = 0,$$

so

$$Q = \frac{10}{2} = 5$$

Thus, their combined output will be 5 gallons per hour.

7. They should set the marginal cost at one firm equal to the marginal cost at each other firm. If firm 1 produces 4 units, firm 2 produces 3 units, and firm 3 produces 4 units, the marginal cost at each firm equals $30. Thus, this seems to be the optimal distribution of output.

8. To earn 20 percent on its total investment of $250,000, its profit must equal $50,000 per year. Thus, if it operates at 80 percent of capacity (and sells 10,000 units), it must set a price of $15 per unit. (Since average cost equals $10, profit per unit will be $5, so total profit per year will be $50,000.) However, based on the information that is given, there is no assurance that it can sell 10,000 units per year if it charges a price of $15 per unit.

9. It meant that the holders of these inventories were unlikely to sell them (and depress the price).
   Yes, by holding output off the market, producers could maintain prices.
   No.

10. The price leaders tend to be the largest firms. Also, historical factors play a role, and there is sometimes a tendency for low-cost (or medium-cost) firms to be leaders.

11. Oligopoly is a market characterized by a small number of firms and a great deal of interdependence, actual and perceived, among firms.
    Oligopoly can arise from economies of scale, or barriers to entry of various kinds.
    A pure oligopoly produces a homogeneous product, whereas a differentiated oligopoly produces a differentiated product.

12. The Cournot model assumes that each firm believes that, regardless of what output it produces, the other firm will hold its output constant at the existing level. This is not a very reasonable assumption under a wide set of circumstances.

13. The Edgeworth model assumes that each firm believes that its rivals will hold price, rather than quantity, constant. This too is not a very reasonable assumption under a wide set of circumstances.

14. The Chamberlin model assumes that firms, conscious of their interdependence, feel that the best they can do is to share the monopoly level of profit. This is more reasonable because it recognizes that firms learn and recognize their interdependence.

15. The kinked oligopoly demand curve is more elastic for price increases than for price decreases. It does not explain the level of price, but it does help to explain the rigidity of price.

16. The basic elements are the players, the rules of the game, the payoffs of the game, and the information conditions that exist during the game. Generally, markets contain more than two firms, and it is not a zero-sum game.

17. Firm I will choose strategy A.
   Firm II will choose strategy 2.

18. Two-person zero-sum games are not very realistic descriptions of market conditions, and the theory of more complicated and realistic games is not well developed.
   These criticisms are important. Nonetheless, game theory is a suggestive framework for analysis.

19. When a collusive arrangement is made openly and formally, it is called a cartel.
   A perfect cartel will determine the marginal cost curve for the cartel as a whole. Then it will produce the output where marginal cost equals marginal revenue, and it will charge the price at which it can sell that output.
   No.

20. Because members have a great incentive to "cheat." This tendency existed among the electrical equipment manufacturers. One collusive agreement after another was drawn up in the 1950s, but after a while some firms began in each case to pursue an independent price policy.

21. The dominant-firm model assumes that the dominant firm sets the price for the industry, but that it lets the other firms sell all they want at that price.
   On the other hand, the barometric-firm model assumes that there is one firm that is usually the first to make changes in price that are generally accepted by other firms in the industry. The barometric firm may not be the largest or most powerful, but it is a reasonably accurate interpreter of changes in basic cost and demand conditions in the industry as a whole.

22. According to cost-plus pricing, firms estimate the cost per unit of output (at some assumed output level) and add a certain percentage markup to obtain the price.
   No.

23. Smallness of the market relative to optimum size of firm, large capital requirements, unavailability of natural resources, patents, and franchises.

24. Price and profits are likely to be higher than under perfect competition, but lower than under monopoly. Output is likely to be more than under monopoly, but less than under perfect competition (if the demand curve is the same).

25. *a.* Since $Q = 300 - P$, and the demand for the firm's output is $Q - Q_r$, it follows that the firm's demand curve is:

$$Q_b = Q - Q_r = (300 - P) - 49P$$
$$= 300 - 50P ,$$

or

$$P = 6 - 0.02 \, Q_b$$

Thus, the firm's marginal revenue curve is $MR = 6 - 0.04 \, Q_b$. And since its marginal cost curve is $2.96Q_b$

$$6 - 0.04 \, Q_b = 2.96 \, Q_b$$
$$Q_b = 2$$

That is, your output level should be 2 million barrels per week.

b. Since $P = 6 - 0.02\,Q_b$, and $Q_b = 2$, it follows that

$$P = 6 - 0.02\,(2) = 5.96$$

That is, the price should be $5.96 per barrel.

c. Since $Q = 300 - P$, and $P = 5.96$, it follows that

$$Q = 300 - 5.96 = 294.04.$$

That is, the industry output is 294.04 million barrels per week.

26. There really is no way that we can answer this question with any certainty.
27. Yes. Many products are dominated by only a few sellers, and there are substantial barriers to entry.
29. Yes
30. Oligopoly is very likely in tractor manufacturing, but not (for this reason at least) in fresh-meat packing.
31. Yes. Because of possible entry, for one thing.
33. Yes. One might expect that the profit rate would be higher in more concentrated indus-tries. However, a number of prominent economists challenge this conclusion.

higher wages

Completion Questions

1. will, equal to, greater than
2. changes
3. steel (among many others)
4. pure
5. its existing level
6. constant
7. monopoly
8. maintain their present price
9. lower their price too
10. definite optimal pure strategy
11. always exists

True or False

1. True   2. False   3. False   4. True   5. False   6. True   7. False   8. True   9. False
10. False   11. True

Multiple Choice

1. *c*   2. *b*   3. *a*   4. *a*   5. *b*   6. *c*

Part 5   MARKETS FOR INPUTS

CHAPTER 12   Price and Employment of Inputs under Perfect Competition

Case Study: Welfare Payments

The welfare system in the United States has been criticized by both conservatives and liberals. To understand some of the effects of welfare payments, it is instructive to examine the indifference map of a (hypothetical) poor worker, Jean Lapp, shown below.

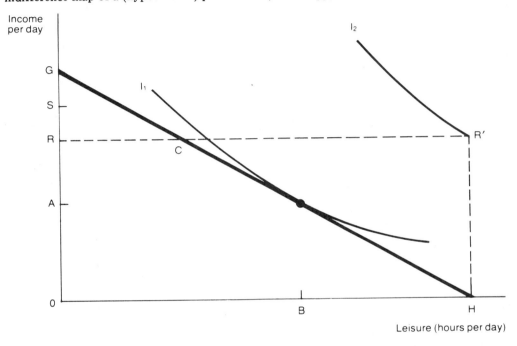

If she holds a job, her aftertax wage rate is minus one times the slope of the line GH, where OH equals 24 hours of leisure. For simplicity, suppose that, if her earnings are less than OR, the welfare system makes up the difference, so she is assured an income per day of OR.

a. If she were to work 24 hours a day, how much would she earn?

b. Given that her indifference curves are I_1 and I_2, how many hours per day would she work in the absence of the welfare program, and how much would she earn per day?

c. Given that the welfare program exists, how many hours per day will she work, and how much will she earn per day?

d. Suppose that this welfare system is replaced by a negative income tax which has the following provisions: A minimum income of OR is guaranteed; if the worker's income exceeds OS, he or she pays taxes; if income is less than OS, he or she receives (negative) taxes. Will this have an effect on the amount of work some workers will do? (Their indifference curves need not be the same as those shown above.) Explain.

Problems and Review Questions

1. The Krakow Manufacturing Company is a member of a perfectly competitive industry. The relationship between various amounts of labor input and the firm's output is shown below:

Product price (dollars)	Units of labor	Units of output	Marginal product of labor	Value of marginal product (dollars)
20	0	0		
20	1	2½		
20	2	5		
20	3	7		
20	4	8		

a. Fill in the blanks.

b. If you are told that the Krakow Manufacturing Company is hiring 3 units of labor, you can establish a range for the value of the wage rate prevailing in the labor market (assuming that the firm maximizes profit). What is this range? Specifically, what is the minimum value that the wage (for a unit of labor) may be? What is the maximum value? Why?

2. Henry George, an influential nineteenth-century economist, argued that land rents should be taxed away by the government. In his view, owners of land were receiving substantial land rents simply because their land happened to be well situated, not because they were doing anything productive. Since this land rent was unearned income and since the supply of land would not be influenced by such a tax, George felt that it was justifiable to tax away such land rent. Indeed, he argued that a tax of this sort should be the only tax imposed by the government. What weaknesses can you detect in his views?

3. Since various studies indicated a relationship between cigarette smoking and lung cancer, there has been considerable discussion of ways to reduce cigarette smoking in the United States. Suppose that it was decided to impose a tax of $1 on each ounce of tobacco grown by farmers. In your answers to the following questions, assume that all inputs are supplied by competitive input markets, that land has alternative uses, and that the land which can be used for tobacco production is not fixed.

a. Will the tax have any effect on the equilibrium price of tobacco land? Explain.

b. Will the tax have any effect on the equilibrium price of machinery used to raise tobacco? Explain.

c. Is the return to tobacco land an economic rent from the point of view of the tobacco industry? Explain.

d. Suppose that the tax was imposed only on one small tobacco farmer, rather than on all farmers. What would be its effect on the equilibrium price of tobacco land and the equilibrium price of tobacco machinery?

4. A textile mill uses labor and capital. The price of a unit of labor is $5 and the price of a unit of capital is $6. The marginal product of a unit of labor is the same as the marginal product of a unit of capital. Is this firm (which is a perfect competitor) maximizing its profit?

5. A perfectly competitive firm can hire labor at $30 per day. The firm's production function is as follows:

Number of days of labor	Number of units of output
0	0
1	8
2	15
3	21
4	26
5	30

If each unit of output sells for $5, how many days of labor should the firm hire?

6. Suppose that the ratio of the price of capital to the price of labor decreases by 1 percent in 1985, with the result that the capital-labor ratio increases by 0.5 percent.
   a. What is the elasticity of substitution?
   b. If the elasticity of substitution remains at this value, and if the ratio of the price of capital to the price of labor decreases by 1 percent again in 1986, will the ratio of capital's total income to labor's total income rise in 1986, or will it fall? Explain.

7. Suppose that you own a car wash and that its production function is

$$Q = -0.8 + 4.5L - 0.3L^2$$

where Q is the number of cars washed per hour and L is the number of men employed. Suppose that you receive $5 for each car washed and that the wage rate for each person you employ is $4.50. How many people should you employ to maximize profit? What will your hourly profit amount to? (Assume that labor is the only input.)

8. Suppose once again that you own the car wash described in the previous problem. How many people will you employ if the wage rate is $1.50? How many if it is $7.50? Based on these results, draw three points on your firm's demand curve for labor below.

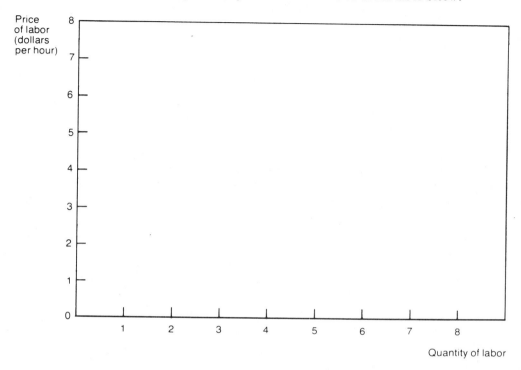

9. What factors determine the distribution of income? What role do input prices play?

10. Show that the cost-minimizing perfectly competitive firm will set

$$\frac{P_x}{MP_x} = \frac{P_y}{MP_y} = \cdots = \frac{P_z}{MP_z} = MC,$$

where P_x, P_y, and P_z are prices of inputs, MP_x, MP_y, and MP_z are marginal products of inputs, and MC is marginal cost.

11. Show that a profit-maximizing perfectly competitive firm will set an input's price equal to the value of its marginal product.

12. Suppose that labor is the only variable input, and that the marginal product of labor is as follows:

Amount of labor per year	Marginal product of labor
1	9
2	8
3	7
4	6
5	5
6	4

(Figures concerning the marginal product pertain to the interval between the indicated amount of labor and one unit less than this amount.) If the price of the product is $2 per unit and the firm is perfectly competitive, plot the firm's demand curve for labor in the graph below. (Assume that labor can only be hired in integer amounts.)

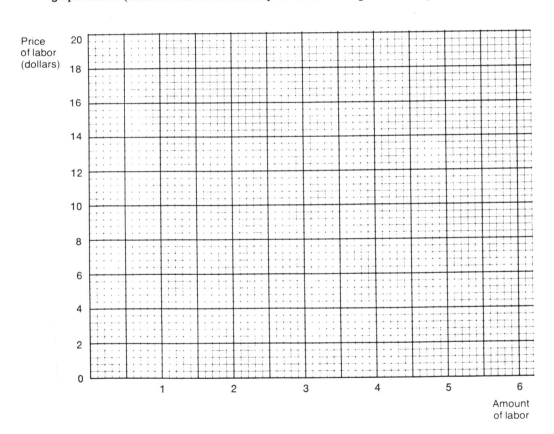

13. Describe and discuss the factors that influence the elasticity of demand for an input.

14. Describe the conditions that can result in a backward-bending supply curve for an input.

15. Why is a price of OP_0 not an equilibrium price? If OP_0 is the price, what forces will be set in motion to change it? Similarly, why is OP_1 not an equilibrium price? What is the equilibrium price for this input? (DD' and SS' are the demand and supply curves of the input.)

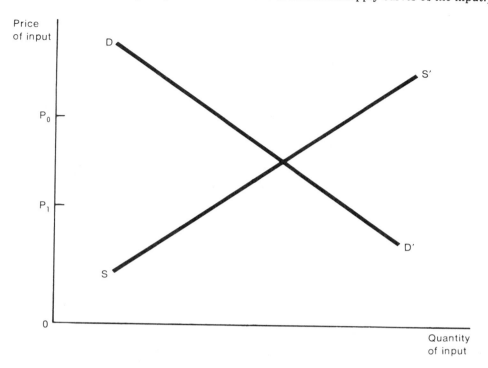

16. Show that a reduction of a payment to an input will not influence the availability and use of the input if the payment is a rent. Why is this important?

17. Describe what is meant by a quasi-rent.

18. Show that the differential in wages between skilled and unskilled plumbers should be equal to the differential in their marginal products.

19. Discuss some of the factors that could cause wage differentials even if labor were homogeneous.

20. What is the elasticity of substitution? How is it related to the ratio of capital's total income to labor's total income?

21. (*Advanced*) Suppose that a textile plant's production function in 1985 is $Q = L^8 K^2$. If it takes the product price as given and the input prices as given, show that total wages paid by the firm will equal 80 percent of its revenues.

22. Economists used microeconomic analysis to estimate the costs to the Department of Defense of an all-volunteer army. Can you guess how they went about doing this?

23. According to Elliot Berg, "the quantity of wage labor offered by the individual African tends to be inversely related to changes in village income and changes in wage rates." What does this imply about the shape of the supply curve for labor? How do you explain this shape?

24. Using the conventional supply and demand apparatus, show why black labor receives lower wages than white labor. What would happen to black wages, white wages, and total output if discrimination were to cease?

Completion Questions

1. In competitive firm A, the marginal product of the first unit of labor is 4 units of output, the marginal product of the second unit of labor is 3 units of output, and the marginal product of the third unit of labor is 2 units of output. If the price of a unit of output is $20, the firm will demand _____ units of labor when the price of a unit of labor is $75, _____ units of labor when the price of a unit of labor is $59, and _____ units of labor when the price of a unit of labor is $45.

2. If the ratio of each input's marginal product to its price is not the same for all inputs, the firm can _____ its costs by using some other input combination.

3. If a firm is maximizing profit under perfect competition, the ratio of the marginal product to the price of each input equals _____.

4. The value of the marginal product of an input equals the marginal product of the input times _____.

5. The price of an input in fixed supply is called _____ .

6. The elasticity of substitution measures the extent to which the ratio of capital to labor changes in response to changes in _____ _____.

7. If the elasticity of substitution is less than one, the effect of an increase in the price of labor relative to the price of capital is to _____ the ratio of capital's share (of total income) to labor's share (of total income).

8. A quasi-rent is paid to an input which is temporarily _____ in _____.

9. The price elasticity of demand for an input is generally greater in the _____ run than in the _____ run.

10. If an input's supply curve is backward-bending, beyond some point increases in its price bring forth _____ amounts supplied.

11. Wage differentials among labor of similar quality will arise to offset _____ _____.

True or False

_____ 1. If an innovation occurs which increases the marginal productivity of labor, and if at the same time the supply curve of labor shifts to the right, the price of labor must fall.

_____ 2. A backward-bending supply curve for labor implies that labor is an inferior good.

_____ 3. So long as the supply of land in a country is inelastic with regard to its price, economic efficiency does not require payments for land.

_____ 4. If more than one input is variable in quantity, the value-of-marginal-product curve will be the demand curve for an input.

_____ 5. Changes in the amounts used of other inputs will generally change the value-of-marginal-product curve for an input.

_____ 6. Under perfect competition, the supply of an input to an individual firm is perfectly inelastic.

_____ 7. Euler's theorem states that, if there are constant returns to scale, the total physical output of a firm will be identically equal to the sum of the amount of each input used multiplied by the input's marginal product.

_____ 8. Euler's theorem holds even if there are increasing returns to scale.

_____ 9. The more easily other inputs can be substituted for a certain input, the less price elastic is the demand for this input.

_____ 10. In the case of a backward-bending supply curve for labor, the income effect more than offsets the substitution effect.

_____ 11. An intermediate good is a good that is produced neither by agriculture nor by manufacturing.

_____ 12. The price elasticity of demand for an input depends on the price elasticity of the good the input produces.

Multiple Choice

1. The production function of firm Z, a perfectly competitive firm, is as follows:

Number of workers employed per day	Output per day
1	0
2	5
3	20
4	35
5	38

If the value of the marginal product of a worker is $150 when between 2 and 3 workers are employed per day, the price of a unit of output must be:

a. $1,000.

b. $100.
c. $20.
d. $10.
e. $5.

2. The traditional factors of production are:
   a. land and labor.
   b. land and capital.
   c. land, labor, and capital.
   d. air, land, and capital.
   e. none of the above.

3. (*Advanced*) If one minimizes cost subject to the constraint that a certain output is produced, the Lagrange multiplier turns out to equal
   a. marginal revenue.
   b. average cost.
   c. marginal cost.
   d. all of the above.
   e. none of the above.

4. The share of income going to labor in the United States has been
   a. declining markedly over time.
   b. relatively constant.
   c. subject to great variation.
   d. none of the above.
   e. all of the above.

5. The elasticity of substitution for the Cobb-Douglas production function is
   a. less than one.
   b. one.
   c. greater than one.
   d. undefined.
   e. dependent on the exponent of labor.

Key Concepts for Review

Land
Labor
Capital
Rent
Wages
Profits
Firm's demand curve for an input
Value of marginal product
Market demand curve for an input

Derived demand
Price elasticity of demand for an input
Market supply curve for an input
Intermediate goods
Backward-bending supply curve
Quasi-rents
Qualitative differences in inputs
Wage differentials
Elasticity of substitution

Answers

Case Study: Welfare Payments

   a. OG.

   b. She would work *BH* hours per day, and she would earn *OA* per day.

   c. Under the welfare program, she can attain point *R'* without working. Since this point lies on her highest attainable indifference curve, she will choose it; that is, she will not work, but receive the assured daily income of *OR.*

   d. Yes.

Problems and Review Questions

1. *a.*
     2½ $50
        2½   50
        2   40
        1   20

   b. $20 to $40.

2. Critics of George's views pointed out that land of many kinds can be improved, with the result that the supply is not completely price inelastic. The supply of such land really is not fixed, and it may be influenced by the tax. (The return from such land, although called "land rent," is not really rent, as we have defined it.) Moreover, they argued that if land rents are "unearned" so are many other types of income. Further, they claimed that it is unrealistic to expect such a tax to raise the needed revenue.

3. *a.* Because the tax is likely to reduce the output of tobacco, it may shift the demand curve for tobacco land to the left, thus reducing its equilibrium price.

   b. Because the tax is likely to reduce the output of tobacco, it may shift the demand curve for such machinery to the left, thus reducing its equilibrium price.

   c. No, because the supply curve for such land is not vertical.

   d. This farmer would be driven out of business, and there would be little or no effect on the equilibrium price of tobacco land and the equilibrium price of such machinery.

4. No. It should set the marginal product of labor divided by $5 equal to the marginal product of capital divided by $6.

5. The value of the marginal product is shown below:

Number of days of labor	Output	Marginal product	Value of marginal product (dollars)
0	0		
1	8	8	40
2	15	7	35
3	21	6	30
4	26	5	25
5	30	4	20

Thus, if the daily wage of labor is $30, the firm should hire 2 or 3 days of labor.

6. a. 0.5.
   b. The ratio of capital's total income to labor's total income will decrease, since the elasticity of substitution is less than one. This is explained in the text.
7. Your hourly profit equals $5Q - 4.5L$. Substituting for Q, your profit equals

$$5[-0.8 + 4.5L - 0.3L^2] - 4.5L = -4 + 18L - 1.5L^2$$

If you plot profit against L, you will find that it is a maximum at $L = 6$. Thus, you should employ 6 men.
$50.
8. 7 men.
   5 men.

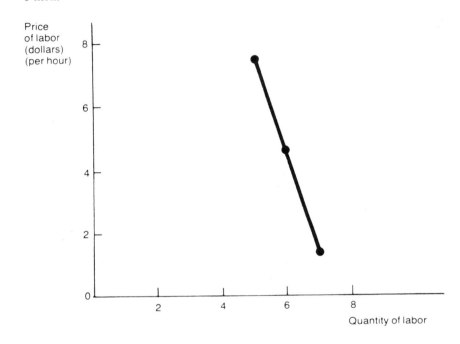

Price of labor (dollars) (per hour)

Quantity of labor

9. A person's income depends largely on the quantity of inputs he owns and the prices of these inputs. Input prices play a very important role.
10. It follows from the fact that the marginal rate of technical substitution must equal the input price ratio that

$$\frac{P_x}{MP_x} = \frac{P_y}{MP_y} = \ldots = \frac{P_z}{MP_z}$$

Also, the extra cost of producing an extra unit of product, if the extra production comes about by increasing the use of any input, must equal the ratio of the price of the input to its marginal product. Consequently, each of the ratios shown above equals marginal cost.
11. This follows from problem 10. Since MC = Price under perfect competition, it follows that

$$\frac{P_x}{MP_x} = \frac{P_y}{MP_y} = \ldots = \frac{P_z}{MP_z} = \text{Price.}$$

Thus, MP_x times Price = P_x; MP_y times Price = P_y; and so forth.

12. The demand curve for labor is:

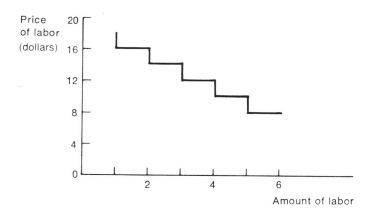

13. First, the more easily other inputs can be substituted for a certain input, the more price-elastic is the demand for this input.

    Second, the larger the price elasticity of demand for the product that the input helps to produce, the larger the price elasticity of demand for the input.

    Third, the greater the price elasticity of supply of the other inputs, the greater is the price elasticity of demand for this input.

    Fourth, the price elasticity of demand for an input is likely to be greater in the long run than in the short run.

14. A backward-bending supply curve can occur when the person supplying the input can use it himself. As the price of the input increases, the person supplying the input becomes richer. If the income effect more than offsets the substitution effect, the result will be that the person supplies less of the input.

15. OP_0 is not an equilibrium price because at this price the quantity supplied exceeds the quantity demanded. If the input is a good (like coal), inventories of the input would build up and sellers would begin to reduce the price.

    OP_1 is not an equilibrium price because at this price the quantity demanded exceeds the quantity supplied. Since this is the case, inventories would fall and shortages might develop, with the result that the price would be bid up.

    The equilibrium price is at the intersection of DD' and SS'.

16. This is because a rent is, by definition, a payment to an input that is in fixed supply. It is important because, if the government imposes a tax on rents, there will be no effect on the supply of resources to the economy.

17. A quasi-rent is a payment to any input that is in temporarily fixed supply.

18. If a firm maximizes profit, it hires each type of plumber in such amounts that:

$$MP_s \cdot MR = P_s$$
$$MP_u \cdot MR = P_u$$

where MP_s is the marginal product of skilled plumbers, MP_u is the marginal product of unskilled plumbers, MR is marginal revenue, P_s is the wage of skilled plumbers, and P_u is the wage of unskilled plumbers. Thus, $P_s \div P_u = MP_s \div MP_u$.

19. Differences in costs of training, occupational expenses, stability of employment, geographical differences in the cost of living, and so forth.

20. The elasticity of substitution measures the extent to which the capital–labor ratio changes in response to changes in the ratio of the price of capital to the price of labor. Whether or not an increase in the price of labor relative to the price of capital will decrease the ratio of capital income to labor income depends on the elasticity of substitution.

21. The wage, P_L, will equal the price of the product, P, times the marginal product of labor, which equals

$$\frac{\partial Q}{\partial L} = 0.8L^{-.2}\, K^{.2} = \frac{0.8Q}{L}$$

Thus $P_L = \dfrac{0.8Q}{L} \cdot P$, which means that

$$\frac{P_L L}{PQ} = 0.8$$

Since $P_L \cdot L$ equals the total wages paid by the firm and PQ equals its revenues, this completes the proof.

22. On the basis of cross-section data, Stuart Altman and Alan Fechter estimated the supply curve for manpower to the defense establishment. Then on the basis of independent estimates of the necessary size of the armed forces, they estimated the wage required to obtain this much labor. The total cost to the Department of Defense was this wage times the number of people in the armed forces.

23. It is backward-bending. See answer to question 14 above.

Completion Questions

1. one, two, two
2. reduce
3. the reciprocal of the price of the product
4. the price of the product
5. rent
6. the ratio of the price of capital to the price of labor
7. decrease
8. fixed; supply
9. long; short
10. smaller
11. differences in training costs, occupational expenses, cost of living, stability of employment, and so forth.

True or False

1. False   2. False   3. False   4. False   5. True   6. False   7. True   8. False   9. False
10. True   11. False   12. True

Multiple Choice

1. *d*   2. *c*   3. *c*   4. *b*   5. *b*

CHAPTER 13 Price and Employment of Inputs under Imperfect Competition

Case Study: A Statistical Study of the Salaries of Baseball Players

Economist Gerald Scully* estimated the contribution of baseball players of varying quality on a team's gross revenues. For hitters, his results were as follows:

Lifetime hitting average of player	Marginal revenue product		
	Gross	Net	Salary
255	$121,200	−$ 39,100	$ 9,700
283	135,000	− 25,300	20,000
338	256,600	128,300	29,100
427	405,800	290,500	42,200

The gross marginal revenue product is an estimate of the player's gross contribution to the team's revenues. The net marginal revenue product deducts the costs of player development and training, as well as other costs, from the gross marginal revenue product. The average 1969 salary of players with each batting average is shown in the last column. These data pertain to the period when the reserve clause was in effect.

  a. According to these results, were all baseball players exploited?

  b. When the courts allowed players to become free agents, the salaries of star players skyrocketed. Why?

Problems and Review Questions

1. The Pennsylvania Widget Company uses capital and labor to produce widgets. The price of a unit of capital is $10 per unit and the price of labor is $5 per unit. The marginal product of capital is 20 units and the marginal product of labor is 10 units. Is this firm maximizing profit if it is:

  a. a perfectly competitive firm in perfectly competitive input markets?
  b. a monopolist that buys inputs in perfectly competitive input markets?
  c. a monopsonist?

Explain your answer in each case.

*G. Scully, "Pay and Performance in Major League Baseball," *American Economic Review* (December 1974).

2. Firm M, a monopsonist, confronts the supply curve for labor shown below:

Wage rate per hour (dollars)	Number of units of labor supplied per hour	Cost of adding an additional unit of labor per hour (dollars)
3	1	
4	2	
5	3	
6	4	
7	5	
8	6	

a. Fill in the blanks.
b. Firm M's demand curve for labor is a horizontal line at a wage rate of $8 per hour. What quantity of labor will firm M demand?
c. What will be the equilibrium wage rate?

3. a. Suppose that the market supply schedule for input Y is as follows:

Quantity of Y	Price of Y (dollars)
10	1
11	2
12	3

Plot the marginal expenditure curve for Y in the relevant range in the graph below.

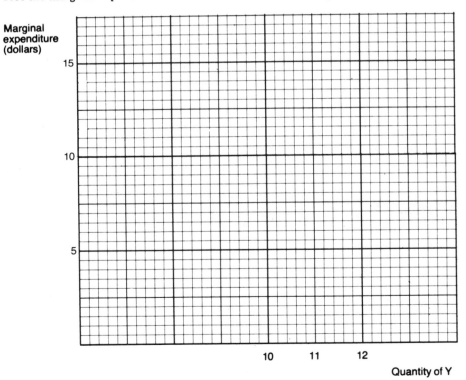

b. If the market supply curve for an input is a horizontal line, will the marginal expenditure curve for this input differ from the market supply curve? Explain.

4. Suppose that labor is the only input used by the Bijou Manufacturing Company, a hypothetical producer of tea kettles. This firm's production function is

Quantity of labor (workers)	Number of tea kettles produced per day
0	0
1	5
2	10
3	15
4	19
5	22

The demand schedule for its product is

Price (dollars per tea kettle)	Number of tea kettles demanded per day
1	22
2	19
3	15
4	10
5	5
6	0

What is the marginal revenue product of labor when:

a. between 0 and 1 laborers are hired?
b. between 1 and 2 laborers are hired?
c. between 2 and 3 laborers are hired?
d. between 3 and 4 laborers are hired?
e. between 4 and 5 laborers are hired?

5. In the previous problem, how many laborers will the Bijou Manufacturing Company hire if:
a. the wage of a laborer is $30 per day?
b. the wage of a laborer is $25 per day?
c. the wage of a laborer is $15 per day?
d. laborers can be obtained free of charge?

6. A craft union is formed which forces employers to hire only union members. The union membership is restricted by high initiation fees and a variety of other devices. What are the effects on the demand curve, supply curve, and price of labor?

7. According to Albert Rees, "A union will almost always insist on maintaining the current wage even at the cost of severe contraction in employment, whereas it would not insist on increasing the money wage if the consequences for employment were anything like as severe."* How can this fact be incorporated into our models of union behavior? What is the implication of this statement for classical theories of unemployment, which assumed that prices and wages are flexible?

*Albert Rees, *The Economics of Work and Pay* (New York: Harper and Row, 1973), p. 131.

8. Lloyd Reynolds has pointed out that the union sometimes presents demands that it does not expect to be acted on immediately. As he puts it, "It is the normal opening move in the chess game." * Give some examples of demands that were first met by outraged opposition by management, but which ultimately came to be accepted.

9. Describe how a profit-maximizing firm under imperfect competition will determine how much of each input to employ. Prove that this does indeed result in maximum profit.

10. *a.* Suppose that the demand curve for a firm's product is as follows:

Output	Price of good (dollars)
23	$5.00
32	4.00
40	3.50
47	3.00
53	2.00

Also, suppose that the marginal product and total product of labor at this firm is:

Amount of labor	Marginal product of labor	Total output
2	10	23
3	9	32
4	8	40
5	7	47
6	6	53

(Note that the figures regarding marginal product pertain to the interval between the indicated amount of labor and one unit less than the indicated amount of labor.) Given these data, how much labor would the firm employ if labor costs $12 a unit?

b. How much labor will the firm employ if labor costs $13 a unit?

c. How much labor will the firm employ if labor costs $10 a unit?

d. How much labor will the firm employ if labor costs $1 a unit?

e. Assuming labor is the only variable input, plot the firm's demand curve for labor in the graph on the opposite page.

*Lloyd Reynolds, *Labor Economics and Labor Relations* (Englewood Cliffs, N.J.: Prentice Hall, 1970), p. 435.

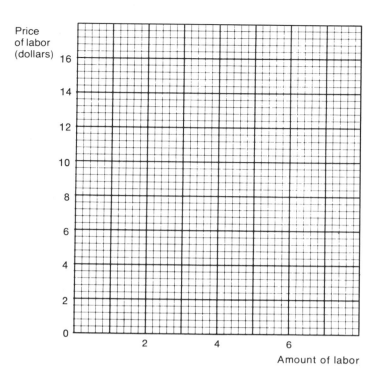

Price of labor (dollars)

Amount of labor

11. Prove that the marginal revenue product is the product of the marginal product and marginal revenue.

12. Discuss what is meant by monopsony. Give some cases in the real world where monopsony seems to be present.

13. If you were a laborer, would you prefer the labor market to be perfectly competitive or monopsonistic?

14. If you wanted your area to become a low-wage area, would you prefer the labor market to be perfectly competitive or monopsonistic? Why?

15. Describe the conditions determining how much of each input a profit-maximizing monopsonist will employ.

16. How can unions influence the wage rate paid to their members? Describe at least three ways that they can influence the wage.

17. Discuss the nature of union objectives. Give a few plausible kinds of union motivation and describe their implications for the wage rate and employment.

18. What do we know about the economic effects of unions? Describe the sorts of empirical studies that have been made, and summarize their results.

19. According to Ruth Greenslade, the ratio of average hourly earnings in the bituminous coal industry to that in general manufacturing rose from 1:1 at the turn of the century to about 2:1 at the peak of post-World-War-I union strength in the industry in 1922. Then as union strength declined in the industry, the ratio declined to 1.07 in 1933. But as union strength increased subsequently, the ratio increased too, and reached 1.7:1 in 1957. What do these findings seem to indicate about the economic effects of unionism?

20. Joseph Garbarino studied the behavior of wages in 34 manufacturing industries in 1923–40. He found that wages were directly related to degree of concentration of output, changes in output per man-hour, and extent of unionism. But the extent of unionism seemed least important and was not statistically significant. Comment on these findings.

21. According to Allan Cartter and F. Ray Marshall, the impact of unionism on wage levels of organized workers is most noticeable during periods of recession. Why?

22. According to Simon Rottenberg, in his discussion of the labor market for baseball players: "The reserve rule, which binds a player to the team that contracts him, gives a prima facie appearance of monopsony to the market."* Do you agree? What are the likely effects of this rule?

23. Allan Cartter and F. Ray Marshall (former U.S. Secretary of Labor) state, "Reviewing the data from 1919 to the present, and particularly the last 15 years, there seems to be no indication that trade unions in general have increased labor's share of income."† How can one reconcile this finding with the feeling that unions in some industries have raised wages substantially?

Completion Questions

1. To a monopsonist in the labor market, the cost of hiring an additional laborer (increases, decreases) _____ as it hires more and more labor. The cost of hiring an additional laborer (exceeds, equals, is less than) _____ the wage that must be paid this worker. If the monopsonist can hire 10 workers at a daily wage of $40 and 11 workers at a daily wage of $45, the daily cost of hiring the eleventh worker is _____, as compared with the daily wage of the eleventh worker, which is _____.

2. The condition for profit maximization under imperfect competition is that the firm should set the price of the input equal to _____
   _____.

3. The marginal revenue product of an input differs from the value of the marginal product in the following way: _____
   _____.

*Simon Rottenberg, "The Baseball Players' Labor Market," *Journal of Political Economy* (June 1956).
†Allan Cartter and F. Ray Marshall, *Labor Economics* (Homewood, Ill.: Irwin, 1967).

4. If marginal revenue is equal to price, the marginal-revenue-product schedule becomes precisely the same as the _____ .

5. If all firms are monopolists in their product markets, the market demand curve for an input would simply be the _____ of the demand curves of the individual firms.

6. Monopsony is a case where there exists _____ .

7. The classic case of monopsony is _____

   _____ .

8. The marginal expenditure curve for an input lies _____ its supply curve, if its supply curve slopes upward to the right.

9. If a monopsonist maximizes profit, he sets the marginal expenditure on an input equal to

   _____ .

10. The monopsonist employs _____ of the input than if the input market were perfectly competitive.

11. The monopsonist pays a _____ price for the input than if the input market were perfectly competitive.

True or False

_____ 1. If a union shifts the supply curve of labor to the left, and if the price elasticity of demand for labor is infinite, the price of labor will rise.

_____ 2. If a union wants to maximize the total payments to labor, it will operate in the inelastic portion of the demand curve for labor.

_____ 3. Under perfect competition, the marginal expenditure for an input equals its price.

_____ 4. A monopsonist will hire inputs so that the ratio of the marginal product to the marginal expenditure for each input is the same for all inputs.

_____ 5. If a labor union tries to maximize its wage bill, it will try to operate at the point where its marginal revenue is zero.

_____ 6. In recent years, union wages have increased much more rapidly than nonunion wages.

_____ 7. The initial asking figure concerning wages put forth by a union in collective bargaining is likely to be lower than its real expectations.

_____ 8. The marginal-revenue-product curve for an input often has a positive slope.

_____ 9. The marginal revenue product of an input is equal to marginal revenue divided by marginal product.

_____ 10. Oligopsony occurs when there are few buyers.

_____ 11. The theory of bilateral monopoly, when applied to collective bargaining, assumes that the union wants to maximize the difference between the total wages that are paid to (employed) workers and the amount of money required to bring this amount of labor onto the market if each unit of labor were paid only the price necessary to induce it to work.

Multiple Choice

1. It makes perfectly good sense for a labor union to want to
   a. maximize the wage rate.
   b. maximize its marginal revenue.
   c. keep its members fully employed.
   d. all of the above.
   e. none of the above.

2. If the price of labor is $1 a unit, its marginal product is 2 tons of output, and the firm's marginal revenue is $5 per ton, the firm (which is not a monopsonist) is
   a. minimizing cost.
   b. maximizing profit.
   c. not maximizing profit.
   d. at a corner solution.
   e. a monopolist.

3. If there is only one variable input, the firm's demand curve for an input is obtained by multiplying
   a. marginal cost and marginal revenue curves.
   b. marginal product and marginal revenue curves.
   c. average cost and marginal revenue curves.
   d. average cost and average revenue curves.
   e. none of the above.

4. Under imperfect competition in the product market, the equilibrium price of an input is given by
   a. the intersection of the product demand and supply curves.
   b. the intersection of the input demand and supply curves.
   c. the intersection of the product demand and input supply curves.
   d. all of the above.
   e. none of the above.

5. Monopsony often stems from the fact that:
   a. an input is not mobile.
   b. an input is extremely mobile.
   c. an input is an intermediate good.
   d. an input has a wide variety of uses.
   e. none of the above.

6. The marginal expenditure for an input will always be
   a. higher than the input's price.
   b. higher than the input's price if its supply curve is upward-sloping
   c. higher than the input's price if its supply curve is horizontal.
   d. all of the above.
   e. none of the above.

Key Concepts for Review

Marginal revenue product
Firm's demand curve for an input
Market demand curve for an input
Market supply curve for an input
Monopsony
Oligopsony
Monopsonistic competition

Marginal expenditure curves
Labor unions
Collective bargaining
Bilateral monopoly
Union objectives
Economic effect of unions

Answers

Case Study: A Statistical Study of the Salaries of Baseball Players

a. No. The players with low batting averages seemed to be paid more than the net contribution they made to their team's profit.

b. According to Scully's estimates, the star hitters contributed much more to their team's profit than they were being paid when the reserve clause was in effect. This was also true of the star pitchers.

Problems and Review Questions

1. a. and b. Under the conditions set forth in parts a and b of this question, a necessary condition for profit maximization is that the price of each input be proportional to its marginal product. This condition is fulfilled in this case. However, this is not a sufficient condition for profit maximization. Even though this condition is satisfied, the firm may not be maximizing profit.
   c. Unless the price of each input is proportional to the marginal expenditure for this input, the firm is not maximizing profit. If they are proportional, the firm may not be maximizing profit. See the answer to 1. a and b.

2. a. $5.
       7.
       9.
       11.
       13.
   b. 3 units of labor per hour.
   c. $5 per hour.

3. *a.*

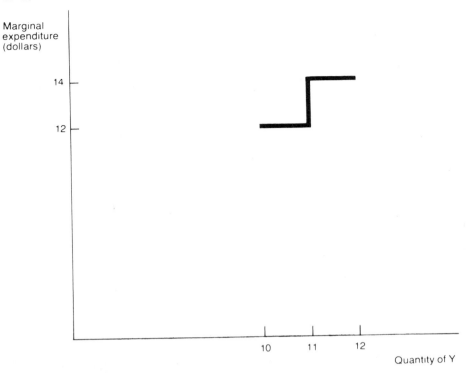

b. No. The additional expenditure for an additional unit of the input equals its price under these circumstances.

4.

Quantity of labor	Number of tea kettles	Price (dollars)	Total revenue (dollars)	Marginal revenue product (dollars)
0	0	6	0	
				25
1	5	5	25	
				15
2	10	4	40	
				5
3	15	3	45	
				−7
4	19	2	38	
				−16
5	22	1	22	

  a. $25.
  b. $15.
  c. $ 5.
  d. −$7.
  e. −$16.

5. *a.* None.
  b. Zero or 1.
  c. 1 or 2.
  d. 3.

6. The supply curve for labor is shifted to the left, with the result that the price of labor will increase. There may be no effect on the demand curve for labor, unless employers are forced to hire more labor at a given wage than they otherwise would have.

7. It can be incorporated by asserting that the current wage is a floor that almost never will be penetrated in the course of collective bargaining. It implies that an assumption of downward wage flexibility is unrealistic.

8. The Auto Workers and Steel Workers asked for a "guaranteed" annual wage in the 1940s. Also, pensions and health and welfare funds are other examples.

9. The firm will set the marginal revenue product of each input equal to the input's price. Since the former measures the extra revenue derived from an extra unit of input and the latter measures the extra cost of an extra unit of input, profit cannot be a maximum if the latter is less than the former—or more than the former. It can only be a maximum when they are equal.

10. *a.* 3 or 4 units of labor. For reason, see below:

Amount of labor	Total product	Marginal product	Price of good (dollars)	Total revenue (dollars)	Marginal revenue product (dollars)
2	23	10	5.00	115	n.a.
3	32	9	4.00	128	13
4	40	8	3.50	140	12
5	47	7	3.00	141	1
6	53	6	2.00	106	-35

b. 2 or 3 units of labor.

c. 4 units of labor.

d. 4 or 5 units of labor.

e. The demand curve is:

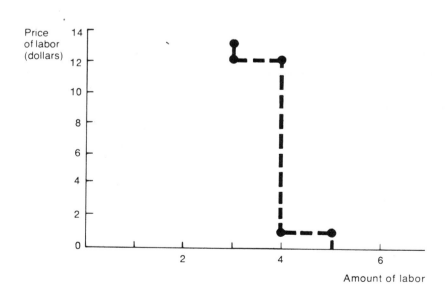

11. By definition, the marginal revenue product is $\Delta R \div \Delta I$, where ΔR is the change in total revenue and ΔI is the change in the quantity of the input. Since marginal revenue (MR) equals $\Delta R \div \Delta Q$, where ΔQ is the change in output, it follows that the marginal revenue product equals $MR \, \Delta Q \div \Delta I$. And since marginal product (MP) equals $\Delta Q \div \Delta I$, it follows that the marginal revenue product equals $MR \cdot MP$.

12. Monopsony is a case where there is a single buyer. Company towns or mill towns are some-times examples of monopsony with respect to labor.

13. Perfectly competitive, because the wage will be higher.

14. Monopsonistic, because the wage will be lower.

15. A profit-maximizing monopsonist will hire an input up to the point where its marginal product times the firm's marginal revenue equals the marginal expenditure for the input.

16. They can shift the supply curve for labor to the left, try to get the employer to pay a higher wage while allowing some of the supply of labor forthcoming at this higher wage to find no opportunity for work, or try to shift the demand for labor upward and to the right.

17. The union might want to maximize the wage, subject to the constraint that a certain num-ber of its members be employed. Or it might want to maximize the wage bill. It is difficult to summarize union goals adequately and simply.

18. Far too little is known about their effects. Empirical studies have generally been based on comparisons of wage increases in unionized industries with those in nonunion industries. Such evidence is difficult to interpret, and the findings have not been clear-cut.

19. They seem to indicate that the strength of the union was directly related to the relative height of wages in the industry.

21. Because union contracts tend to introduce rigidity in wage structures.

22. Wages of baseball stars may be lower than in a competitive market.

23. Although unions may have raised wages in some industries, they may not have done so in others. Moreover, this finding depends on things other than the wage rate.

Completion Questions

1. increases, exceeds, $95, $45
2. the input's marginal revenue product
3. $MRP = MR \cdot MP$, whereas $VMP = P \cdot MP$
4. value-of-marginal-product schedule
5. horizontal summation
6. a single buyer
7. a company town where a single firm is the sole buyer of labor.
8. above
9. the input's marginal revenue product
10. less
11. lower

True or False

1. False   2. False   3. True   4. True   5. True   6. False   7. False   8. False   9. False
10. True   11. True

Multiple Choice

1. *c*   2. *c*   3. *b*   4. *b*   5. *a*   6. *b*

Part 6 GENERAL EQUILIBRIUM, WELFARE ECONOMICS, AND POLITICAL ECONOMY

CHAPTER 14 General Equilibrium Analysis and Resource Allocation

Case Study: Can Boretania's Targets Be Met?

Boretania, a hypothetical country with a very simple economy, produces only two goods: food and machinery. The amount of each input used per dollar of output is shown below.

	Type of output	
	Food	Machinery
Type of input	(dollars)	(dollars
Food	0.10	0.20
Machinery	0.40	0.70
Labor	0.50	0.10
Total	1.00	1.00

The Boretania government has set consumption targets of $100 million of food and $50 million of machinery. There is available in the Boretania economy sufficient capacity to produce $200 million of food and $400 million of machinery, but no more. Can the consumption targets be met?

Problems and Review Questions

1. According to some observers, population growth is a tremendous problem and Zero Population Growth is a desirable objective. In their view, population growth is a problem because the private cost of children to parents is less than the social cost imposed on society. To deal with this problem, it has sometimes been suggested that we take one of the following actions. (1) Limit each woman to two children. (2) Issue two tickets to each woman, and allow her to sell one or more of them to other women. Each ticket entitles its owner to bear one child. (3) Hold an auction where such tickets are sold by the government to the highest bidders.

   a. Using the Edgeworth box diagram, show, in the graph on page 212, that the first proposal is likely to lead to a less satisfactory outcome than the second proposal.
   b. Do you agree that the private cost of children to parents is less than the social cost imposed on society? Explain.
   c. What factors help to determine whether the third proposal is preferable to the second proposal?
   d. Many religious and other groups disagree with the proponents of Zero Population Growth. Do microeconomic principles prove that Zero Population Growth is the proper objective of our present-day society? Explain.

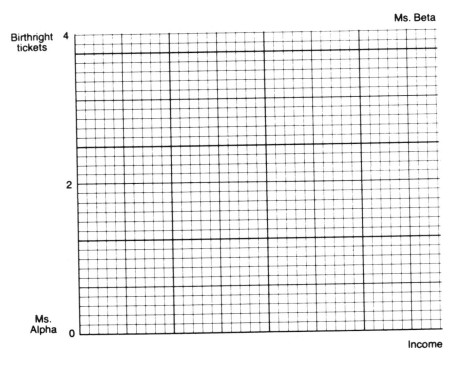

2. Country X contains two industries, agriculture and machinery. The input-output matrix is:

| | Output (dollars) | |
Input	Agriculture	Machinery
Agriculture	0.10	0.00
Machinery	0.30	0.30
Labor	0.60	0.70
	1.00	1.00

  a. If this country sets consumption targets of $90 million of agriculture and $40 million of machinery, how much will each industry have to produce to meet these targets?

  b. How much labor will be required to meet these targets?

3. Suppose that Tom and Harry are the only consumers and that the marginal rate of product transformation between food and medicine is two, while Tom's marginal rate of substitution is one. Prove that, if this is the case, Harry can be made better off without hurting Tom. (Assume that firm *A* produces both food and medicine.)

4. Suppose that there are only two industries, the food industry and the clothing industry, in the economy, and that the Edgeworth box diagram showing the isoquants of both industries is as follows:

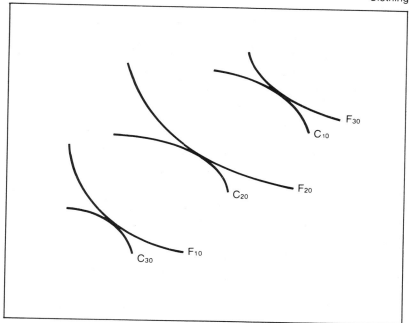

Clothing

Food

The isoquant F_{30} shows input combinations that can produce 30 units of food per year, the isoquant C_{30} shows input combinations that can produce 30 units of clothing per year, and so on. Using the graph below, draw three points on this economy's product transformation curve.

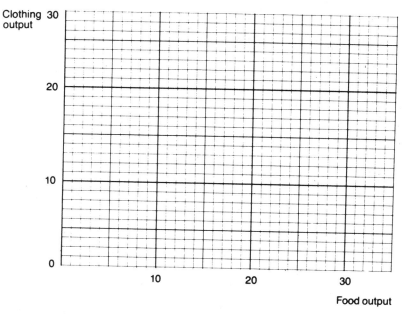

-213-

5. In the diagram provided at the top of the previous page, what is being measured along each of the axes?

6. In the case of the following Edgeworth box diagram, curves 1 and 2 are indifference curves of one consumer, and curves I and II are indifference curves of the second consumer. Is it optimal for the first consumer to receive OX units of good X and OY units of good Y, the second consumer receiving $(OC - OX)$ units of good X and $(OB - OY)$ units of good Y? What allocations would be better?

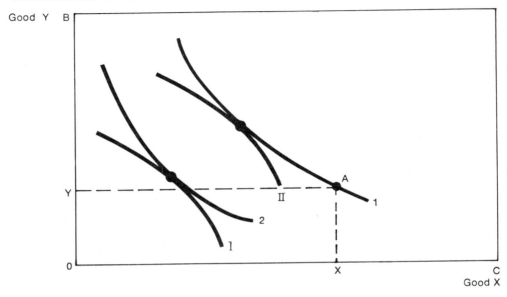

7. John takes a date, Joan, to a Chinese restaurant, and they order a portion of lemon chicken and a portion of sweet and sour pork. When the food arrives, they divide each portion between them.

   a. Indicate below how the Edgeworth box diagram might be used to analyze the way in which they should divide the food.

-214-

b. Is it reasonable to assume that John's satisfaction depends only on the amount of food he consumes and not on the amount Joan consumes too?

8. Suppose that you have six bottles of beer (and no potato chips) and your roommate has four bags of potato chips (and no beer). It is late at night, and the stores are closed. You decide to swap some of your beer for some of her potato chips. The Edgeworth box diagram is the following:

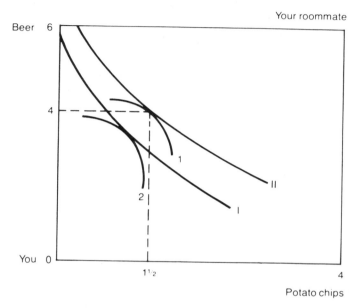

Label the point on the diagram which represents your pretrade situation.

9. In Question 8, suppose that you offer to swap 2 bottles of your beer for 1 ½ bags of your roommate's potato chips.
   a. Will your roommate agree to this?
   b. Is this a rational offer for you to make; that is, will it make you better off?

10. According to Robert Dorfman, Paul Samuelson, and Robert Solow, input-output analysis "rejects as unrealistic the Austrian economists' view that you can identify certain industries as being in 'earlier' stages of production and certain other industries as being in 'later' stages."* What do they mean? Do you agree? Why or why not?

11. Robert Dorfman, Paul Samuelson, and Robert Solow point out that "a system which leaves many supply and demand functions (or the utility and production functions which lie one step further back) almost completely unspecified as to shape can yield only incomplete results."† Explain the significance of this fact for general equilibrium analysis.

---

*R. Dorfman, P. Samuelson, and R. Solow, *Linear Programming and Economic Analysis* (New York: McGraw-Hill, 1958), p. 205.
† Ibid., p. 349.

12. What is general equilibrium analysis? How does it differ from partial equilibrium analysis?

13. When should one use general equilibrium analysis? When should one use partial equilibrium analysis?

14. Define a state of general equilibrium. Can we be sure that a state of general equilibrium can be achieved?

15. Describe the conditions given by Kenneth Arrow and Gerard Debreu that are sufficient for the existence of general equilibrium. Are these conditions necessary for its existence?

16. Construct a simple general equilibrium model. Count up the number of equations and the number of variables.

17. Describe the nature and purposes of input-output analysis. Be sure to specify its key assumptions.

18. Suppose that the following table shows the amount of each type of input used per dollar of output:

Type of input	Output (dollars)		
	Electric power	Coal	Chemicals
Electric Power	$0.1	$0.3	$0.0
Coal	0.5	0.1	0.0
Chemicals	0.2	0.0	0.9
Labor	0.2	0.6	0.1
TOTAL	1.0	1.0	1.0

Suppose that this economy has set consumption targets of $100 million of electric power, $50 million of coal, and $50 million of chemicals. Given these targets, how much labor must be used?

19. What factors might cause changes over time in the technical coefficients in input-output analysis?

20. How can one derive the contract curve in an Edgeworth box diagram representing exchange between two consumers? What is the significance of the contract curve?

21. Describe how a product transformation curve can be derived from an Edgeworth box diagram representing production of two goods.

22. Given the amount of each commodity to be produced, how should this output be allocated and how should inputs be allocated in the two-good, two-input, two-consumer case?

23. Describe how input-output analysis might be used to analyze the effects of disarmament on the American economy.

24. Describe how input-output analysis might be of use to an economist interested in forecasting the sales of the IBM Corporation next year.

25. According to an input-output table prepared by the Bureau of Labor Statistics for 1947, the chemical industry produced $14 billion of output.* This table also shows that the biggest purchaser of this output is the chemical industry. How can this be? Isn't there a contradiction here?

26. Werner Hirsch constructed an input-output model that included local government as an "industry."† How would you go about doing this? What sorts of problems are there in this approach?

Completion Questions

1. Three inputs are used to make a chair: labor, wood, and electric power. The value of labor used per dollar of output is twice the value of wood used per dollar of output, and the value of electric power used per dollar of output is 3.5 times the value of labor used per dollar of output. The column of an input-output table corresponding to this product equals _____, _____, and _____, where the first figure pertains to labor input, the second figure pertains to wood input, and the third figure pertains to electric power input.

2. Partial equilibrium analysis is adequate in cases where the effect of a change in market conditions in one market has _____ repercussion on prices in other markets.

3. _____ is the branch of microeconomics that deals with the interrelations among various decision-making units and various markets.

4. A state of _____ can be achieved under a wide set of circumstances in a _____ economy.

5. _____ puts general equilibrium analysis in a form that is operationally useful.

6. Input-output analysis emphasizes the _____ of the economic system.

7. Wassily Leontief, the founder of _____ , assumes that production coefficients are _____ .

8. It is impossible for a combination of outputs lying outside the _____ _____ to be produced.

*Wassily Leontief, "Input–Output Economics," *Scientific American* (October, 1951).
+Werner Hirsch, "Input–Output Techniques for Urban Government Decisions," *American Economic Review* (May 1968).

9. If we connect the points of tangency of one person's indifference curves with the other person's indifference curves in an Edgeworth box diagram, we obtain the _____ _____ .

10. Consumer satisfaction will not be maximized unless the marginal rate of product transformation between two goods is equal to the _____ _____ .

11. The contract curve is an optimal set of points in the sense that, if the consumers are off the contract curve, it is always preferable for them to _____ _____ .

True or False

_____ 1. Input-output analysis assumes that inputs are used in varying proportions, so that demand theory is an important part of the analysis.

_____ 2. There is only one set of absolute prices that results in general equilibrium.

_____ 3. It is very difficult to find reasonable conditions under which a perfectly competitive economy is in a state of general equilibrium.

_____ 4. The complexity of input-output models is not substantially increased if the assumption of fixed production coefficients is relaxed.

_____ 5. If commodities are allocated optimally, the marginal rate of substitution between a pair of commodities must be the same for all consumers that consume both.

_____ 6. If commodities are allocated optimally, the marginal rate of substitution between any pair of commodities must be the same for all pairs of commodities.

_____ 7. In the case of production, it is not optimal for producers to move to a point on the contract curve.

_____ 8. A point that is inside the product transformation curve is an efficient point.

_____ 9. Input-output analysis involves the solution of a number of simultaneous linear equations.

_____ 10. Changes in the relative prices of inputs may result in changes in production coefficients.

_____ 11. A product transformation curve often has a positive slope.

Multiple Choice

1. An input-output table for nation A is given below. All inputs and outputs are included.

Type of input	Type of output		
	Steel	Coal	Trucks
Steel	.20	.10	.30
Coal	.40	.20	___
Trucks	.05	___	.10
Labor	___	.65	.50

The figures in the blank spaces
a. are .35, .05, and .10.
b. are .25, .15, and .10.
c. sum up to .60.
d. sum up to .40.
e. none of the above.

2. No market can adjust to a change in conditions without
   a. a change in other markets.
   b. other markets remaining unchanged.
   c. governmental aid.
   d. violating the assumption of general equilibrium analysis.
   e. none of the above.

3. Whether or not there is a solution to a set of equations can
   a. never be determined by comparing the number of variables with the number of equations.
   b. always be determined by comparing the number of variables with the number of equations.
   c. under certain circumstances be determined by comparing the number of variables with the number of equations.
   d. be determined by the method of least squares.
   e. none of the above.

4. Input-output analysis has been used to
   a. analyze problems of defense and mobilization.
   b. determine the relationship of imports and exports to domestic production.
   c. analyze problems of underdeveloped countries.
   d. all of the above.
   e. none of the above.

5. Compared with a certain point on the contract curve, a point off the contract curve
   a. may be better.
   b. is certainly better.
   c. is never better.
   d. is always equally good.
   e. none of the above.

6. If a point is off the contract curve, we can find
   a. a point on the contract curve that is better.
   b. no point on the contract curve that is better.
   c. a point on the contract curve that is better, if and only if the contract curve is a straight line.
   d. a point on the contract curve that is better, if and only if the contract curve goes through the origin.
   e. none of the above.

Key Concepts for Review

Partial equilibrium analysis
General equilibrium analysis
General equilibrium
Existence of general equilibrium
Uniqueness of general equilibrium
Numeraire
Input-output analysis
Input-output table

Production coefficients
Edgeworth box diagram
Exchange
Contract curve
Product transformation curve
Production and exchange in a two-
    good, two-consumer, two-input
    economy

Answers

Case Study: Can Boretania's Targets Be Met?

No. To meet these targets,

$$F = 100 + 0.1\,F + 0.2\,M$$
$$M = 50 + 0.4\,F + 0.7\,M,$$

where F is the food output and M is the machinery output needed to meet the targets (both F and M are expressed in millions of dollars). Solving these two equations simultaneously, we find that $F = 211$ and $M = 448$; so, to meet these targets, $211 million of food and $448 million of machinery would have to be produced.

Problems and Review Questions

1. *a.* Suppose that two women, Ms. Alpha and Ms. Beta, have indifference maps shown below, where income is plotted along the horizontal axis and birthright tickets are plotted along the vertical axis.

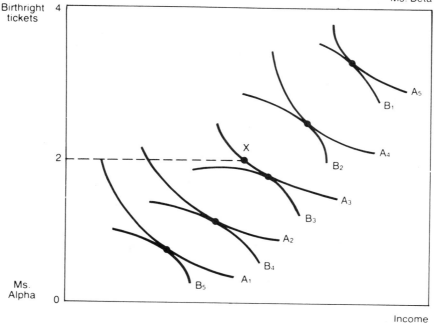

Birthright tickets

Ms. Alpha

Income

Indifference curves $A_1, \ldots, A_5$ are Ms. Alpha's; indifference curves $B_1, \ldots, B_5$ are Ms. Beta's. The first proposal says that the allocation must be that represented by point X, but in general one or both women can increase utility by moving to the contract curve. The second proposal would enable them to move to the contract curve.

b. This may be true because of external diseconomies; however, there also may be external economies.

c. One important consideration here is what the government does with the proceeds of the auction.

d. No. As stressed repeatedly, economics is no substitute for religion, ethics, or politics. It does not tell us what our objectives or values should be.

2. a. $100 million of agricultural goods and $100 million of machinery will have to be produced.

   b. $130 million of labor.

3. Because the marginal rate of product transformation is 2, firm A can produce 2 extra units of food if it reduces its production of medicine by 1 unit. Suppose that it does this and that it provides Tom with 1 less unit of medicine (since it produces 1 unit less). At the same time, suppose that it gives him 1 extra unit of food to compensate for his loss of medicine. There is 1 unit of food left over (since firm A produced 2 extra units), which can make Harry better off without hurting Tom.

4.

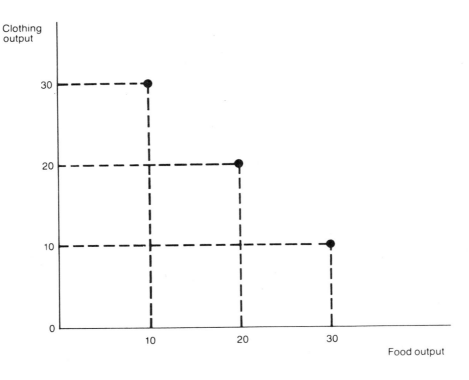

5. The quantity of labor input is measured along one axis; the quantity of capital input is measured along the other axis.

6. No.

   The allocation corresponding to the point where indifference curve 1 is tangent to indifference curve II would be better.

7. *a*. The quantity of lemon chicken might be measured along the horizontal axis; the quantity of sweet and sour pork might be measured along the vertical axis. The indifference curves of each person (A_1, A_2, A_3 for Joan; B_1, B_2, B_3 for John) might be inserted, as shown on the next page:

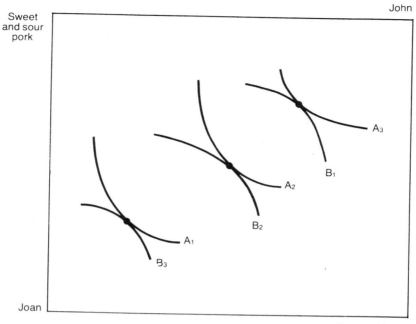

The optimal point would be on the contract curve.

    b. Probably not, since he probably gets satisfaction from her well-being (and hopefully she feels the same way).

8. Point Y represents your pretrade position.

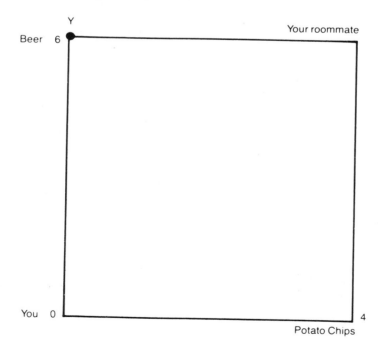

9. *a.* This trade would put her on her indifference curve 1, which is a higher indifference curve than that going through point *Y*. (To identify point *Y*, see the answer to Question 8.) Thus, she should agree to this.

   b. This trade would put you on your indifference curve II, which is a higher indifference curve than that going through point *Y*. Thus, the trade will make you better off.

10. In input-output analysis, it is recognized that industries often use each other's products. Yes.

11. Unless one is willing to specify something about their shape, many important questions simply cannot be answered.

12. An analysis that takes account of the interrelationships among prices in various markets is called a general equilibrium analysis. This is in contrast to partial equilibrium analysis, which assumes that changes in price can occur in whatever market is being studied without causing significant changes in price in other markets, which in turn affect the market being studied.

13. Partial equilibrium analysis is adequate in cases where the effect of a change in market conditions in one market has little repercussion on prices in other markets. However, if the effects of a change in market conditions in one market result in important repercussions on other prices, a general equilibrium analysis may be required.

14. A state of general equilibrium is achieved when consumers are maximizing utility (subject to budget constraints), resource owners are providing as much of various inputs as they choose, firms are maximizing profit (subject to technological constraints), and all markets are cleared. Modern work has established that in a perfectly competitive economy a state of general equilibrium can be achieved under a fairly wide set of conditions.

15. Arrow and Debreu assume that there are not increasing returns to scale, at least one primary input must be used to produce each good, each consumer can supply all primary inputs, the amount supplied by a consumer must not exceed his or her initial stock, each consumer's utility function is continuous, his or her wants cannot be satiated, and his or her indifference curves are convex. These conditions are sufficient but not necessary.

17. Recognizing the interdependence among various parts of the economy, input-output analysis attempts to determine the amount that each industry must produce in order to fulfill certain targets for the economy as a whole. It assumes that production coefficients are fixed.

18. $0.2E + 0.6X + 0.1C = 200$. Thus, $200 million of labor, since $C = 818$, $E = 159$, $X = 144$. (*E* is output of electric power, *X* is output of coal, and *C* is output of chemicals.)

19. Changes in input prices and changes in technology.

20. Find those points where one consumer's indifference curve is tangent to the other consumer's indifference curve. The contract curve is an optimal set of points in the sense that, if the consumers are at a point off the contract curve, it is always preferable for them to move to a point on the contract curve, since one or both can gain from the move while neither incurs a loss.

21. Each point on the contract curve in such a box diagram corresponds to a certain level of production of each good. Plot these pairs of production levels, one against the other. The result is the product transformation curve.

22. Construct an Edgeworth box diagram where the upper right-hand corner of the box is the point on the product transformation curve corresponding to the amount of each commodity to be produced. Then find the point on the contract curve where the consumers' indifference curves have a common slope equal to that of the product transformation curve at the point corresponding to the amount of each commodity produced. This point on the contract curve indicates the optimal distribution of commodities between the consumers. The optimal allocation of inputs is indicated by the point on the production contract curve corresponding to the specified point on the product transformation curve.

25. No.

Completion Questions

1. 0.2, 0.1, 0.7
2. little
3. general equilibrium analysis
4. general equilibrium; perfectly competitive
5. input-output analysis
6. interdependence
7. input-output analysis; fixed
8. product transformation curve
9. contract curve
10. marginal rate of substitution between the goods
11. move to a point on the contract curve

True or False

1. False 2. False 3. False 4. False 5. True 6. False 7. False 8. False 9. True
10. True 11. False

Multiple Choice

1. *a* 2. *a* 3. *c* 4. *d* 5. *a* 6. *a*

CHAPTER 15 Welfare Economics

Case Study: The Lackawanna Social Club

The Lackawanna Social Club, which contains 20 resident members, keeps a refrigerator stocked with soda and beer. Each can of soda or beer is obtained from a local distributor for 30 cents per can. Each member has free access to the refrigerator and can consume as many cans of soda or beer as he or she likes. At the end of each month, the total cost of the soda and beer is divided evenly among the members.

    a. If one member of the club drinks a can of beer, what is its cost to him or her?

    b. What is the cost of this beer to the rest of the members of the club?

    c. From the point of view of the club, what is the total social cost of the beer?

    d. Is the amount of beer and soda consumed by the club's members likely to depart from the amount that is socially optimal? If so, why?

    e. What would be the social advantages and disadvantages of having each member buy and store his or her own soda and beer?

    f. What would be the social advantages and disadvantages of having a bartender with a key to the refrigerator who will open it during certain hours and sell soda and beer at 30 cents per can?

    g. What would be the social advantages and disadvantages of having the refrigerator open and asking each member to sign on a sheet (and later pay) for each can of soda or beer he or she consumes?

    h. If the Lackawanna Social Club contained 400 resident members, rather than 20, do you think that the relative advantages and disadvantages of these and other ways of handling this problem would be unaffected? Explain.

    i. Do you think that the sort of problem taken up in this case study arises frequently within households? Explain.

Problems and Review Questions

1. A perfectly competitive industry produces cotton. The demand and supply curves for cotton are as follows:

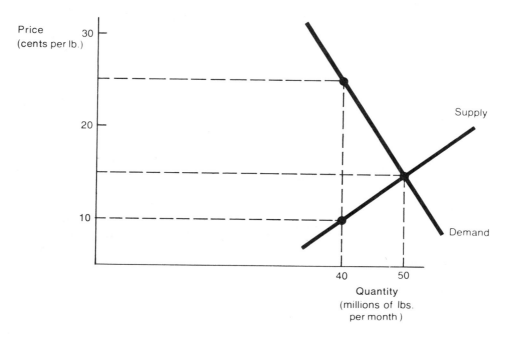

If 40 million pounds (rather than 50 million pounds) of cotton are produced per month, how much is the loss to society?

2. The diagram below shows the average cost curve, AA′, of a regulated monopoly. It produces OQ units of output and sets a price of OP.
   a. Is the firm engaged in marginal cost pricing? Why or why not?
   b. Does existing regulatory practice in the United States generally lead to marginal cost pricing?

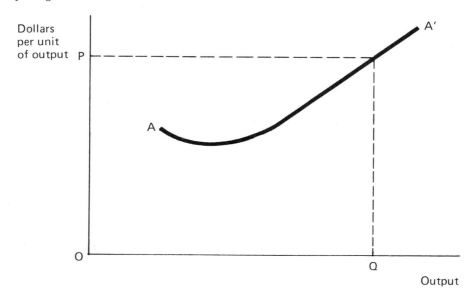

3. A poor man receives $10 per day in cash income. In addition, a kind neighbor provides him with three free meals a day, the cost to the neighbor of these three meals being $6. The man's preferences between meals and cash are shown in the following indifference map.

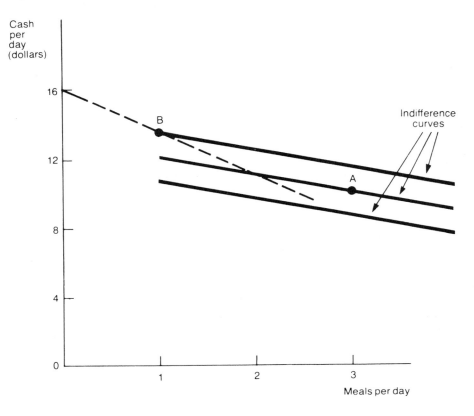

A social worker suggests to the neighbor that she give the man the $6 per day and let him spend it as he pleases. If he can buy a meal for $2.50, would such a change be an improvement, according to the Pareto criterion?

4. The antitrust laws prohibit many forms of "tying," which is a procedure whereby a consumer has to buy one product to get another product. It has been argued that: "If a group of parts or subassemblies are used together, and if they can be manufactured more cheaply together than separately, there is good reason from both society's and the manufacturer's viewpoint in their being made and sold as a unit." Evaluate this statement on the basis of the precepts of welfare economics.

5. For many years, the United States used a draft to obtain military personnel. Did this procedure violate any of the rules for optimal resource allocation? Explain.

6. Suppose that two consumers, after swapping goods back and forth, have arrived at a point on the contract curve. In other words, neither can be made better off without making the other worse off.

a. Does this mean that neither of them can find a point *off* the contract curve which he or she prefers to the point at which they have arrived?

b. If it does not mean this, why do economists claim that points on the contract curve are to be preferred?

7. In recent decades there has been considerable talk in government circles about tax reform. For example, former President Jimmy Carter suggested that lavish business lunches should no longer be completely tax deductible.

a. If this suggestion were carried out, what segments of the population would it hurt? What segments might it help?

b. Is there any way to tell on purely scientific grounds whether, on balance, it would be good or bad for society?

8. A small private jet lands at Kennedy Airport in New York at the busiest time of day. It pays a nominal landing fee. What divergences may exist between the private and social costs of this plane's landing there at that time? What policies might help to eliminate such divergences?

9. Suppose that the market for men's neckties is in disequilibrium; that is, the actual price does not equal the equilibrium price. If all industries in the economy are perfectly competitive (including neckties), will the necessary conditions for optimal resource allocation be met? Explain.

10. William Baumol has pointed out that the cafes in the Piazza San Marco in Venice "hire bands to serenade their customers. But, being outdoors, they cannot avoid providing music to the patrons of adjoining bistros. Unfortunately, however, with four or five of these going at once it becomes impossible to hear the music anywhere."* Analyze this situation, using the concepts of external economies and diseconomies.

11. According to William Baumol, "The idea of external economies and diseconomies has taught us to beware of policies which yield optimal results for each of the various divisions of a firm taken by themselves."† What is so dangerous about such policies? Suppose that you were hired by a large corporation to write a report on the pitfalls involved in such policies. What points would you stress?

12. Discuss the difficulties involved in making interpersonal comparisons of utility. Is it possible at all? What implications does this have for objective analysis of the optimal distribution of income?

13. State the three necessary marginal conditions for optimal resource allocation. Are these conditions sufficient as well as necessary for optimality?

*W. Baumol, *Economic Theory and Operations Analysis* (Englewood Cliffs, N.J.: Prentice Hall, 1977), p. 519.
† Ibid., p. 535.

14. Suppose that I regard an extra unit of peanut butter as having the same utility as 2 extra units of jelly, but you regard an extra unit of peanut butter as having the same utility as 3 extra units of jelly. Is this an optimal situation? If not, how can it be improved?

15. If the marginal rate of technical substitution between labor and capital is not the same for two producers, show how output can be increased by reallocating labor and capital.

16. Prove that, for optimal resource allocation, the marginal rate of substitution between any two commodities must be the same as the marginal rate of transformation between these two commodities for any producer.

17. Show that, if marginal cost varies from firm to firm, industry output must be produced inefficiently. Relate this fact to agricultural price supports.

18. Show how one can derive a utility-possibility curve in the two-commodity, two-input, two-consumer case.

19. What is a social welfare function? Show how a social welfare function, coupled with the utility-possibility curve, can enable us to get a complete solution to the two-commodity, two-input, two-consumer case.

20. Can we be sure that the three necessary conditions for welfare maximization are satisfied under perfect competition? Are they satisfied under monopoly?

21. Discuss the advantages of marginal cost pricing.

22. According to Thomas Marschak, marginal cost pricing has resulted in savings in the French nationalized electricity industry. For example, he states that there seems to have been a leveling of consumption between the daytime and nighttime periods. Why do you think this occurred?

23. Discuss the meaning and importance of external economies and diseconomies, both of consumption and production. How do they alter the optimality of perfect competition?

24. Indicate how the theory of external economies and diseconomies sheds light on public policy toward basic research.

25. What is a public good? Will perfect competition result in an optimal allocation of such goods?

26. Describe Arrow's impossibility theorem and its significance.

27. Describe the theory of the second best and its significance.

28. According to William Vickrey, "By far the most important of the considerations that conflict with the strict application of marginal cost pricing is the need for revenues." Why is this the case? How can one get around this difficulty?

29. According to Milton Friedman, significant external economies are gained from the education of children: "The gain from the education of a child accrues not only to the child or its parents but also to other members of the society." * Moreover, "it is not feasible to identify the particular individuals (or families) benefited and so to charge for the services rendered." What kind of government action is justified by these considerations?

30. Milton Friedman states, "One argument frequently made for public housing is based on an alleged neighborhood effect: slum districts in particular, and low quality housing to a lesser degree, are said to impose higher costs on the community in the form of fire and police protection. This literal neighborhood effect may well exist. But insofar as it does, it alone argues, not for public housing, but for higher taxes on the kind of housing that adds to social costs since this would tend to equalize private and social cost."† Comment on this statement.

31. According to Ronald Coase, "Analysis in terms of divergencies between private and social products concentrates attention on particular deficiencies in the system and tends to nourish the belief that any measure which will remove the deficiency is necessarily desirable. It diverts attention from those other changes in the system which are inevitably associated with the corrective measure, changes which may well produce more harm than the original deficiency."‡ Do you agree? Comment on this statement.

32. According to a study done by Jack Hirshleifer, James De Haven, and Jerome Milliman, water rights sometimes cannot be freely traded in the United States. What effect will this have on the efficiency of the allocation of water supplies?

Completion Questions

1. If resources are allocated optimally, the amount of money a consumer will give up to obtain an extra unit of water must be (different, the same) _____ for all consumers.

2. There is _____ on which we can validly measure pleasure or pain so that interpersonal comparisons can validly be made.

3. Whether or not one income distribution is better than another is a _____

   _____ .

4. The marginal conditions for optimal resource allocation imply that consumers are on their

   _____ .

5. The marginal conditions for optimal resource allocation imply that producers are on their

   _____ .

*Milton Friedman, *Capitalism and Freedom* (Chicago: University of Chicago Press, 1962).
† Ibid.
‡Ronald Coase, "The Problem of Social Cost," reprinted in Edwin Mansfield, *Microeconomics: Selected Readings*, 5th ed. (New York : Norton, 1985).

6. If there were only one consumer, the marginal conditions for optimal resource allocation would imply that his or her indifference curve be tangent to the _____ _____ .

7. Under perfect competition, the marginal rate of substitution between two goods is the same for any pair of consumers because they pay _____ for the goods.

8. Under perfect competition, the marginal rate of technical substitution between two inputs is the same for any pair of producers because they pay _____ _____ for the inputs.

9. A firm that is polluting a stream without incurring any cost is an example of an _____ _____ .

10. When one firm benefits from another firm's research, this is an example of an _____ _____ .

11. National defense and a lighthouse are examples of _____ goods.

True or False

_____ 1. In a perfectly competitive economy, a change that pushes the economy away from equilibrium will make everyone better off.

_____ 2. According to the Pareto criterion, a change that harms no one and improves the lot of at least one person is an improvement.

_____ 3. According to the Pareto criterion, a dollar taken from a rich man and given to a poor man is an improvement.

_____ 4. Kaldor's criterion does not require that compensation actually be paid by the gainers to the losers.

_____ 5. Under certain circumstances, the Kaldor criterion will indicate that a change is an improvement, but it will also indicate that a change back to the original state of affairs is an improvement.

_____ 6. Bergson's criterion does away with any reliance on a social welfare function.

_____ 7. Kenneth Arrow's impossibility theorem showed that it was impossible to escape dictatorship if society's allocation of resources was to be efficient.

_____ 8. The attainment of a Pareto optimum does not require the fulfillment of all of the marginal conditions for optimal resource allocation.

_____ 9. The theory of the second best implies that the reduction of the number of monopolies in the economy from 12 to 8 may not be a good thing.

_____ 10. A social welfare function can rather easily be estimated for the United States by fitting curves to historical data.

_____ 11. Perfect competition results in an optimal allocation of resources. Public goods will be allocated the right amount of resources without government intervention or other nonmarket mechanisms.

Multiple Choice

1. A road is built which is maintenance-free and which is so wide (relative to the available traffic) that no person or car interferes with the movement of another person or car. The cost of the road is entirely a fixed cost. If marginal cost pricing is adopted:
   a. the receipts from the road will be no less than the road's total profit.
   b. the receipts from the road will not depend on the number of autos using the road.
   c. the receipts from the road will be no greater than the road's fixed cost.
   d. all of the above.
   e. none of the above.

2. Suppose that the product transformation curve looks as in the diagram below: This is due to
   a. decreasing returns.
   b. external economies.
   c. increasing returns.
   d. all of the above.
   e. none of the above.

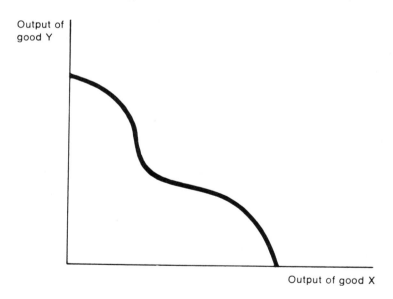

Output of good Y

Output of good X

3. Scitovsky's criterion is intended to meet a weakness in
   a. the Bergson criterion.
   b. the Kaldor criterion.
   c. the Pareto criterion.
   d. all of the above.
   e. none of the above.

4. The marginal conditions for optimal resource allocation
   a. depend on interpersonal comparisons of utility.
   b. help to determine the optimal distribution of income.
   c. are silent concerning the optimal distribution of income.
   d. all of the above.
   e. none of the above.

5. Marginal cost pricing is automatically the rule under
   a. monopoly.
   b. oligopoly.
   c. monopolistic competition.
   d. perfect competition.
   e. none of the above.

6. If a perfectly competitive industry is monopolized, the result is that
   a. the marginal conditions for optimal resource allocation are no longer fulfilled.
   b. the marginal conditions for optimal resource allocation are still fulfilled.
   c. more of the marginal conditions for optimal resource allocation are fulfilled than was formerly the case.
   d. the marginal conditions for optimal resource allocation are no longer applicable.
   e. none of the above.

7. The theory of the second best shows that piecemeal attempts to fulfill the marginal conditions for optimal resource allocation
   a. are bound to be worthwhile.
   b. can easily be a mistake.
   c. are always a mistake.
   d. are all that can be achieved.
   e. none of the above.

Key Concepts for Review

Welfare economics
Interpersonal comparison of utility
Distribution of income
Marginal conditions for optimal
  resource allocation
Utility-possibility curve
Social welfare function
Marginal cost pricing
External economies of production
External diseconomies of production

External economies of consumption
External diseconomies of consumption
Public goods
Pareto criterion
Kaldor criterion
Scitovsky criterion
Bergson criterion
Arrow's impossibility theorem
Theory of the second best

Answers

Case Study: The Lackawanna Social Club

    a. 30 cents ÷ 20, or 1.5 cents.

    b. 28.5 cents.

    c. 30 cents.

    d. It is likely to exceed the optimal amount because the private cost is much less than the social cost.

    e. It would result in the private and social costs' being brought into equality, but it would result in more inconvenience (to buy and store and refrigerate the soda and beer) to the members.

    f. It would push the private cost toward the social cost, but it would increase cost because a bartender would have to be hired. The price would have to be increased to cover the cost of the bartender.

    g. If strictly observed, this procedure would eliminate the gap between private and social costs, and it would eliminate the cost involved in hiring a bartender. But cheating could occur.

    h. The bigger the club, the smaller the cost (per can of beer or soda) of having a bartender, and the more difficult it would be to police schemes such as the one in part (*g*).

    i. Yes. For example, a family frequently has a refrigerator stocked with food or some other group of goods that the family members can draw on. The cost to a particular family member of consuming some of these items is frequently very small because other members of the family pay for the food or the group of goods. Thus a teen-ager may consume much more soda or ice cream than if he or she had to pay the full cost of these items.

Problems and Review Questions

1. The extra 10 million pounds are worth $\frac{1}{2}$ (25 + 15) cents times 10 million, or $2 million. This is the area under the demand curve from 40 to 50 million pounds. If the extra 10 million pounds were produced, it would cost $\frac{1}{2}$ (10 + 15) cents times 10 million, or $1.25 million. This is the area under the supply curve from 40 to 50 million pounds. Thus, the net loss is $2 million minus $1.25 million, or $0.75 million.

2. *a.* No. Price equals average cost, not marginal cost.

    b. No.

3. Yes, because the man would be better off and his neighbor would be no worse off. If the neighbor gives him $6 per day, the man's budget line is shown by the dashed line. This budget line enables him to choose a point like *B*, which is on a higher indifference curve than *A*, the point corresponding to his present situation. The neighbor is no worse off since the cost is the same to her.

4. It certainly is reasonable that, if less resources are needed to produce and distribute a group of parts or assemblies as a unit, they should be made and distributed as a unit, if they are used together and consumers are not inconvenienced by this procedure.

5. The draft involved price control, since the maximum price that could be set by the military services was established by law. The number of people of many types who were willing to serve at these prices was less than the number demanded by the defense establishment, and a compulsory draft was used to obtain the number demanded. So long as military manpower

of various types were underpriced, there was an incentive to use these manpower in other than a socially optimal way.

6. *a.* No.
   b. Because, if the two consumers arrive at any point off the contract curve, they can find a superior point on the contract curve, in the sense that one of them can be made better off without making the other worse off.

7. *a.* It would be likely to hurt restaurants, hotels, and other businesses that cater to the demand for such lunches. It would help those whose tax bills might be reduced as a consequence of this tax reform.
   b. It is very difficult to say, without being able to make interpersonal comparisons of utility. One's answer is likely to depend on his or her political and ethical values.

8. The plane's landing at that time may delay large commercial jets and impose substantial costs (in terms of delay and inconvenience) on the passengers carried by these commercial aircraft. Increases in the landing fees paid by small private aircraft could help to eliminate such divergences.

9. No.

10. When one band is playing, there may be external economies accruing to customers of other cafes. But when lots of them play, there may be external diseconomies because it is impossible to hear any of them properly.

11. By not taking account of the effects on other parts of the firm, policies which produce optimal results—looking at the division alone—may yield results that are far from optimal for the whole firm.

12. There is no scientifically meaningful way to compare the utility levels of different individuals. Consequently, we cannot tell whether one distribution of income is better than another.

13. First, the marginal rate of substitution between two commodities must be the same for any two consumers consuming both commodities.
    Second, the marginal rate of technical substitution between two inputs must be the same for any pair of producers using both inputs.
    Third, the marginal rate of substitution between any two commodities must be the same as the marginal rate of transformation between these two commodities for any producer.
    These conditions are necessary but not sufficient for optimality.

14. No. I should trade you some peanut butter in exchange for some jelly.

15. For example, suppose that, for the first producer, the marginal product of labor is twice that of capital, whereas for the second producer the marginal product of labor is three times that of capital. Then, if the first producer gives one unit of labor to the second producer in exchange for 2.5 units of capital, both firms can expand their output.

16. Suppose for simplicity that there is only one consumer. The optimal point on the product transformation curve is the point on the consumer's highest indifference curve. This is a point where the product transformation curve is tangent to an indifference curve. Thus, the slope of the product transformation curve—the marginal rate of transformation (times minus one)—must equal the slope of the indifference curve—the marginal rate of substitution (times minus one).

17. If marginal cost varies, it is possible to reduce the total cost of the existing output by transferring production from firms with high marginal cost to firms with low marginal cost. Quota schemes related to agricultural price supports can result in differences among firms in marginal cost.

18. For each point on the product transformation curve, find the optimal allocation of output between the two consumers. Then plot the utility of one consumer against the utility of the other consumer.

19. A social welfare function shows society's evaluation of various states of the world. Given a social welfare function, one can obtain social indifference curves to couple with the utility-possibility curve. The optimal distribution of income is at the point on the utility-possibility curve that is on the highest social indifference curve.

20. Yes.

No.

22. Because of price changes.

23. An external economy occurs when an action taken by an economic unit results in uncompensated benefits to others. An external diseconomy occurs when an action taken by an economic unit results in uncompensated costs to others. Too little is produced of goods generating external economies; too much is produced of goods generating external diseconomies.

24. Basic research results in important external economies. Consequently, there seems to be a good case for the government (or some other agency not motivated by profit) to support basic research. Too little would be supported by a perfectly competitive economy.

25. A public good is a good that one person can enjoy without reducing the enjoyment it gives others. Also, the consumer frequently cannot be made to pay for a public good, because he cannot be barred from using it (whether or not he pays) or because it is obligatory for everyone to use it.

No.

26. Arrow showed that, under conditions that seem to be a sensible basis for democratic community decision-making, it is impossible to make a choice among all sets of alternatives without violating some of the conditions. His work has led to a much clearer understanding of the relationships between individual preferences and social choice.

27. The theory of the second best shows that piecemeal attempts to force fulfillment of the optimality conditions can easily be a mistake. So long as some conditions remain unfulfilled, there is no assurance that a reduction of the number of unfulfilled conditions will result in increased welfare.

28. If average costs decline with output, marginal cost is below average cost, the result being that marginal-cost pricing will result in a deficit. Public subsidy is one possible answer under these circumstances.

29. Government requirement of minimum schooling, probably accomplished through government subsidy.

31. Yes. Economists recognize that this is an important point.

32. It prevents water rights from being transferred from less valuable to more valuable uses, thus interfering with the optimal allocation of water.

Completion Questions

1. the same
2. no scale
3. value judgment
4. contract curve
5. contract curve
6. product transformation curve

7. the same prices
8. the same prices
9. external diseconomy of production
10. external economy of production
11. public

True or False

1. False   2. True   3. False   4. True   5. True   6. False   7. False   8. False   9. True
10. False   11. False

Multiple Choice

1. *d*   2. *c*   3. *b*   4. *c*   5. *d*   6. *a*   7. *b*

CHAPTER 16 Public Goods, Externalities, and the Role of Government

Case Study: The Fable of the Bees

Some economists have argued that beekeeping is a case where external economies abound. Owners of fruit trees benefit from the presence of honeybees, since the bees pollinate the blossoms, thus resulting in an increased yield of fruit per acre. On the other hand, the bee-keeper benefits from the presence of the fruit trees since the trees provide nectar for the bees. Because of these externalities, it has been argued that the competitive market, without government intervention, will not result in the proper behavior by the orchard owner or by the bee-keeper.

a. According to this argument, the orchard owner will grow fewer nectar-yielding blossoms than would be socially optimal. Why would this seem to be true?

b. According to the same argument, the beekeeper will provide too few pollination benefits to the orchard owner. Why would this seem to be true?

In fact, Steven Cheung has shown that the beekeepers and orchard owners are aware of these external benefits and that they incorporate them within their private decision-making.* In some cases, the beekeeper pays an "apiary rent" for the right to situate his bees on the orchard owner's land. In some cases, the orchard owner pays "pollination fees" for the right to have the bees situated on his land. Some of the pricing arrangements in the state of Washington during 1970-71 were as follows:

Crop	Surplus honey (pounds per hive)	Pollination fees (dollars)	Apiary rent per hive (cents)
Almond	0	5-8	—
Cherry	0	6-8	—
Apples	0	9-10	—
Alfalfa	60	—	13-60
Mint	70-75	—	15-65
Pasture	60	—	15-65

c. Why do you think that there is a pollination fee, but no apiary rent, in cases where the honey yield is low and there is no surplus honey?

d. Why do you think that there is an apiary rent, but no pollination fee, in cases where the honey yield is high and surplus honey exists?

*S. Cheung, "The Fable of the Bees: An Economic Investigation," *Journal of Law and Economics* (April 1973).

Problems and Review Questions

1. Individuals A and B are the only two people that demand good X. Each individual's demand curve for good X is shown below:

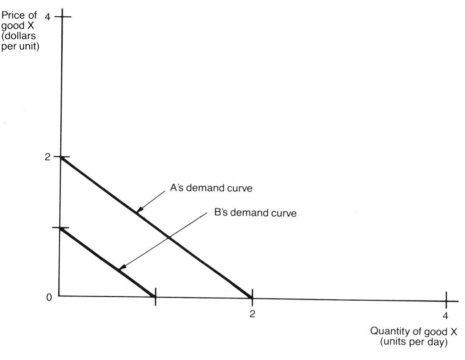

   a. If good X is a private good, draw its market demand curve.
   b. If good X is a public good, draw its market demand curve.

2. The town of Erewhon is faced with a serious smog problem. The smog can be dispelled if an air treatment plant is installed at an annual cost of $1 million. There is no way to clean up the air for some but not all of the town's population. Each of the town's families acts independently, and no single family can afford to carry out the project by itself. Why doesn't a private firm build the air treatment plant and sell its services to the town's families (acting individually)?

3. Nearly 95 percent of all families in the United States have television sets.
   a. For these families, is a television program a public good?
   b. Is it possible for firms to exclude some of these families from viewing certain programs?
   c. Who pays for ordinary TV programs?
   d. Must there be any commercials on "pay TV"?

4. Discuss the advantages and disadvantages of the following policies for dealing with air pollution due to gas emission from cars:
   a. Ban the internal combustion engine after 1990.
   b. Impose a tax on each car which varies with the amount of noxious gas it emits.
   c. Subsidize research to develop better antipollution devices that can be used by cars.

5. "Public goods have marginal costs of zero. In other words, they can be provided as cheaply for one as for all. Consequently, it is foolish to attempt to compare the benefits of public goods with their costs. Any public good is worth producing because it benefits so many people." Comment and evaluate.

6. Suppose that there are only three citizens of a (very small) nation and that the amount of national defense each would demand (at various prices) is as follows:

Price of a unit of national defense (dollars)	Citizen A	Citizen B	Citizen C
	(Number of units demanded)		
1	10	8	12
2	9	7	9
3	8	6	7
4	7	5	5

If the marginal cost of a unit of national defense is $9, what is the optimal amount of national defense for this nation?

7. "All public goods must be provided by the government." Comment and evaluate.

8. C. N. Parkinson presents the following data concerning the British Admiralty in 1914 and 1928:

	1914	1928
Capital ships in commission	62	20
Officers and men in Royal Navy	146,000	100,000
Dockyard workers	57,000	62,439
Dockyard officials and clerks	3,249	4,558
Admiralty officials	2,000	3,569

a. Did the number of civil servants in the Admiralty vary in proportion to the size of the Royal Navy?
b. What factors might have accounted for these results?

9. What is the exclusion principle? Does this principle hold for private goods? For public goods?

10. What is meant by rivalry in consumption? Is this characteristic found among private goods? Public goods?

11. Why is it that people often fail to reveal their true preferences concerning public goods?

12. Do you sum individual demand curves vertically or horizontally to get the market demand curve for a *private* good? Why?

13. Do you sum individual demand curves vertically or horizontally to get the market demand curve for a *public* good? Why?

14. Suppose that the Department of Transportation has a budget of $10 million to spend on roads and that the costs and benefits from all proposed roads are as follows:

Road	Benefits (dollars)	Costs (dollars)
X to Y	20 million	10 million
X to Z	5 million	3 million
Y to Z	6 million	7 million

How should the department spend its $10 million? Why?

15. In Question 14, suppose that the Office of Management and Budget says that the Department of Transportation can spend all that it wants (up to $20 million) on roads. Which roads should the department build? Why?

16. According to Roland McKean, "It is in connection with comparatively narrow problems of choice that cost-benefit analysis can sometimes play a more significant role." What does he mean? Do you agree? Why or why not?

17. According to A. R. Prest and Ralph Turvey, savings of time by drivers and passengers "often form a very high proportion of total estimated benefits of road improvements. . . . Unfortunately, [estimates of the value of these savings] . . . have not so far been very satisfactory." How would you go about making such estimates? What problems would you encounter? How accurate do you think your results would be?

18. A. R. Prest and Ralph Turvey point out that the benefit-cost ratio for a cross-Florida barge canal was estimated to be 1.20 by the Corps of Engineers, but only 0.13 by some consultants retained by the railroads. What factors might account for the difference in these results?

19. On the basis of the benefit-cost analyses carried out by the Department of the Interior and the Federal Power Commission (since 1977 the Federal Energy Regulatory Commission), would you be in favor of building a dam on the Middle Snake river? Why or why not?

20. What are the basic causes of environmental pollution in our society?

21. What is an effluent fee? How can it be used to reduce pollution to more satisfactory levels? Have effluent fees been used elsewhere?

22. The Environmental Protection Agency has pointed out that a fundamental problem is, "At what point do the additional costs of controlling all sources of pollutants exceed the additional benefits of improved water quality?" EPA responds to this question by saying, "Clearly the current societal concern for environmental quality indicates that the public believes that there are significant benefits yet to be attained."* Do you agree? Do you think that this answers the question? How can the question be answered?

---

*The Economics of Clean Water, EPA (1973), p. 8.

23. The 1972 Amendments to the Federal Water Pollution Control Act required industries to use "best practicable" water pollution control technology by mid-1977 and "best available" technology by mid-1983. Do you think that this was proper public policy? Why or why not?

24. According to EPA, "Individual plants in certain industries will experience difficulties in meeting the requirements."* Why? In what industries would you expect the difficulties to be greatest? What kinds of firms were most affected?

25. Should a person living in the Mojave Desert take the same pains to reduce air pollution as someone living in Pasadena? According to Larry Ruff, California law makes no distinction between these situations. Should it?

26. Some people ask, "If we can go to the moon, why can't we eliminate pollution?" How would you answer this question?

Completion Questions

1. Public goods generally (are, are not) _____ sold in the private marketplace.

2. A "free rider" is _____ .

3. The demand curve for a _____ good will not be revealed.

4. If the total budget is fixed, projects should be chosen that have the highest

   _____ ratios.

5. If the total budget is not fixed, projects should be chosen where the

   _____ ratio exceeds _____ .

6. If projects are divisible, a government agency should allocate funds so that the

   _____ from an extra dollar of expenditure on each project equals

   the _____ from an extra dollar of expenditure in the private sector.

7. _____ benefits and costs arise because of changes in relative prices.

8. Marginal social cost equals marginal _____ cost plus marginal

   _____ cost.

9. The more an industry cuts down on the amount of wastes it discharges, the

   _____ are its costs of pollution control.

10. The more untreated waste an industry dumps into the environment, the _____ the cost of pollution.

11. The optimal level of pollution is generally not _____ .

* Ibid., p. 6.

12. An _____ is a fee that a polluter must pay to the government for discharging waste.

13. _____ have been used successfully in the Ruhr Valley.

True or False

_____ 1. Tickets to a concert by the Cleveland Symphony Orchestra are an example of a public good.

_____ 2. Fifty independent fishing companies attempt to catch fish in the same lake. One company buys up all of the others. The number of fishermen sent out each day by the one company will be the same as the number that was sent out by the fifty companies.

_____ 3. Public goods will be provided in the right amount by the market mechanism.

_____ 4. Goods where there is rivalry in consumption are called public goods.

_____ 5. An uncrowded bridge is an example of a public good.

_____ 6. National defense is not a public good.

_____ 7. For a public good, the market demand curve is the horizontal summation of the individual demand curves.

_____ 8. Benefit-cost analysis has been used only in the past ten years.

_____ 9. Pecuniary benefits do not influence the distribution of income.

_____ 10. The Department of the Interior's study of the Middle Snake hydroelectric project was accepted by the staff of the Federal Power Commission.

_____ 11. In large part, environmental pollution is due to external economies.

_____ 12. The price paid by polluters for water and air is often less than the true social costs.

_____ 13. Pollution is tied inextricably to national output.

_____ 14. The only way to reduce pollution is to reduce population.

Multiple Choice

1. Which of the following is *not* a public good?
   a. a smog-free environment.
   b. the services of the Supreme Court.
   c. blood donated to the Red Cross.
   d. the Apollo space program.
   e. national defense.

2. Technological change
   a. has made people more interdependent.
   b. has brought about more and stronger external diseconomies.
   c. has resulted in some harmful ecological changes.
   d. is a powerful positive force in the fight against pollution.
   e. all of the above.

3. If SS′ shows the marginal social cost of a product and *DD′* is the product's demand curve, the optimal output of the product is
   a. less than 500.
   b. 500.
   c. 600.
   d. more than 600.
   e. none of the above.

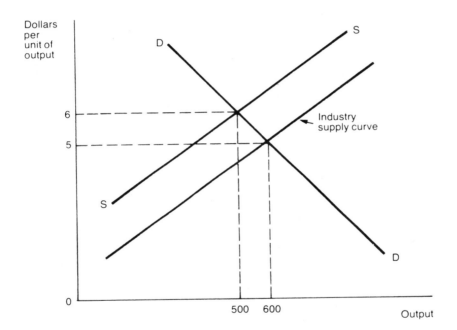

4. In the previous problem, the market mechanism, left to its own devices, would result in an output of
   a. less than 500.
   b. 500.
   c. 600.
   d. more than 600.
   e. none of the above.

5. Continuing the previous problem, at the output that would result from the market mechanism, the marginal social cost of the product would be _____ its marginal social value.
   a. greater than
   b. equal to
   c. less than
   d. either less than or equal to
   e. none of the above.

6. In general, there is _____ between an industry's output and the amount of pollution it generates.
   a. a proportional relationship
   b. no fixed or proportional relationship
   c. no relationship whatsoever
   d. an inverse relationship
   e. none of the above.

7. To reduce pollution, the government can
   a. institute effluent fees.
   b. enact direct regulations.
   c. both a and b.
   d. cut back on the use of scrubbers.
   e. all of the above.

8. Economists tend to prefer effluent fees over direct regulation because such fees are more likely to
   a. achieve a reduction in pollution more cheaply.
   b. require less information on the part of government agencies.
   c. both a and b.
   d. reduce monopoly.
   e. all of the above.

Key Concepts for Review

Public good
Exclusion principle
Rivalry in consumption
Benefit-cost analysis
Real benefits
Pecuniary benefits
Externalities

Air pollution
Water pollution
Thermal pollution
Direct regulation
Effluent fee
Coase's theorem

Answers

Case Study: The Fable of the Bees

   a. It has been argued that the orchard owner will not take proper account of the external benefit to beekeepers.
   b. It has been argued that the beekeeper will not take proper account of the external benefit to the orchard owner.
   c. The beekeeper receives part of his return in money (the pollination fee) and part in honey. Since the honey yield is low, the beekeeper must receive a monetary return in addition to the honey yield to make it worthwhile to maintain the bees.
   d. If the beekeeper receives a relatively large honey yield, the orchard owner can and does ask for an apiary rent. In the absence of such a rent, the beekeeper would be making supernormal profits.

Problems and Review Questions

1. *a.*

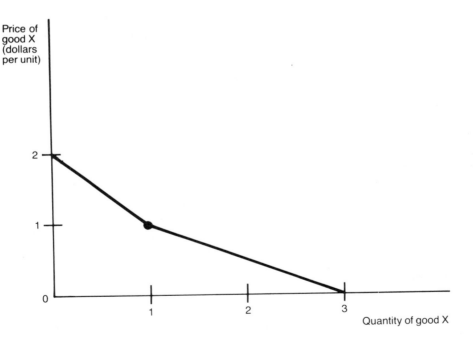

b.

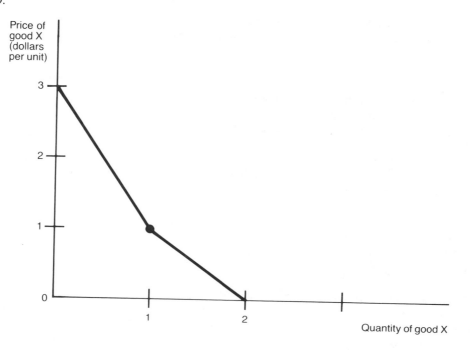

2. If any family buys smog-free air, it automatically buys it for others too, whether the latter pay for it or not. And since no family can afford the cost, so long as families act independently, it will be unprofitable for a private firm to carry out this project.
3. *a.* Yes, because once the program is put on the air, an extra family can watch it without depriving others of the opportunity to do so. In other words, once the program is broadcast to some viewers, others can watch it at no (or trivial) extra cost.
   b. Yes. A means has been devised to "scramble" the signal so that, unless a viewer's TV set is equipped to unscramble it, the viewer cannot get the program. Viewers rent this equipment or operate it by means of coins. This is called "pay TV."
   c. Advertisers pay for the broadcasts in order to air their commercials. In addition, listeners pay something, if they don't like commercials!
   d. No, because the viewers pay directly for the broadcasts.
4. *a.* This is unlikely to be the optimal way to handle the problem, since it would be very difficult to develop effective substitutes for the internal combustion engine by 1990.
   b. An effluent fee of this sort might be useful but it might be difficult to measure the amount of pollution caused by a particular car and to make sure that each car pays the tax. Also, it might be reasonable to set different levels of the tax, depending on where the car is driven.
   c. This step would help to improve matters, but it contains no incentive for people to switch to less polluting transportation techniques in the short run.
5. It is not true that any public good is worth producing. The optimal output of a public good can be determined by summing the individual demand curves vertically and by finding the intersection with the supply curve. In many instances, the optimal output may be zero.
6. 7 units of national defense.

7. It is not true that all public goods must be provided by the government. As pointed out in the text, some quantity of public goods may be provided privately, particularly if the number of people in the society is small. But the amount provided privately is likely to be less than the optimal amount.

8. *a.* No.

    b. According to Parkinson, the bureaucracy tends to grow, regardless of whether there is a decline in the amount of work it must perform.

9. The exclusion principle operates when whether or not a person consumes a good is contingent on whether or not he or she pays the price.

    Yes.

    Frequently not.

10. Rivalry in consumption holds for goods where, if one person consumes them, someone else cannot consume them too.

    Yes.

    No.

11. Because a person is likely to feel that the total output of the good will not be affected significantly by his or her action. He or she will be likely to make no contribution to supporting the good, although he or she will use whatever output of the good is forthcoming.

12. Horizontally, because each unit of output can be consumed by only one person.

13. Vertically, because each unit of output can simultaneously be consumed by all consumers in the market.

14. Build the road from X to Y, because it will maximize the benefits to be derived from the fixed budget of $10 million.

15. Build the roads from X to Y and from X to Z, because these projects have benefit–cost ratios exceeding one.

16. In broad problems of choice, it frequently is more difficult to quantify benefits and make them comparable.

    Yes.

17. You might try to estimate how much people could make if they could use the time saved in various alternative pursuits, but this is difficult to estimate. See the article by Prest and Turvey in Mansfield, *Microeconomics: Selected Readings*, 5th ed., New York: Norton, 1985.

18. The Corps of Engineers included many kinds of benefits that the railroad consultants did not include, such as enhancement of waterfront land values. Also, the Corps of Engineers made a lower estimate of the costs. To some extent, as Prest and Turvey point out, the difference may be "due to the facts that the Corps likes to build canals and that the consultants were retained by the railroads."

20. External diseconomies from waste disposal.

21. An effluent fee is a fee that a polluter must pay to the government for discharging waste. It brings the private cost of waste disposal closer to the social cost.

    Yes, for example, in the Ruhr Valley.

22. The fact that the public is concerned is not a proof that the extra benefits exceed the extra costs. Unfortunately, however, it is extremely difficult to answer this question in any definitive sense.

23. A better criterion would be one that is based on a comparison of costs and benefits, assuming that these costs and benefits can be measured, at least roughly.

24. Because of increases in cost, some plants would have to shut down.
    Some industries that would be affected are beet sugar, dairies, electroplating, leather, meat packing, timber, and chemicals.
    The older and small firms would be likely to be most affected.
25. No.
    It probably should make a distinction.

Completion Questions

1. are not
2. someone who makes no contribution to a public good, but who uses whatever amount of it that is provided
3. public
4. benefit-cost
5. benefit-cost; one
6. marginal benefit; marginal benefit
7. Pecuniary
8. private; external
9. greater
10. greater
11. zero
12. effluent fee
13. Effluent fees

True or False

1. False 2. False 3. False 4. False 5. True 6. False 7. False 8. False 9. False
10. False 11. False 12. True 13. False 14. False

Multiple Choice

1. *c* 2. *e* 3. *b* 4. *c* 5. *a* 6. *b* 7. *c* 8. *c*

Part 7 INTERTEMPORAL CHOICE AND DECISION-MAKING INVOLVING RISK

CHAPTER 17 Intertemporal Choice and Technological Change

Case Study: Technological Change in Energy Production

In recent years, there has been considerable emphasis in the United States on the development of new sources of clean fuel. Ever since the Arab oil embargo of late 1973, both the private and public sectors have been engaged in a great many projects to develop new ways to power our economy. In this case, we consider three possible ways of producing energy: (1) shale oil, (2) oil from tar sands, and (3) coal gasification. Of course, these are only a sample of the new technologies that have been explored, but they are among the more important ones.

Shale, found in large amounts in Colorado, Utah, and Wyoming, is a potentially important source of synthetic oil. But this source has not been used because others were cheaper. As conditions and prices change, this may no longer be the case. However, one problem with shale is that it involves a waste-disposal program. The spent shale could fill an enormous volume, and the danger of environmental damage must be considered.

Another potentially important source of synthetic oil is the tar sands located in Alberta, Canada. Great Canadian Oil Sands, Ltd. (GCOS), 96 percent owned by Sun Oil Company, has invested about $750 million in learning how to obtain oil from these tar sands, which are estimated to be a potential source of as much as 30 billion barrels of synthetic crude oil. GCOS has been the innovator, and the risks have been high. (J. Howard Pew, chairman of Sun Oil, even went against the advice of his own engineers when he set the innovation in motion.) Based on its 45,000 barrel-a-day plant, opened in 1967, it has reported some success in reducing the cost of synthetic crude oil. One factor influencing the rate of adoption of this technique is the Canadian government's policies concerning the exploitation of this natural resource. In 1980, the Canadian government reduced the price that Sun was allowed to receive for its synthetic crude oil from $32 (the world oil price) to $14. In 1981, it allowed the price to rise somewhat.

Finally, coal gasification is another potentially important source of energy. The United States is endowed with huge deposits of coal (about 20 percent of the world's supply), but there is no commercially successful way of burning much of it cleanly. One way to get around the environmental problems involved in using coal as a fuel is to convert coal to a clean gas. At present, much of this work is still in the stage of research and development. A substantial portion of this R and D has been funded in part by the government. Since there is so much uncertainty concerning the relative merits of various processes, the government has helped to finance a number of parallel approaches to the problem. It will be some time before anyone can tell which of these processes, if any, is economically viable.

a. If any of these technologies were to be successfully commercialized, would this result in an increase in productivity? If so, how quickly would such an increase occur?

b. Does the government have a legitimate role in the development of new energy technologies? If so, what is this role?

Problems and Review Questions

1. The following excerpt from congressional testimony by executives of the Armstrong Cork Company describes the procedure it has used to decide which investment projects to undertake:

Effective evaluation of capital appropriation requests is essential to maintaining a satisfactory return on investment, both short-term and long-term. Such evaluation should be planned to follow the concept and terminology in use for budgetary controls and operating reports: otherwise the evaluation will fail to answer the questions that arise in the minds of top management when considering the advisability of granting an appropriation request.

Faced with these considerations, a system for evaluating capital appropriation requests has been developed by the Armstrong Cork Company which, we believe, gives management the information it needs to make sound decisions. This system is based on the same concept of costs used in reporting budgets and operating results.

The more important aspects of the Armstrong Cork Company system can be summarized as follows:

1. The economics of proposed capital appropriation requests are examined by the controller's office in consultation with the interested staffs like central engineering, research, industrial engineering, economic and marketing research, purchasing, and so forth, before presentation to top management.

2. The basic evaluation is made in return on investment terms.

3. An evaluation of risk is made, based on the length of time required to recover the cash to be expended.

4. Management relies on these valuations in making appropriation decisions.

5. Follow-up reports of the in-process status and actual results of capital appropriations granted are made annually by the controller's office to top management, which, in turn, discuss the results with the accountable persons.

"Return on investment" or, as we use the phrase, "return on capital employed," (ROCE) is nothing more than the ratio of net profit after tax to total book assets. In the Armstrong Cork Company, ROCE is accepted as the basis for measuring operating management performance; the success or failure of all our individual and collective efforts to improve operations is reflected in our ROCE results.

Our internal ROCE concept is designed around our operations general managers. These men are responsible for the production and sale of all products within the major market areas assigned to them. They are expected to use the capital they are allocated by the board to obtain the best possible return on it. Furthermore, and this is important, these line men are also responsible for recommending opportunities for the employment of additional capital to improve or expand existing businesses and to enter new businesses. The operations managers, therefore, occupy key positions in our company. The principal function of our staff departments is to help these line men fulfill their responsibilities; that is, to obtain higher returns on more capital, or, in other words, to obtain superior performance as measured by ROCE, coupled with growth in and into businesses having high ROCE potentials.

All matters related to financing are reserved to a staff vice-president. The determination of what shall be financed is reserved, depending upon the amounts involved, for the executive committee of our board of directors or the board itself. In practice, the board of directors and its executive committee control "what shall be financed" almost entirely through our system of capital appropriation requests. This control of capital expenditures automatically controls the basic level of working capital. The general level of cash, accounts receivable, and inventories required by operations is determined basically by the types of businesses in which we operate. Since we are primarily a manufacturing company, the types of businesses we operate are established by the plant, property, and equipment we buy. Therefore, the board of directors and its executive committee, in controlling such purchases, indirectly but effectively control the types of business we operate and, consequently, the basic levels of cash, accounts receivable, and inventories.

Our procedures for reviewing capital appropriation requests are designed specifically to fit the needs of our organization. They do this by profit and loss statements expressed in terms of ROCE. We place our emphasis on accuracy of perspective rather than on accuracy of detail. Our aim is to discover the best of the many potential expenditures. We don't attempt to provide the figure that makes approval or disapproval of a request automatic. The figures we develop are relative, not absolute. One of the most valuable results of our system will never be measured since it is the elimination of projects of low ROCE potential from consideration before an undue amount of valuable technical and management effort is expended upon them.*

   a. Does this procedure attempt to accomplish the same objective as the present-value rule? Explain.

   b. What differences can you detect between this procedure and the present-value rule?

2. The Milwaukee Manufacturing Company is trying to determine whether to buy a type A or type B machine tool. The price of a type A machine tool is $80,000, while the price of a type B machine tool is $50,000. Each machine tool will last 6 years, after which its scrap value will be zero. Each machine tool produces the same quantity and quality of output, but the type A machine tool requires 2,000 man-hours of labor per year, whereas the type B machine tool requires 5,000 man-hours of labor per year.

   a. If the interest rate is 10 percent, how big must the hourly wage of labor be for the firm to find it worthwhile to make the extra investment in the type A machine (relative to the type B machine)?

   b. Based on the above data, can we be sure that the firm should buy either machine tool?

3. In recent years, there has been an enormous amount of interest in the availability and pricing of mineral resources like oil and tin. Suppose that the Tonawanda Mining Company has found a deposit of tin, and that it has the option of selling all or part of it now or some time in the future. For simplicity, suppose that the cost of mining and producing the tin is zero.

   a. If the price per ton of tin is $100 this year and if it is expected to be $120 next year, will the firm sell its tin this year if the interest rate is 10 percent?

   b. By how much must next year's price exceed this year's price in order to induce firms not to sell all of their tin this year?

   c. In equilibrium, the firm must be content with the amount it is selling now and in the future. In other words, the firm must be indifferent between selling now and selling later. By how much must the price increase from one year to the next if equilibrium is to be maintained?

*Testimony before the Joint Economic Committee of Congress, 89th Cong., 2d Sess., February 9–10, 1966.

d. If the demand curve for tin remains as shown below, will the consumption of tin increase or decrease over time, if an equilibrium of this sort is maintained?

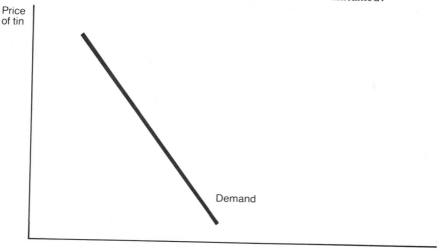

e. Does this analysis take account of the fact that firms may discover new deposits of tin and that technological change is likely to occur in tin production and use? If not, how will this affect your answer to part *d* of this question?

4. If Firm Z buys a particular machine in 1985, the effect will be that (1) the firm's cash inflow will be reduced by $10,000 in 1985, and (2) the firm's cash inflow will be increased by $2,000 annually in 1986–92. If the interest rate is .10, should the firm buy this machine?

5. An automobile manufacturer is trying to develop an improved engine that will emit fewer pollutants. There are two possible approaches to this technical problem. If either one is adopted, there is a 50-50 chance that it will cost $2 million to develop the engine and a 50-50 chance that it will cost $1 million to do so. The expected cost of development is the sum of the total costs of development if each possible outcome occurs times the probability of the occurrence of this outcome.
   a. If the firm chooses one of the outcomes and carries it to completion, what is the expected cost of developing the engine?
   b. If the two approaches are run in parallel and if the true cost of development using each approach can be determined after $150,000 has been spent on each approach, what is the expected cost of developing the engine? (More will be said about parallel approaches in the cross-chapter case(at the end of Chapter 18) in the text.)

6. A government program involves the training of disadvantaged teenagers. The cost of training each person is $8,000. With this training, he or she makes $500 more each year than he or she otherwise would. If this income differential is an adequate measure of the social benefit, and if the interest rate is 10 percent, is this program worthwhile?

7. John Miller is trying to decide whether to install aluminum siding on his house. As matters stand, his house has wood siding, which must be painted every year at an annual cost of $500. If he installs aluminum siding now, it will cost $2,000, and the need for painting will be eliminated. If he does not install aluminum siding, he will paint the house now, a year from now, 2 years from now, 3 years from now, and 4 years from now. Then he plans to sell

the house. He believes that he will be able to get no more for the house if he installs the aluminum siding than if he does not. If Mr. Miller can get 8 percent on alternative investments, should he install the aluminum siding?

8. Suppose that Mary Brown's situation is as follows, where AB is her budget line.

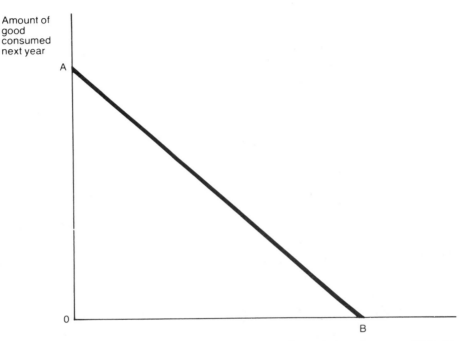

a. If $OA = 10$ units of the good, and the interest rate equals 0.08, what does OB equal?

b. What is Mary Brown's endowed wealth?

9. A government bond pays $10 per year and has no due date; that is, the interest payment of $10 per year goes on forever. If the interest rate is 0.05, how much would you be willing to pay for the bond?

10. Technological change is called labor-saving if it results in a decrease in the marginal rate of technical substitution of labor for capital. Under these circumstances, does technological change result in a greater increase in the marginal product of capital than in the marginal product of labor (at a given capital-labor ratio)? Does it result in the firm's using more capital relative to labor?

11. According to F. M. Scherer, "Some of the most blatant price fixing schemes in American economic history were erected on a foundation of agreements to cross-license complementary and competing patents."* How could such schemes come about? What were some of the industries where such schemes occurred?

*F. M. Scherer, *Industrial Market Structure and Economic Performance*, second edition (Chicago: Rand McNally, 1980), p. 452.

12. In recent decades, there has been a great deal of concern over the acquisition of coal firms by petroleum firms. Four of the nation's ten biggest coal companies—Pittsburgh and Midway, Consolidation, Island Creek, and Old Ben—were acquired by oil firms in the 1960s. What effect do you think this will have on the rate of technological change in coal?

13. Define technological change. In principle, how can certain types of technological change be measured? Can this technique deal with new products?

14. What is the difference between a change in technique and technological change? Can the former occur without the latter? Can the latter occur without the former?

15. What is the difference between capital-embodied and disembodied technological change? Give some examples of each type of technological change.

16. Is the growth of output per man-hour a complete measure of the rate of technological change? If not, why not? Is it commonly used for this purpose?

17. What is the total productivity index? What advantages does it have over output per man-hour? Under what circumstances is it precisely the proper measure of the rate of technological change?

18. What are some of the difficulties in practically all indirect estimates of the rate of technological change based on "residuals" or unexplained productivity change?

19. What are some of the principal determinants of the rate of technological change in a particular industry?

20. What is research and development? In what sense is R and D a learning process?

21. What determines how much a particular development project will cost?

22. What is meant by an innovation? How does it differ from an invention? Is there commonly a long lag between invention and innovation? Why is innovation economically important?

23. Summarize the arguments of J. K. Galbraith and Joseph Schumpeter to the effect that imperfect competition stimulates economic progress. Also summarize the arguments of their critics.

24. Does the evidence indicate that an industry dominated by a few giant firms is generally more progressive than one composed of a larger number of smaller firms? Summarize the evidence.

25. Describe the disadvantages of the patent system from the viewpoint of static efficiency.

26. According to John Kendrick, output per unit of labor input increased by 5.1 percent per year in the tobacco industry during 1899–1953 and by 3.5 percent per year in the chemical

industry during 1899–1953. The chemical industry spends much more on research and development than does the tobacco industry. Does this mean that R and D has relatively little impact on an industry's rate of technological change?

27. The annual rate of increase of the total productivity index during 1899–1953 was 3.5 percent in the transportation equipment industry and 1.6 percent in the beverage industry. What sorts of factors may be able to explain this difference?

28. Figures provided by the Bureau of Labor Statistics show that output per man-hour in blast furnaces using the most up-to-date techniques was about twice as large as the industry average in 1926. How can such large differences exist at a given point in time? Why don't all firms adopt the most up-to-date techniques at every point in time? Do differences of this sort persist today?

29. According to John Enos, about nine years passed between the time when catalytic cracking was invented by Eugene Houdry and the time when it was first introduced commercially. What factors may be able to account for this long lag?

30. According to Robert Solow, "Invention is the historical answer to the law of diminishing returns." Explain this statement.

31. Data gathered by the National Science Foundation show that in 1961 drug firms employing 5,000 or more people spend 4.4 percent of sales on research and development, while drug firms employing 1,000–4,999 people spent 5.8 percent of sales on research and development. Do these data concerning the drug industry support John Kenneth Galbraith's thesis concerning the technical progressiveness of giant firms?

Completion Questions

1. The decision-maker should carry out any investment project with a _____ present value.

2. Technology is _____ regarding the industrial arts.

3. Technological change results in a _____ in the production function.

4. If there are _____, there is at a given point in time a unique relationship between capital input per unit of output and labor input per unit of output.

5. The total productivity index is _____

_____.

6. An invention, when applied for the first time, is called an _____

_____.

True or False

_____ 1. If an investment yields $100 per year indefinitely into the future, and the interest rate is .10, the present value of this investment is $500.

_____ 2. A firm almost never is wise to wait more than a few weeks in introducing an innovation.

_____ 3. Learning takes place among the users of an innovation but not among the producers of an innovation.

_____ 4. The marginal conditions for optimal resource allocation in Chapter 15 assume that the level of technology is fixed.

_____ 5. If an imperfectly competitive economy has a higher rate of technological change and productivity growth than a perfectly competitive economy, this may offset its static inefficiency.

_____ 6. Practically all economists agree that an economy composed of monopolies would have the highest rate of technological change and productivity growth.

_____ 7. The available evidence indicates that an industry dominated by a few giant firms is always more progressive than one composed of a large number of smaller firms.

_____ 8. The patent system has the disadvantage that new knowledge is not used as widely as it should be from the viewpoint of static efficiency.

_____ 9. The patent system results in marginal-cost pricing for new information.

Multiple Choice

1. Firm R buys a painting for $1,000 in 1985. If maintenance of the painting is costless, and if the interest rate is 0.10, how much must it sell the painting for in 1988 if the present value of the investment in the painting is to be non-negative?
   a. At least $(1.10)^3 \times \$1,000$.
   b. At least $(1.30) \times \$1,000$.
   c. At least $1,000.
   d. At least $\$1,000 + (.30)^3 \times \$1,000$.
   e. None of the above.

2. All changes in technique
   a. result from technological change.
   b. result from changes in input prices.
   c. mean that a change occurs in utilized methods of production.
   d. all of the above.
   e. none of the above.

3. The diesel locomotive was an example of
    a. disembodied technological change.
    b. capital-embodied technological change.
    c. cost-increasing technological change.
    d. all of the above.
    e. none of the above.

4. The rate of growth of output per man-hour is
    a. an adequate measure of the rate of technological change.
    b. influenced by the rate of technological change.
    c. independent of the rate of technological change.
    d. constant in the United States.
    e. none of the above.

5. The Schumpeter-Galbraith hypothesis
    a. is wrong in its entirety.
    b. is right in saying that a perfectly competitive industry would be unlikely to be able to carry out the R and D required for a high rate of technological change in many parts of the economy.
    c. is right in saying that an industry composed of a very few giant firms is the best market structure from the point of view of promoting technological change and rapid acceptance of innovations.
    d. is concerned with the present-value rule.
    e. none of the above.

Key Concepts for Review

Interest rate
Present value
Endowed wealth
Maximization of wealth
Saving
Investment
The present-value rule

Technology
Technological change
Change in technique
Patent system
Productivity growth
Total productivity index

Answers

Case Study: Technological Change in Energy Production

    a. To the extent that these technologies use less input per unit of output than the technologies they replace, productivity will increase. But, in general, productivity will not increase merely because new technologies are introduced (because they are new). The first commercial introduction of a new technology may have little effect. How quickly productivity increases in response to a new technology depends on the rate of diffusion, which depends on the profitability of using the technology, among other things.

b. Yes. In the case of R and D where there are very great external economies, most economists would argue that government support may be worthwhile. This is more likely to be true for relatively basic research than for more applied work.

Problems and Review Questions

1. *a.* In crude terms, both seem to attempt to promote the wealth (or something like it) of the firm. The firm's executives are supposed "to use the capital they are allocated by the board to obtain the best possible return on it." However, this decision-making procedure does not focus directly on the wealth of the firm, and is not the same as the present-value rule.
   b. Armstrong Cork used the ratio of net profit (after tax) to investment as a measure of the desirability of an investment project, whereas the present-value rule uses the present value of the investment project.
2. *a.* The annual saving in labor costs with the type A machine equals $3,000W$, where W is the hourly wage rate. If the annual saving in labor costs occurs $1, 2, \ldots, 6$ years hence, and if the extra $30,000 (that must be paid for the type A machine) must be paid now, the extra investment in the type A machine is worthwhile if:

$$\$30,000 < 3,000\,W\left(\frac{1}{1.1} + \frac{1}{1.1^2} + \frac{1}{1.1^3} + \frac{1}{1.1^4} + \frac{1}{1.1^5} + \frac{1}{1.1^6}\right)$$
$$< 3,000(.9091 + .8264 + .7513 + .6830 + .6209 + .5645)\,W$$
$$< 13,065.6W,$$

   or if $W > \$30,000/13,065.6 = \$2.30$. Thus, if the wage rate exceeds $2.30, the extra investment is worthwhile.
   b. No. All that the above analysis tells us is whether the extra investment in the type A machine is worthwhile. No data are presented to indicate the profitability of the investment in either machine tool, relative to the profitability of other uses of the funds.
3. *a.* No. The present value of $120 per ton next year equals $120 ÷ 1.10, or $109. This is more than this year's price of $100. Thus, the firm will sell its tin next year rather than this year.
   b. Next year's price must be at least 10 percent above this year's price. To see this, let P_1 be next year's price and P_0 be this year's price. For firms not to sell all of their tin this year, the present value of next year's price must be at least equal to this year's price. Since the present value of next year's price equals $P_1 ÷ 1.10$, this means that firms will not sell all of their output this year if $P_1 ÷ 1.10 \geqslant P_0$—or if $P_1 ÷ P_0 \geqslant 1.10$.
   c. For the firm to be indifferent between selling now and selling later, the present value of the price received in the next year must equal the price received this year. In other words, if the interest rate equals 10 percent, it must be the case that $P_1 ÷ 1.10 = P_0$, which implies that $P_1 ÷ P_0 = 1.10$. Thus, price must increase from one year to the next by a percentage equal to the interest rate (10 percent in this case).
   d. Since the price of tin increases over time, tin consumption will fall over time, if the demand curve remains fixed.

e. No. Recognizing that the cost of mining the tin may in fact be nonzero, these factors may offset or even reverse the tendency for the price of mineral resources to increase over time. Because of these and other factors, the price of natural resources often has fallen (relative to other prices) over extended periods of time.*

4. The present value of the investment is $-10{,}000 + \dfrac{2{,}000}{1.10}$

$$+ \frac{2{,}000}{1.21} + \frac{2{,}000}{1.331} + \frac{2{,}000}{1.464} + \frac{2{,}000}{1.610} + \frac{2{,}000}{1.771} + \frac{2{,}000}{1.948}$$

$= -10{,}000 + 1{,}818 + 1{,}653 + 1{,}503 + 1{,}366 + 1{,}242 + 1{,}129 + 1{,}027$

$= -263$ dollars.

Thus the firm should not buy the machine.

5. *a.* If a single approach is used, the expected costs of development are $0.5 \times \$2$ million $+ 0.5 \times \$1$ million, or $\$1.5$ million, since there is a 0.5 probability that total costs with any single approach will be $\$2$ million and a 0.5 probability that they will be $\$1$ million.

   b. The expected total costs of development are $0.25 \times \$2$ million $+ 0.75 \times \$1$ million $+ \$150{,}000$, or $\$1.4$ million, if each approach is carried to the point at which $\$150{,}000$ have been spent on it, and if the cheaper approach is chosen at that point (and the other approach is dropped.) Why? Because there is a 0.25 probability that total costs with the better of the two approaches will be $\$2$ million and a 0.75 probability that they will be $\$1$ million. In addition, there is the certainty that a cost of $\$150{,}000$ will be incurred for the approach that is dropped. The reason why there is a 0.25 chance that total costs with the better of the two approaches is $\$2$ million is that this will occur only when the total cost of both approaches turns out to be $\$2$ million—and the probability that this will occur is 0.5×0.5, or 0.25.

6. If the benefit continued indefinitely, its present value would be $\$500 \div 0.10$, or $\$5{,}000$. This is an overestimate, since the benefit will not continue indefinitely. Since the cost is $\$8{,}000$, the investment is not worthwhile.

7. The present value of painting costs is

$$\$500 \left\{ 1 + \frac{1}{1.08} + \frac{1}{(1.08)^2} + \frac{1}{(1.08)^3} + \frac{1}{(1.08)^4} \right\} = \$500[1 + 0.926 + 0.857 + 0.794 + 0.735]$$

$$= \$500\,[4.312] = \$2{,}156$$

This must be compared with $\$2{,}000$, the cost of installing aluminum siding now. Since the latter is less than the former, it is cheaper to install the aluminum siding.

8. *a.* $10 \div 1.08 = 9.26$.

   b. $10 \div 1.08 = 9.26$.

9. $\$200$.

10. Yes.

    Yes.

---

*For a classic treatment of this topic, see H. Hotelling, "The Economics of Exhaustible Resources," *Journal of Political Economy* (April 1931). Also see O. Herfindahl and A. Kneese, *Economic Theory of Natural Resources* (Columbus, Merrill, 1974).

11. The patent holders have added to the patent exchange agreements provisions specifying prices, market shares, and so forth.

Electric lights, glass bottles, eyeglasses, magnesium, synthetic rubber, titanium paint pigments, among many others.

12. To the extent that the sizable financial and R and D resources of the oil companies are brought to bear on coal technology, it may result in a more rapid rate of technological change. However, if the oil firms feel that it is not in their interests to advance coal technology, there may be little or no such effect.

13. Technological change is the advance of knowledge concerning the industrial arts, such advance often taking the form of new processes and products.

Certain types of technological change can be measured by the shift in the production function.

Not with new final products.

14. Technological change is an advance in knowledge, whereas a change in technique is a change in the utilized method of production.

Yes.

Yes.

15. Capital-embodied changes in technology must be embodied in new equipment if they are to be utilized. Disembodied technological change consists of better methods and organization that improve the efficiency of both old capital and new.

Examples of capital-embodied technological change are the diesel locomotive and catalytic cracking. Examples of disembodied technological change are various advances in industrial engineering.

16. No.

It is influenced by many factors other than the rate of technological change—for example, changes in capital per worker.

Yes.

17. The total productivity index is the relative increase in output divided by a weighted average of the relative increase in labor input and the relative increase in capital input.

It takes explicit account of capital input as well as labor input.

If the production function is $Q = \alpha (t) [b\, L + c\, K]$.

18. Since they equate the effects of technological change with whatever increase in output is unexplained by other inputs, they may not isolate the effects of technological change alone. They contain the effects of whatever inputs may have been excluded or misspecified.

19. The amount of resources devoted to improving an industry's technology, which in turn depends on the rewards from particular kinds of technological change and on factors that determine their costs. Also, the quantity of resources devoted to improving the capital goods and other inputs it uses. Also, the industry's market structure and its relation to government objectives such as defense.

20. Research is aimed at the creation of new knowledge. Development is aimed at the reduction of research findings to practice. R and D is aimed at the reduction of uncertainty; it is a learning process.

21. The size and complexity of the product being developed, the extent of the advance in performance that is sought, the available stock of knowledge, components, and materials, the development time, and the development strategy used.

22. An innovation is the first application of an invention. There is commonly a lag of ten years or more. An invention has little or no economic significance until it is applied.

23. They argue that firms under perfect competition have fewer resources to devote to research and experimentation than do firms under imperfect competition. Moreover, they argue that, unless a firm has sufficient control over the market to reap the rewards of an innovation, the introduction of the innovation may not be worthwhile.

Defenders of perfect competition retort that there is likely to be less pressure for firms to innovate in imperfect markets. Also, they say that there are advantages in having a large number of independent decision-making units, there being less chance that an important technological advance will be blocked by the faulty judgment of a few men.

24. No. There is no evidence that giant firms are needed in most industries to ensure rapid technological advance and rapid utilization of new techniques.

25. The price of the relevant information should be set equal to marginal cost, which is often practically zero. (Only static efficiency is considered here.)

26. No. Many factors other than technological change also influence output per man-hour.

27. Differences in R and D expenditures and economies of scale, among others.

28. A profit-maximizing firm generally will not scrap existing equipment merely because somewhat better equipment is available. The new equipment must be sufficiently better to offset the fact that the old equipment is already paid for, whereas this is not the case for the new. Yes.

29. Uncertainty concerning the technical and economic feasibility of the process, difficulty in interesting oil firms in the process, the lag involved in disseminating information concerning the existence and characteristics of the process, and so forth.

30. Technological change shifts the production function, thus offsetting the tendency toward diminishing returns.

31. No.

Completion Questions

1. positive
2. society's pool of knowledge
3. change
4. constant returns to scale
5. the relative increase in output divided by a weighted average of the relative increase in labor input and the relative increase in capital input
6. innovation

True or False

1. False   2. False   3. False   4. True   5. True   6. False   7. False   8. True   9. False

Multiple Choice

1. *a*   2. *c*   3. *b*   4. *b*   5. *b*

CHAPTER 18 Decision-Making and Choice Involving Risk

Case Study: Prospecting for Oil

An oil prospector has an option on a particular piece of land. If he drills, he believes that the costs will be $400,000. If he finds oil, he expects to receive $2 million; if he does not find oil, he expects to receive nothing.

a. Construct a decision tree to represent his decision.

b. Can you tell whether he should drill or not on the basis of the available information? Why, or why not?

c. If he applies the minimax rule, should he drill?

The oil prospector believes that the probability of finding oil if he drills on this piece of land is 1/5, and that the probability of not finding oil if he drills here is 4/5.

d. Can you tell whether he should drill or not on the basis of the available information? Why, or why not?

e. Suppose that he can be shown to be a risk lover. Should he drill or not? Why?

f. Suppose that he is indifferent to risk. Should he drill or not? Why?

g. What is the expected value of perfect information concerning whether or not he will find oil?

Problems and Review Questions

1. A newspaper publisher in a small town must decide whether or not to publish a Sunday edition. The publisher thinks that the probability is 0.7 that a Sunday edition would be a success and that it is 0.3 that it would be a failure. If it is a success, he will gain $200,000. If it is a failure, he will lose $100,000.

   a. Construct the decision tree for this problem, and use it to solve the problem, assuming that the publisher is indifferent to risk.

   b. What is the expected value of perfect information?

   c. How would you go about trying to determine whether the publisher is in fact indifferent to risk?

2. A Honolulu restaurant owner must decide whether or not to expand his restaurant. He thinks that the probability is 0.6 that the expansion will prove successful and that it is 0.4 that it will not be successful. If it is successful, he will gain $100,000. If it is not successful, he will lose $80,000.

   a. Construct the decision tree for this problem, and use it to solve the problem, assuming that the restaurant owner is indifferent to risk.

   b. List all forks in the decision tree you constructed, and indicate whether each is a decision fork or a chance fork; and state why.

3. In the previous problem, would the restaurant owner's decision be altered if he felt that:
   a. the probability that the expansion will prove successful is 0.5, not 0.6?
   b. the probability that the expansion will prove successful is 0.7, not 0.6?
   c. What value of the probability that the expansion will prove successful will make the
      restaurant owner indifferent between expanding and not expanding the restaurant?

4. Mary Malone says that she is indifferent between the certainty of receiving $10,000 and a
   gamble where there is a 0.5 chance of receiving $25,000 and a 0.5 chance of receiving
   nothing. In the graph below, plot three points on her utility function.

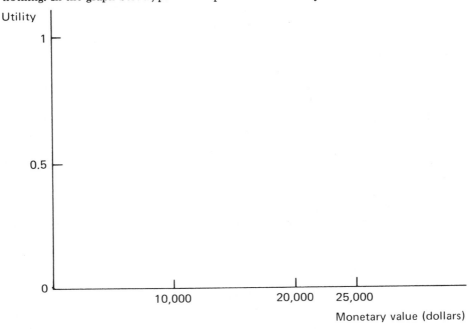

5. John Jones's utility function is shown below:

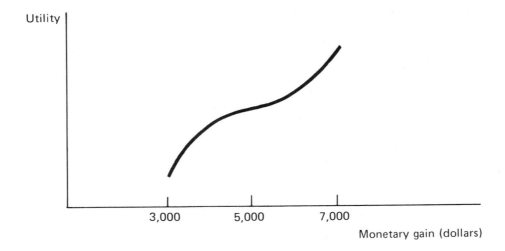

a. Is he a risk averter at all levels of monetary gain?
b. Is he a risk lover at all levels of monetary gain?
c. Does he prefer the certainty of gaining $4,000 over a gamble where there is a 0.5 probability of gaining $3,000 and a 0.5 probability of gaining $5,000?

6. If each card in a standard 52-card deck of playing cards has the same probability of being drawn, what is the probability that a single card that is drawn will be
a. a red 9?
b. a black ace?
c. a black card?
d. neither a red card nor a queen?
e. a queen, king, or ace?

7. The Tremont Corporation is considering the purchase of a firm that produces tools and dies. Tremont's management feels that there is a 50-50 chance, if Tremont buys the firm, that it can make the firm into an effective producer of auto parts. If the firm can be transformed in this way, Tremont believes that it will make $1 million if it buys the firm; if it cannot be transformed in this way, Tremont believes that it will lose $2 million. What is the expected monetary value to Tremont of buying the firm?

8. In fact, the Tremont Corporation decides to purchase the firm described in the previous question. Does this mean that Tremont's management is (a) indifferent to risk, (b) a risk averter?

9. Margaret Murphy is selling her house. She believes that there is a 0.2 chance that each person who inspects the house will purchase it. What is the probability that no more than two people will have to inspect the house before she finds a buyer? (Assume that the probability that each person who inspects the house would buy it is unaffected by the decisions of persons who inspected it previously.)

10. In the previous problem, what is the probability that more than two people will have to inspect the house before Ms. Murphy finds a buyer?

11. A true die is rolled twice. (a) What is the probability of getting a total of 6? (b) Is this a subjective probability?

12. Banker William Martin says that he is indifferent to risk. Suppose that we iet 0 be the utility he attaches to $100,000 and 1 be the utility he attaches to $200,000. If what he says is true, what is the utility he attaches to
a. $300,000?
b. $50,000?
c. -$10,000?

13. Ms. Cherrytree's Neumann-Morgenstern utility function can be represented by the following equation:

$$U = 10 + 2M,$$

where U is utility and M is monetary gain (in thousands of dollars). She has the opportunity to invest $25,000 in Archie Bunker's Bar and Grill. She believes that there is a 0.5 probability that she will lose her entire investment and a 0.5 probability that she will gain $32,000.
   a. If she makes the investment, what is her expected utility?
   b. Should she make the investment?

14. An appliance firm must decide whether or not to offer Warren Whelan a job. If Whelan turns out to be a success, the firm will increase its profits by $100,000; if he turns out not to be a success, the firm's profits will decrease by $80,000. The firm feels that the chances are 50-50 that he will be a success.
   a. What is the expected value of perfect information?
   b. What is the expected monetary value to the firm if it does not hire Whelan?
   c. What is the expected monetary value to the firm if it hires Whelan?

15. The owner of a machine shop says that he is indifferent between the certainty of receiving $7,500 and a gamble where there is a 0.5 chance of receiving $5,000 and a 0.5 chance of receiving $10,000. Also, he says that he is indifferent between the certainty of receiving $10,000 and a gamble where there is a 0.5 chance of receiving $7,500 and a 0.5 chance of receiving $12,500. In the graph below, draw four points on the utility function of the owner of the machine shop.

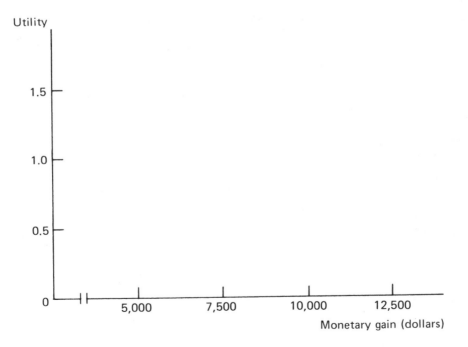

16. Based on the information provided in the previous question, does the owner of the machine shop seem to be a risk averter, a risk lover, or indifferent to risk? Why?

17. A firm must decide whether or not to go forward with an R and D project to develop a new process. If the project is successful, it will gain $5 million; if it is not successful, it will lose $1 million. Suppose that the firm has no idea of what the probabilities of success or failure may be. If the minimax rule is applied, should the firm go forward with the R and D project? Why or why not?

18. Michael McGillicuddy can buy fire insurance on his house, which is worth $80,000. The insurance costs 10 percent of the face value of the insurance.
    a. If he buys $40,000 worth of insurance, how much must he pay for the insurance?
    b. If he buys $60,000 worth of insurance, how much money will he receive (after paying for the insurance) if his house is destroyed by fire?
    c. If he buys $80,000 worth of insurance, what will be the value of his assets if his house is not destroyed by fire? (Assume that his house is his only asset.)

19. Based on the information in the previous question, plot in the graph below the relationship between the value of Mr. McGillicuddy's assets if his house is destroyed by fire and their value if it is not destroyed by fire.

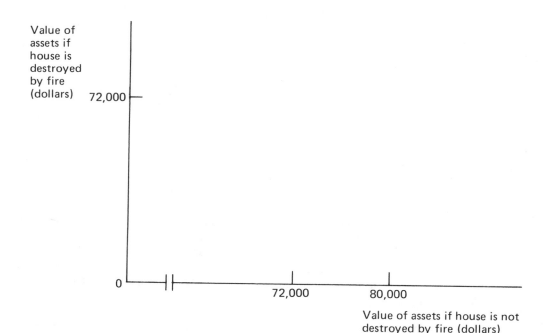

-267-

20. Suppose that Mr. McGillicuddy's Neumann-Morgenstern utility function is
$$U = 5Y$$
where U is utility and Y is the value (in dollars) of his assets. In the graph below, plot the locus of points where expected utility equals 250,000. Assume that Mr. McGillicuddy's house is very susceptible to fire, and that he believes that the probability is 0.5 that it will be destroyed by fire, and 0.5 that it will not be destroyed by fire.

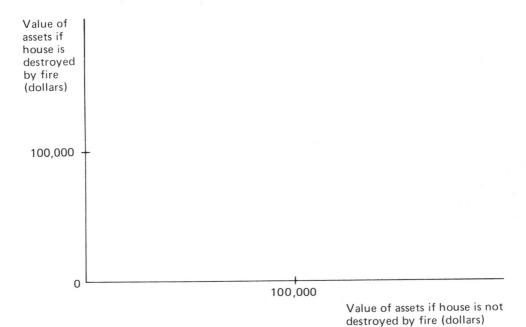

21. Under the circumstances described in questions 18 to 20, how much fire insurance should Mr. McGillicuddy buy on his house? Why?

22. The Martin Engineering Company must decide whether or not to buy a piece of equipment. If it buys this equipment, and if the price of ammonia increases by more than 10 percent in the next year, it will make $3 million; if it buys the equipment and the price of ammonia does not increase by this amount in the next year, it will lose $2 million. If it does not buy the equipment, it gains (and loses) nothing, regardless of what happens to the price of ammonia. Construct a table showing each possible outcome, given that the firm takes each possible course of action.

23. In the previous question, what decision should the Martin Engineering Company make, if it applies the minimax rule? What criticisms can be made of this rule?

Completion Questions

1. If a decision-maker's Neumann-Morgenstern utility function is _____ , the decision-maker maximizes expected monetary value.

2. The Monongahela Company stores spare parts at two warehouses, one in Scranton and one in Cleveland. The number of defective and acceptable spare parts at each warehouse is given below:

Warehouse	Number of Spare Parts		
	Defective	Acceptable	Total
Scranton	200	800	1000
Cleveland	50	450	500

If one of the 1,500 spare parts kept by the firm is chosen at random (i.e., if each spare part has a 1/1,500 chance of being chosen), the probability that it will be defective is _____ .

3. In the previous question, the probability that the chosen spare part will be at the Scranton warehouse is _____ .

4. In question 2, the probability that the chosen spare part will *both* be defective and at the Scranton warehouse is _____ .

5. The Lagrange Corporation can buy theft insurance on a tractor, which is worth \$20,000. The insurance costs 20 percent of the face value of the insurance. If Y_n is the value of the Lagrange Corporation's assets if the tractor is not stolen, and I is the amount of insurance it buys, $Y_n =$ _____ − _____ I. (Assume that the tractor is the firm's only asset.)

6. In the previous question, if Y_T equals the value of the Lagrange Corporation's assets if the tractor is stolen, $Y_T =$ _____ + _____ I.

7. Combining the results of questions 5 and 6, $Y_T =$ _____ − _____ Y_n.

8. In calculating the expected value of perfect information, it is important to recognize that the decision-maker (does, does not) _____ know what this information will be.

9. When a decision-maker applies the minimax rule, he or she assumes that nature (or whatever force determines the outcome of the situation) dictates that if any course of action is taken, the _____ outcome will occur.

10. Sue Smathers is indifferent between a can of peas and a can of corn. She is not indifferent between two lottery tickets that are identical except that one offers a can of peas as a prize while the other offers a can of corn. She does not conform to the _____ axiom.

True or False

_____ 1. The maximization of expected utility results in the same decisions as the minimax rule if the Neumann-Morgenstern utility function is linear.

_____ 2. Under conditions of uncertainty, it is easy to formulate optimal general rules for decision-makers; they should maximize expected utility, using the known probabilities of the relevant outcomes.

_____ 3. Risk and uncertainty are indistinguishable.

_____ 4. According to the subjective definition of probability, the probability of a particular outcome is the proportion of times that this outcome occurs over the long run if this situation exists over and over again.

_____ 5. One problem with the minimax rule is that it ignores the maximum amount that the decision-makers can lose.

_____ 6. The minimax rule is often criticized on the grounds that it is not sufficiently conservative.

_____ 7. Backward induction is the process by which one moves from left to right along a decision tree to solve the decision problem.

_____ 8. To construct James Johnson's Neumann-Morgenstern utility function, we begin by setting the utility attached to three monetary values arbitrarily.

_____ 9. If James Johnson is indifferent between the certainty of a $50,000 gain and a gamble where there is a 0.4 probability of a $40,000 gain and a 0.6 probability of a $60,000 gain, the utility he attaches to a $50,000 gain equals 0.4 $U(40)$ + 0.6 $U(60)$, where $U(40)$ is the utility he attaches to a $40,000 gain and $U(60)$ is the utility he attaches to a $60,000 gain.

_____ 10. If a firm accepts a particular gamble, there is a 0.3 chance that it will gain $1 million and a 0.6 chance that it will lose $2 million. Based on this information, one cannot calculate the expected monetary value of this gamble to the firm.

Multiple Choice

1. If a decision-maker is indifferent to risk, and if the expected value of perfect information is $40,000, the decision-maker should be willing to pay the following for perfect information:
   a. $35,000.
   b. $45,000.
   c. $55,000.
   d. $65,000.
   e. $75,000.

2. If a decision-maker is a risk averter for values of monetary gain above $10,000, then he or she
   a. must be a risk averter for values of monetary gain below $10,000.
   b. must be indifferent to risk for values of monetary gain below $10,000.
   c. must be a risk lover for values of monetary gain below $10,000.

    d. must be either (*a*) or (*b*).

    e. none of the above.

3. John Jerome rolls a true die. If the die comes up a 2, he receives $6,000; if it does not come up a 2, he pays $1,000. The expected monetary value of this gamble to him is

    a. $1,167.

    b. $833.

    c. $167.

    d. -$167.

    e. -$833.

4. John Jerome's Neumann-Morgenstern utility function is $U = 10 + 3M$, where U is utility and M is monetary gain (in dollars). He will prefer the certainty of a gain of $20 over a gamble where there is a 0.3 probability of a $9 gain and a 0.7 probability of

    a. a $31 gain.

    b. a $29 gain.

    c. a $27 gain.

    d. a $25 gain.

    e. none of the above.

5. In the previous question, if John Jerome has a 0.4 probability of receiving $100 and a 0.6 probability of losing $200, the expected utility of this gamble is

    a. -70.

    b. -80.

    c. -230.

    d. -250.

    e. none of the above.

6. The decision tree for a firm's decision of whether or not to increase price is as follows:

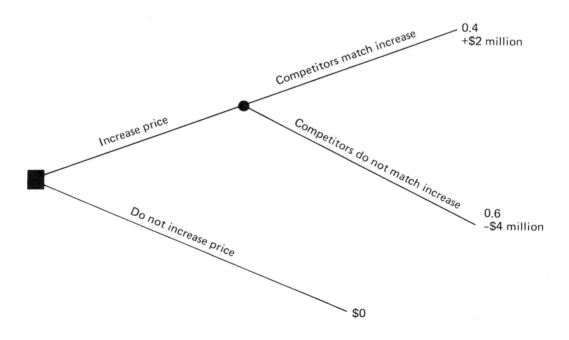

The probability that competitors will match the price increase is
a. 0.
b. 0.4.
c. 0.6.
d. 1.0.
e. none of the above.

7. In the previous question, the expected monetary value if the firm increases price is
a. $800,000.
b. -$1,600,000.
c. -$2,400,000.
d. zero.
e. none of the above.

8. In question 6, the expected value of perfect information concerning whether or not competitors will match the price increase is
a. $2,400,000.
b. $1,600,000.
c. $800,000.
d. $400,000.
e. none of the above.

9. The Neumann-Morgenstern utility function
a. is based on the assumption that the decision-maker's preferences are transitive.
b. is a cardinal utility function of the sort used by nineteenth-century economists.
c. indicates how much extra satisfaction a person receives from consuming an extra unit of various goods.
d. all of the above.
e. none of the above.

10. Theft insurance can be bought on an antique at a cost of 30 percent of the face value of the insurance. Assume that an antique is the decision-maker's only asset. In determining how much theft insurance to buy on this antique, the relationship between the value of the decision-maker's assets if the antique is stolen (Y_T) and the value of his or her assets if it is not stolen (Y_n) is:

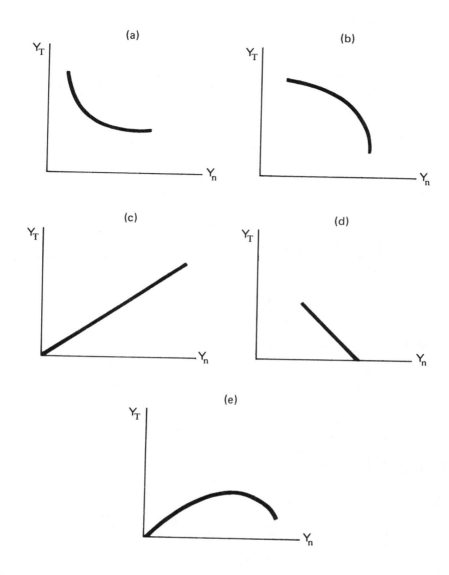

Key Concepts for Review

Risk
Uncertainty
Probability
Frequency definition of probability
Subjective or personal definition of
   probability
Expected monetary value
Decision tree
Decision fork
Chance fork

Backward induction
Neumann-Morgenstern utility function
Utility
Expected utility
Risk averter
Risk lover
Indifference to risk
Expected value of perfect information
Minimax rule

Answers

Case Study: Prospecting for Oil

a.

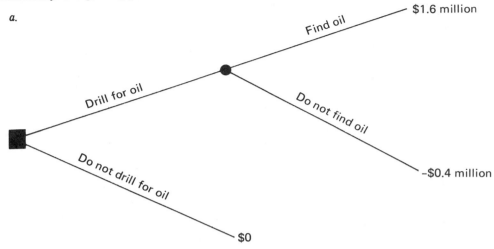

b. Without the probability of finding oil if he drills, it is very difficult to tell whether he should drill.

c. No.

d. No, because his Neumann-Morgenstern utility function is not given.

e. If he drills, the expected monetary value is 1/5 ($1.6 million) + 4/5 (–$0.4 million) = zero. Since the expected monetary value if he drills is the same as the expected monetary value if he does not drill, he should drill because the risk is greater if he drills.

f. He is indifferent between drilling and not drilling.

g. 1/5 ($1.6 million) + 4/5 (zero) – zero = $0.32 million.

Problems and Review Questions

1. a.

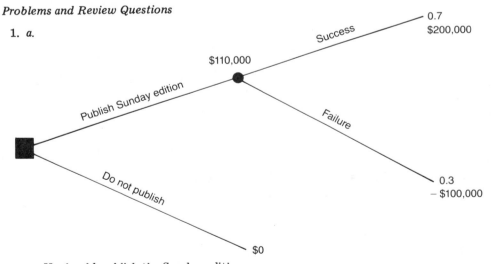

He should publish the Sunday edition.

b. .7($200,000) + .3(0) – $110,000 = $30,000.

c. Construct his Neumann-Morgenstern utility function.

2. a.

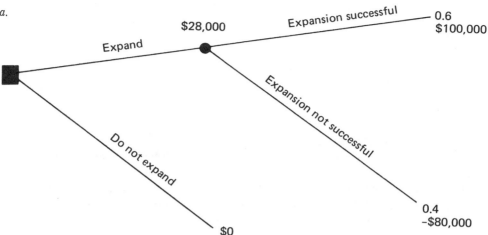

Since the expected monetary value if he expands is 0.6 ($100,000) + 0.4 (–$80,000) = $28,000, he should expand the restaurant.

b. The first fork on the left is a decision fork since the restaurant owner decides whether or not to expand. The next fork is a chance fork, since "chance" decides whether or not the expansion is successful.

3. a. No.
   b. No.
   c. 4/9.

4. Let 0 be the utility of receiving nothing, and 1 be the utility of receiving $25,000. Then, since she is indifferent between the certainty of receiving $10,000 and the gamble described in the problem, the utility of receiving $10,000 must equal

$$0.5(1) + 0.5(0) = 0.5.$$

Thus, three points on her utility function are given below:

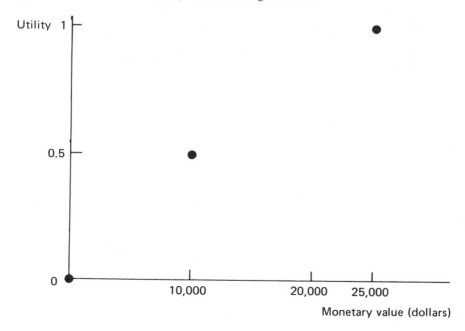

5. *a.* No.
   b. No.
   c. Yes.
6. *a.* 1/26.
   b. 1/26.
   c. 1/2.
   d. 6/13.
   e. 3/13.
7. 0.5($1 million) + 0.5(–$2 million) = –$0.5 million.
8. *a.* No, since it would have chosen not to purchase it if it were indifferent to risk.
   b. No, since it would have chosen not to purchase it if it were risk averse.
9. The probability that the house is bought by the first person who inspects it equals 0.20. The probability that the first person will not buy it but that the second person will buy it equals (0.8)(0.2) = 0.16. Thus, the probability that either the first or second person will buy it equals 0.20 + 0.16 = 0.36.
10. 1 – 0.36 = 0.64.
11. *a.* 5/36.
    b. No.
12. *a.* 2.
    b. –0.5.
    c. –1.1.
13. *a.* The utility of zero equals 10 + 2(0) = 10. The utility of –$25,000 equals 10 + 2(–25) = –40. The utility of +$32,000 equals 10 + 2(32) = 74. Her expected utility equals 0.5(–40) + 0.5(74) = 17.
    b. Since the expected utility if she makes the investment (17) exceeds the expected utility if she does not make it (10), she should make it.
14. *a.* 0.5($100,000) + 0.5(0) – $10,000 = $40,000.
    b. zero.
    c. 0.5($100,000) + 0.5(–$80,000) = $10,000.
15. Let $U(5,000)$ be the utility of receiving $5,000. We arbitrarily set $U(5,000)$ equal to zero and $U(10,000)$ equal to 1. Since $U(7,500) = 0.5\ U(5,000) + 0.5\ U(10,000)$, $U(7,500)$ must equal 0.5. And since $U(10,000) = 0.5\ U(7,500) + 0.5\ U(12,500)$, $U(12,500)$ must equal 1.50. The four points are indicated on the opposite page.

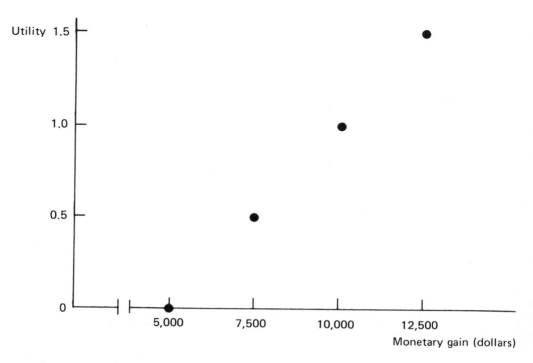

Utility

16. Indifferent to risk, because his Neumann-Morgenstern utility function seems to be a straight line, at least in the range for which data are given.
17. No, because the maximum loss if it goes ahead with the project is $1 million, whereas the maximum loss if it does not go ahead with it is zero.
18. *a.* $4,000.
    b. $60,000 – $6,000 = $54,000.
    c. $80,000 – $8,000 = $72,000.

19.

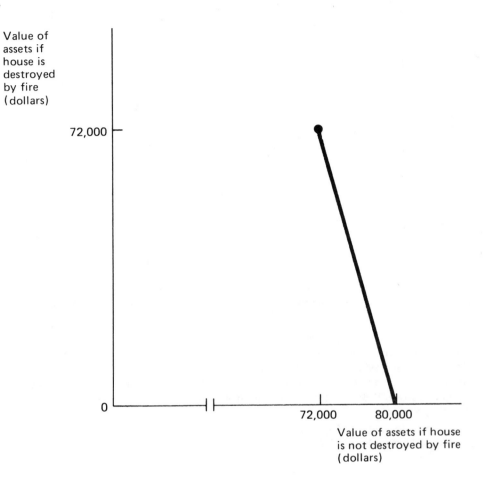

Value of
assets if
house is
destroyed
by fire
(dollars)

72,000

0

72,000   80,000

Value of assets if house
is not destroyed by fire
(dollars)

20. Let Y_T be the value of his assets if the house is destroyed by fire, and let Y_n be the value of his assets if the house is not destroyed by fire. His expected utility equals:

$$0.5(5Y_T) + 0.5(5Y_n) = 250,000.$$

Thus, $Y_T = 100,000 - Y_n$. This relationship is plotted below:

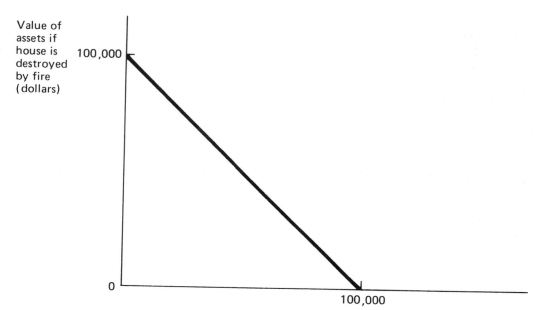

Value of assets if house is destroyed by fire (dollars)

100,000

0

100,000

Value of assets if house is not destroyed by fire (dollars)

21. If we assume various levels of expected utility, we get various curves (in this case, straight lines) parallel to the one in the answer to problem 20. To maximize expected utility, we must find the point on the line shown in the answer to problem 19 that is on the highest of these curves (in this case, straight lines). This point is where both (1) the value of the assets if the house is destroyed by fire and (2) the value of the assets if the house is not destroyed by fire, equal $72,000. To achieve this point, Mr. McGillicuddy should buy $80,000 of insurance.

22.

	Price of ammonia increases by more than 10%	Price of ammonia increases by 10% or less
Martin buys equipment	+$3 million	-$2 million
Martin does not buy equipment	zero	zero

23. It should not buy the equipment. It assumes that the worst outcome will occur, if each action is taken.

Completion Questions

1. linear
2. 250/1500 = 1/6
3. 1000/1500 = 2/3
4. 200/1500 = 2/15
5. $20,000, 0.20
6. zero, 0.80
7. $80,000, 4
8. does not
9. worst
10. independence

True or False

1. False 2. False 3. False 4. False 5. False 6. False 7. False 8. False 9. True 10. True

Multiple Choice

1. *a* 2. *e* 3. *c* 4. *e* 5. *c* 6. *b* 7. *b* 8. *a* 9. *a* 10. *d*

APPENDIX: Linear Programming

Problems and Review Questions

1. A firm can use three processes, A, B, and C, to produce a particular good. To make one unit of the good, Process A requires 2 man-hours of labor and 1 hour of machine time, Process B requires 1.5 man-hours of labor and 1.5 hours of machine time, and Process C requires 1.1 man-hours of labor and 2.2 hours of machine time.

   a. In the graph below, draw the rays corresponding to the three processes.

   b. In the graph below, draw the isoquant corresponding to an output of 100 units of the good.

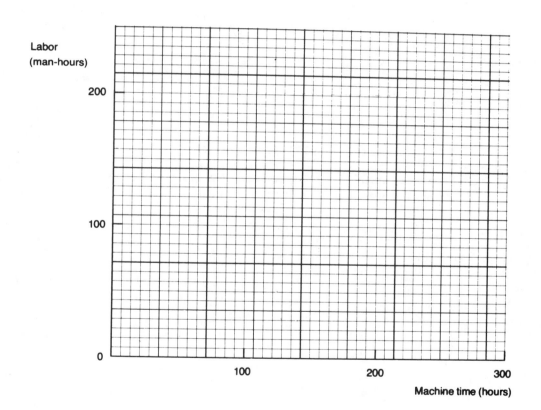

2 Suppose that a firm's product transformation curve is as follows:

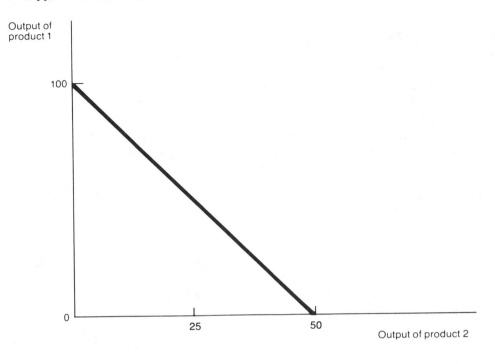

a. If the price of product 1 equals the price of a unit of product 2, draw several isorevenue lines in this graph.
b. What is the optimal amount of each product that the firm should produce?
c. Is the optimal point a point where an isorevenue line is tangent to the product transformation curve?

3. In Example A.1 in the text, suppose that the firm was not constrained to use no more than 120 hours of machine time. Under these circumstances, how many units should it produce with process A? process B? process C?

4. Explain how the firm's production decision can be viewed as a linear programming problem. Describe the advantages of looking at it as a linear programming problem.

5. *a.* Suppose that there are two inputs, machine-hours of finishing capacity and man-hours of labor. If there are at most 2,000 machine-hours and 200 man-hours available per week, draw the set of feasible input combinations in the graph below:

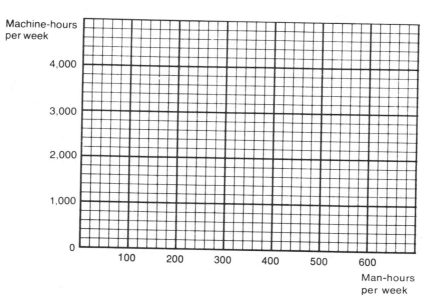

b. Suppose that one process utilizes 1 machine-hour and 1 man-hour to produce a unit of output. Graph the ray depicting this process below:

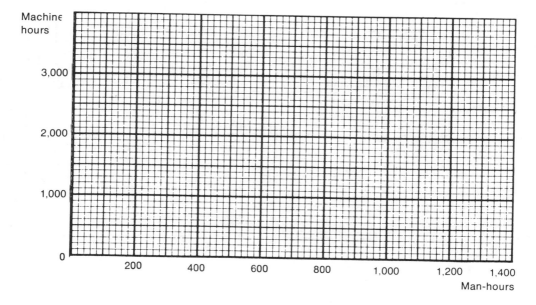

c. Suppose that another process utilizes 1/2 machine-hour and 2 man-hours to produce a unit of output and that still another process utilizes 2 machine-hours and 1/2 man-hours to produce a unit of output. Graph the rays for these additional two processes below.

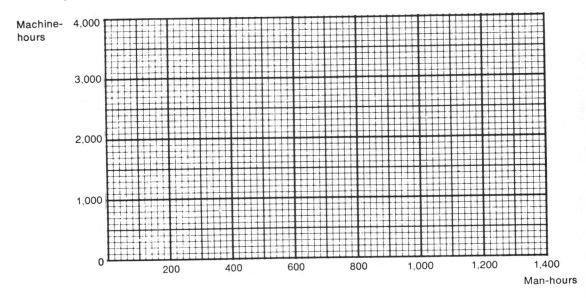

d. Graph the isoquant corresponding to 1,000 units of output below (given the three processes described above).

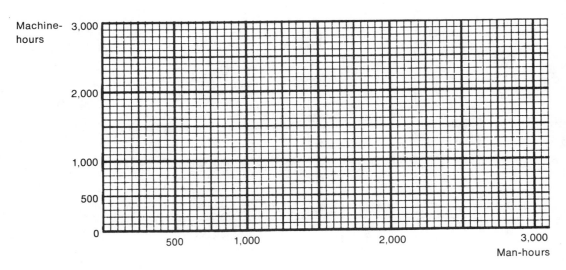

e. Suppose that the firm can rent all of the machine-hours it wants at $1 hour and all of the man-hours it wants at $1 an hour. Which process should it use to produce 1,000 units of output?

6. Describe the meaning and usefulness of shadow prices.

7. Describe one of the ways in which linear programming has been used in the petroleum industry.

8. According to Robert Dorfman, "The essential simplification achieved in mathematical programming is the replacement of the notion of the production function by the notion of the process." Explain this in detail.

9. A family is composed of a husband and wife. The husband needs 3,000 calories per day and the wife requires 2,000 calories per day. The doctor says that these calories must be obtained by eating not less than a certain amount of fats and a certain amount of proteins. The family wants to minimize its food bill, but it does not want to violate the doctor's orders. Is this a linear programming problem? If so, what are the objective function and the constraints?

True or False and Multiple Choice

_____ 1. Linear programming views the technology available to the firm as being a finite number of processes.

_____ 2. Linear programming is a purely mathematical technique.

_____ 3. Linear programming seems to conform more closely than conventional analysis to the way that businessmen tend to view production.

_____ 4. Each process can be operated at only one activity level.

_____ 5. Linear programming works only when there are fewer than 10 constraints.

_____ 6. Isoquants are convex in the case of linear programming.

_____ 7. The optimal solution of a linear programming problem will occur at an extreme point.

_____ 8. The simplex method is a technique designed to determine how many processes the firm should utilize.

_____ 9. To every linear programming problem there corresponds a dual problem.

_____ 10. The solutions to the dual problem are the shadow prices.

_____ 11. In linear programming, each process uses inputs in fixed proportions.

_____ 12. An isoprofit curve contains input combinations resulting in different levels of profit.

13. In linear programming, isoquants are
    a. positively sloped.
    b. smooth.
    c. a series of connected line segments.
    d. all of the above.
    e. none of the above.

14. In linear programming, the objective function is
    a. a summary of the constraints.
    b. what you want to maximize or minimize.
    c. always nonnegative.
    d. all of the above.
    e. none of the above.

Key Concepts for Review

Linear programming
Process
Activity level
Constraints
Objective function

Isoprofit curves
Extreme points
Dual problem
Shadow prices
Simplex method

Answers

Problems and Review Questions

1. Both the rays and the isoquant are shown below:

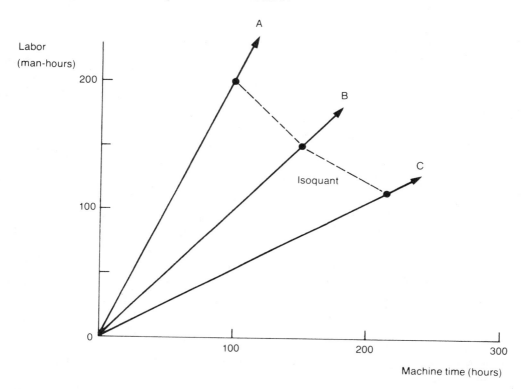

2. *a.* The isorevenue lines are drawn below:

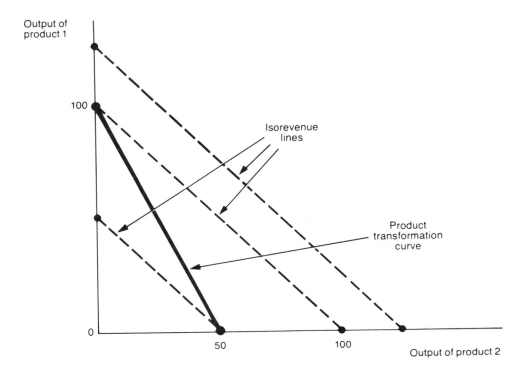

b. It should produce 100 units of product 1 and none of product 2, since this puts the firm on the highest isorevenue line that is attainable.

c. No. This is a corner solution. There is no point where the isorevenue line is tangent to the product transformation curve in this case.

3. The cost of making one unit of the good is $8 with process A, $7.50 with process B, and $7.70 with process C. Thus, all 100 units should be produced with process B since this is the cheapest procedure.

4. The firm has certain fixed amounts of a number of inputs. These limitations are constraints. The firm can use various processes. The amount of profit varies from process to process. Knowing the amount of profit to be made from a unit of output from each process, and bearing in mind the limited amount of inputs at its disposal, the firm must determine the activity level at which each process should be operated to maximize profit.

   This linear programming view has at least two advantages. First, it allows the analyst to get behind the production function. Second, it conforms more closely to the way that businessmen view production.

5. a.

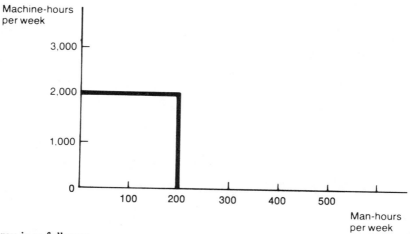

b. The ray is as follows:

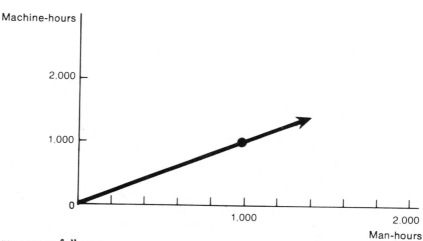

c. The rays are as follows:

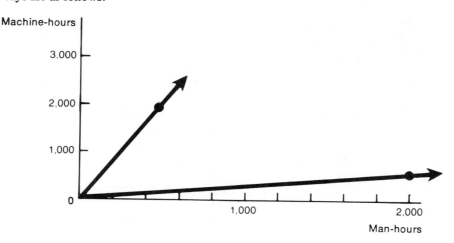

d. The isoquant is as follows:

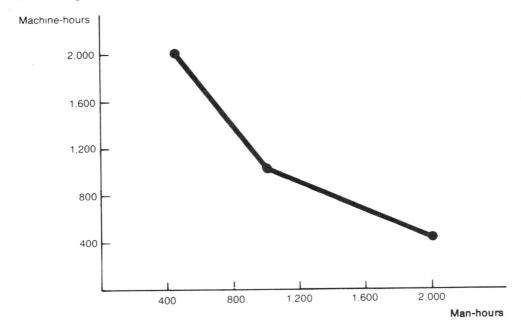

e. It should use the process that uses 1 machine-hour and 1 man-hour to produce a unit of output.

6. The solutions to the dual problem are shadow prices. For example, in the case discussed in this appendix of my *Microeconomics*, the shadow prices show which types of capacity are bottlenecks. They show how much it would be worth to management to expand each type of capacity.

7. Linear programming has been used to determine the schedule of production rates for reservoirs to maximize profit, while meeting various technological constraints as well as commitments to supply oil.

9. Yes. Food cost is the objective function, and the attainment of the proper amount of calories, fats, and proteins is a series of constraints. Also, there are nonnegativity constraints.

True or False and Multiple Choice

1. True   2. True   3. True   4. False   5. False   6. True   7. True   8. False
9. True   10. True   11. True   12. False   13. *c*   14. *b*